Posthumanism

READERS IN CULTURAL CRITICISM

General editor: *Catherine Belsey*

Readers in Cultural Criticism
Series Standing Order
ISBN 0–333–78660–2 hardcover
ISBN 0–333–75236–8 paperback
(*outside North America only*)

You can receive future titles in this series as they are published by placing a
standing order.
Please contact your bookseller or, in case of difficulty, write to us at the address below
with your name and address, the title of the series and the ISBN quoted above.

Customer Services Department, Macmillan Distribution Ltd, Houndmills, Basingstoke,
Hampshire RG21 6XS, England

Readers in Cultural Criticism

Posthumanism

Edited by Neil Badmington

palgrave

First published 2000 by
PALGRAVE
Houndmills, Basingstoke, Hampshire RG21 6XS and
175 Fifth Avenue, New York, N. Y. 10010
Companies and representatives throughout the world

PALGRAVE is the new global academic imprint of
St. Martin's Press LLC Scholarly and Reference Division and
Palgrave Publishers Ltd (formerly Macmillan Press Ltd).

ISBN 0–333–76537–0 hardback
ISBN 0–333–76538–9 paperback

This book is printed on paper suitable for recycling and
made from fully managed and sustained forest sources.

A catalogue record for this book is available
from the British Library.

Library of Congress Cataloging-in-Publication Data
Posthumanism/edited by Neil Badmington
        p. cm
    Includes bibliographical references and index.
    ISBN 0–333–76537–0 — ISBN 0–333–76538–9 (pbk.)
    1. Philosophical anthropology. 2. Humanism. I. Badmington,
    Neil, 1971–

BD450.P585 2000
144—dc21
                                                    00—033320

10   9   8   7   6   5   4   3   2   1
09   08   07   06   05   04   03   02   01   00

Printed and bound in Great Britain by
Creative Print and Design (Wales), Ebbw Vale

Bob Dylan:	We're different. We come from two different worlds. You come from England; I come from the United States.
Interviewer:	That's true, that's true, but we're still human beings, so there's some sort of connection between us.
Bob Dylan:	No, I'm just a guitar player, that's all.

From the film Don't Look Back

Contents

General Editor's Preface

Culture is the element we inhabit as subjects.

Culture embraces the whole range of practices, customs and represent-ations of a society. In their rituals, stories and images, societies identify what they perceive as good and evil, proper, sexually acceptable, racially other. Culture is the location of values, and the study of cultures shows how values vary from one society to another, or from one historical moment to the next.

But culture does not exist in the abstract. On the contrary, it is in the broadest sense of the term textual, inscribed in the paintings, operas, sculptures, furnishings, fashions, bus tickets and shopping lists which are the currency of both aesthetic and everyday exchange. Societies invest these artefacts with meanings, until in many cases the meanings are so 'obvious' that they pass for nature. Cultural criticism denaturalises and defamiliarises these meanings, isolating them for inspection and analysis.

The subject is what speaks, or, more precisely, what signifies, and sub-jects learn in culture to reproduce or to challenge the meanings and values inscribed in the signifying practices of the society that shapes them.

If culture is pervasive and constitutive for us, if it resides in the docu-ments, objects and practices that surround us, if it circulates as the mean-ings and values we learn and reproduce as good citizens, how in these circumstances can we practise cultural *criticism*, where criticism implies a certain distance between the critic and the culture? The answer is that cultures are not homogeneous; they are not even necessarily coherent. There are always other perspectives, so that cultures offer alternative positions for the subjects they also recruit. Moreover, we have a degree of power over the messages we reproduce. A minor modification changes the script, and may alter the meaning; the introduction of a neg-ative constructs a resistance.

The present moment in our own culture is one of intense debate. Sexual alignments, family values, racial politics, the implications of econ-omic differences are all hotly contested. And positions are taken up not only in explicit discussions at political meetings, on television and in the pub. They are often reaffirmed or challenged implicitly in films and advertisements, horoscopes and lonely-hearts columns. Cultural criticism analyses all these forms in order to assess their hold on our consciousness.

There is no interpretative practice without theory, and the more sophisticated the theory, the more precise and perceptive the reading it makes possible. Cultural theory is as well defined now as it has ever been, and as strongly contested as our social values. There could not, in consequence, be a more exciting time to engage in the theory and practice of Cultural Criticism.

Catherine Belsey
Cardiff University

Preface

I owe thanks to the many people whose influence helped *Posthumanism* to take shape. My greatest intellectual debt is to Catherine Belsey, who first proposed the volume, oversaw the project from start to finish, and knew what I was trying to say long before I did.

Margaret Bartley at the publishers was always there in moments of crisis. Clare Birchall traded ideas. The Eatons provided so much more than just a roof. Diane Elam continually pushed my thinking in new directions. Art Evans at *Science-Fiction Studies* and Annie Taylor at the *Guardian* helped with contacts. Ruth Evans talked cyborgs. Alan Grossman and Chris Hilton provided after-hours discussion. N. Katherine Hayles kindly allowed me, a complete stranger, to see an advance copy of her wonderful book on posthumanism. Matthew Herbert and Richard Vine sent me posthumanist soundtracks by which to work. Judy Marshall made perfect sense of the original typescript. Emma Mason lent cabaret to proceedings. Jane Moore restored faith in the title. Karen O'Brien reminded me that humanism has many faces. Carl Plasa suggested Fanon. The students of my course on Posthumanism at Cardiff University, Autumn 1998, made Thursday afternoons both a pleasure and an education. Julia Thomas shared neuroses and a wall, and generously commented on my introduction. Thomas Vargish spoke and wrote words of wisdom about a longer version of my essay on Haraway and Piercy.

The seeds of this project lie in my parents' decision to allow me to watch weekly episodes of *The Six Million Dollar Man* as a small child in the mid-1970s. I thank them for their impeccable foresight.

Posthumanism is dedicated to Maria, for showing me what spring is like on Jupiter and Mars.

NB
Bath, March 1999

Acknowledgements

The editor and publishers wish to thank the following for permission to use copyright material:

Louis Althusser, for 'Marxism and Humanism' from *For Marx* by Louis Althusser, trans. Ben Brewster (1996), pp. 227–31, by permission of Verso; Neil Badmington, for 'Posthumanist (Com)Promises: Diffracting Donna Haraway's Cyborg Through Marge Piercy's *Body of Glass*, by permission of the author; Roland Barthes, for 'The Great Family of Man' from *Mythologies* by Roland Barthes, ed. and trans. Annette Lavers, Jonathan Cape, pp. 100–2. Translation copyright © 1972 Jonathan Cape, by permission of Random House UK and Hill and Wang, a division of Farrar, Straus and Giroux, LLC; Jean Baudrillard, for 'Prophylaxis and Virulence' from *The Transparency of Evil: Essays on Extreme Phenomena*, by Jean Baudrillard, trans. James Benedict (1994), pp. 60–70, by permission of Verso and Editions Galilée; Scott Bukatman, for 'Postcards from the Posthuman Solar System', *Science-Fiction Studies*, 18:3 (1991), 343–57, by permission of *Science-Fiction Studies*; Rosalind Coward, for 'The Instinct' from *Female Desire: Women's Sexuality Today* by Rosalind Coward (1994), pp. 233–43, by permission of HarperCollins Publishers; Frantz Fanon, for material from *The Wretched of the Earth* by Frantz Fanon, trans. Constance Farrington (1976), pp. 251–5. Copyright © 1963 by Presénce Africaine, by permission of HarperCollins Publishers and Grove/Atlantic, Inc; Michel Foucault, for material from *The Order of Things: An Archaeology of the Human Sciences* by Michel Foucault, trans. Alan Sheridan-Smith, Tavistock (1989), pp. 385–7. Copyright © 1970 by Random House, Inc, by permission of Routledge and Pantheon Books, a division of Random House, Inc; Judith Halberstam, for 'Skinflick: Posthuman Gender in Jonathan Demme's *The Silence of the Lambs*', *Camera Obscura*, 27 (1991), 37–52. Copyright © 1991, by permission of Duke University Press; Donna Haraway, for 'A Cyborg Manifesto: Science, Technology, and Socialist Feminism in the Late Twentieth Century', *Socialist Review*, 80 (1985), 65–108, by permission of the author; Jean-François Lyotard, for 'Can Thought Go On Without a Body?' included in *The Inhuman: Reflections on Time* by Jean-François Lyotard, trans. Bruce Boone and Lee Hidrith, Polity Press (1991), pp. 8–23, first published in *Discourse*, 2:1 (1987).

Copyright © Editions Galilée, by permission of Editions Galilée; Paula Rabinowitz, for 'Soft Fictions and Intimate Documents: Can Feminism be Posthuman?' from *Posthuman Bodies*, ed. Judith Halberstam and Ira Livingston (1995), pp. 97–112, by permission of Indiana University Press; Bill Readings, for 'Pagans, Perverts or Primitives?: Experimental Justice in the Empire of Capital' from *Judging Lyotard*, ed. Andrew Benjamin (1992), pp. 168–91, by permission of Routledge.

Every effort has been made to trace the copyright holders but if any have been inadvertently overlooked the publishers will be pleased to make the necessary arrangement at the first opportunity.

1

Introduction: Approaching Posthumanism

Neil Badmington

I

He is young, reliable, quiet, clean and intelligent. He is good with numbers and will teach or entertain the children without a word of complaint. He is, according to *Time* magazine's tradition, Man of the Year, 1982.

Well, almost. 'He' is actually a computer. Breaking with more than half a century of convention, the cover of the first issue of *Time* to appear in 1983 featured a different type of star. 'Several human candidates might have represented 1982', wrote the magazine's publisher in an address to his readers, 'but none symbolised the past year more richly, or will be viewed by history as more significant, than a machine: the computer.'[1] This time, it seemed, humans had failed to leave their mark. In fact, the 'Man of the Year' award was no longer applicable, for the cover was emblazoned with a new headline: 'Machine of the Year'. At the centre of the page stood the victorious machine, its screen alive with information. A ragged and lifeless sculpture of a human figure looked on, its epitaph the four words beneath the main title: 'The computer moves in.'

What would it mean to view this as an example of *posthumanism*?

The use of such a term is, of course, far from straightforward. Writing in 1947, Martin Heidegger drew attention to the paradoxical status of any '-ism', observing that, while such terms 'have for a long time now been suspect ... the market of public opinion continually demands new ones'.[2] More than half a century later, the fate of '-isms' appears to be even more acute. 'We'[3] cannot live with them (why else would 'we' need to keep inventing new ones?), but neither can 'we' live without them (why else would 'we' need to keep inventing new ones?). My decision to name this book *Posthumanism* was continually troubled by Heidegger's words. Was I in danger of giving currency to yet another '-ism' devoid of clarity, coherence and credibility? Would the volume be viewed as a

1

cynical attempt by an academic under the age of thirty to enhance his
career potential by exploiting millennial fears about the future of humanity? After all, as Umberto Eco has pointed out, in the contemporary cultural climate nothing sells quite like a crisis.[4]

The anxiety provoked by Heidegger's words was eventually allayed
when chance led me back to several sentences written by Ihab Hassan
(who certainly knew Heidegger's work) more than twenty years ago:

> At present, posthumanism may appear variously as a dubious neolo-
> gism, the latest slogan, or simply another image of man's recurrent
> self-hate. Yet posthumanism may also hint at a potential in our
> culture, hint at a tendency struggling to become more than a trend ...
>
> We need to understand that five hundred years of humanism may
> be coming to an end, as humanism transforms itself into something
> that we must helplessly call posthumanism.[5]

Hassan's use of 'helplessly' seems to imply that 'posthumanism' is not
necessarily used by the critic because it is a word that unproblematically
conveys its meaning. And yet, while it may even be 'a dubious neologism', I want to suggest that it has the potential to serve as a convenient
shorthand for a general crisis in something that 'we' must just as helplessly call 'humanism'.

I approach this latter term with similar caution, for, as both Kate Soper
and Tony Davies have pointed out in their fine introductions to the
subject, humanism can be a wonderfully vague concept.[6] While Davies
playfully invokes Lewis Carroll's Humpty Dumpty, for whom a word
'means just what I choose it to mean – neither more nor less',[7] Soper
observes that the understanding of the term is likely to depend upon cultural context. To the British or American reader, she writes, humanism is
invariably 'more or less synonymous with atheism':

> In the English-speaking world, in fact, 'humanism' has become so
> closely identified with the promulgation of secularism, that one comes
> to any work containing the word in its title with the suspicion that it
> must belong to that rather earnest genre of writing, much of it
> American, in which 'humanism' is itself presented as a kind of
> religion – the progressive cult for today's broadminded rationalist.[8]

However, she continues, there is a quite different approach. From a perspective informed by recent continental philosophy, humanism is
viewed not as progressive but as reactionary, on account of the manner
in which it 'appeals (positively) to the notion of a core humanity or
common essential feature in terms of which human beings can be
defined and understood'.[9] This latter definition is what is at stake in the

present volume's engagement with posthumanism. Postponing my engagement with the 'post-' for a little longer, I want to develop Soper's outline by turning to the philosophy of René Descartes.

If Descartes is, as Bertrand Russell once declared, 'the founder of modern philosophy',[10] he might also – and by the same token – be seen as one of the principal architects of humanism, for, in the seventeenth century, he arrived at a new and remarkably influential account of what it means to be human. At the very beginning of the *Discourse on the Method*, Descartes proposes that reason is 'the only thing that makes us men [sic] and distinguishes us from the beasts... .'[11] This innate 'power of judging well and distinguishing the true from the false ... is naturally equal in all men'.[12] Rational thought, quite simply, makes humans human. While Descartes certainly retains his Christian faith, God is no longer as central a figure as in previous times. Centre-stage is now occupied by the human, by the figure of Man [sic], the cogitating 'I': 'I think, therefore I am'.[13]

Reason not only grants the subject the power of judgement; it also helps 'us' to tell the difference between the human and the non-human. In a remarkable passage of the *Discourse* that might be read as science fiction *avant la lettre*, Descartes asserts that if there were a machine with the organs and appearance of a monkey, 'we' would not be able to distinguish between the real monkey and the fake – at the level of essence – precisely because, as far as Descartes is concerned, the fact that neither animal nor machine could ever possess reason means that *there would be no essential difference*. If, however, machines were to attempt to mimic human beings, 'we' would always be able to tell the difference, to preserve the firm distinction between the human and the inhuman. This judgement could be made (and, moreover, made correctly) on the grounds of two distinctly human capabilities, for dialogue and for action based on understanding:

> The first is that they could never use words, or put together other signs, as we do in order to declare our thoughts to others. For we can certainly conceive of a machine so constructed that it utters words, and even utters words which correspond to bodily actions causing a change in its organs (e.g. if you touch it in one spot it asks what you want of it, if you touch it in another it cries out that you are hurting it, and so on). But it is not conceivable that such a machine should produce different arrangements of words so as to give an appropriately meaningful answer to whatever is said in its presence, as the dullest of men can do. Secondly, even though such machines might do some things as well as we do them, or perhaps even better, they would inevitably fail in others, which would reveal that they were acting not through understanding but only from the dis-

position of their organs. For whereas reason is a universal instru-
ment which can be used in all kinds of situations, these organs need
some particular disposition for each particular action; hence it is for
all practical purposes impossible for a machine to have enough
different organs to make it act in all the contingencies of life in the
way in which our reason makes us act.[14]

There is, in other words, an absolute difference between the human and
the inhuman: only the former has the capacity for rational thought.
Reason belongs solely to the human and, as such, serves to unite the
human race. 'We' may have different types of bodies, but because reason
is a property of the mind (which, for Descartes, is distinguishable from
the body), deep down 'we' are all the same.

This understanding of what it means to be human was, of course,
developed more than 350 years ago. I want to suggest, however, that the
basic model articulated by Descartes – a model which might be called
humanist, precisely because, to return to Soper's words, it 'appeals
(positively) to the notion of a core humanity or common essential feature
in terms of which human beings can be defined and understood' –
continues to enjoy the status of 'common sense' in contemporary
Western culture. To mark the fiftieth anniversary of the Universal
Declaration of Human Rights in 1999, one of Britain's best-known book-
sellers produced a pocket-sized edition of the document with an introduction that reaffirmed the relevance of the Declaration at the close of
the twentieth century. Meanwhile, the text itself reveals a fundamental
Cartesian humanism at work. The first Article, for instance, asserts that
all human beings 'are endowed with reason and conscience and should
act towards one another in a spirit of brotherhood'. Despite the differences of religion, class, nationality, ethnicity, sexuality and language
alluded to in the subsequent Article, fundamentally 'we' are all the same.
To accept the principles of the Declaration – a document that continues
to govern, as common sense, the thinking of ethical and political
responsibilities – is to assert that there is, at the end of the day, a basic
human essence.

II

If this is humanism, what motivates posthumanism? How did 'we' arrive
in a space where it is possible to discuss such a subject? Although I have
no desire to posit an absolute point of origin, I do want to suggest that
the concept in question becomes a distinct possibility with the work of
Marx and Freud. I recognise that this is a decidedly unfashionable claim
to make. Time has not been kind to either figure: Marxism has become

synonymous with the gulag and a dream that crumbled with the Berlin Wall, while Freud is habitually dismissed as a phallocentric misogynist who saw sex everywhere he looked. Marx and Freud, 'we' are so often told, are no longer relevant, no longer credible. And yet, it seems to me that they triggered, to take a phrase from Althusser and Balibar, an 'immense theoretical revolution',[15] opening up a space for what would become posthumanism.

The German Ideology is the work of two young philosophers determined to overturn traditional ways of thinking about the human subject. The opening sentence of the Preface sets the tone for what follows: 'Hitherto men [sic] have always formed wrong ideas about themselves, about what they are and what they ought to be'.[16] The principal target of *The German Ideology* is the humanist belief in a natural human essence which exists outside history, politics, and social relations. Such a model dominated the philosophical climate within (and against) which Marx and Engels were writing. The idealist philosophers, taking their cue principally from Hegel, believed that an authentic consciousness was the point from which everything else proceeded: first there is the idea, then comes the material world. Marx and Engels certainly never abandoned Hegel *tout court* – much of their methodology and vocabulary is indebted to his work – but they did set out to rethink completely his approach. Consciousness, they insisted, does not determine a person's social life; it is, rather, social life that determines consciousness.[17] Hegel (and, indeed, Descartes) had been turned upside down: idealism had been replaced by materialism. Subjectivity, in the Marxist account, is not the cause but the effect of an individual's material conditions of existence. The subject is not a given. Eternal Man is no more; 'he' now has a history and a contingency denied by humanism. Marx and Engels make possible a '*theoretical anti-humanism*'[18] in which there is an awareness that radically different material conditions of existence produce incompatible subjectivities. Despite the exhibition which prompted the essay by Roland Barthes in this volume, there can be no Family of Man.

Sixteen years after the Russian revolution, Freud observed that 'although practical Marxism has mercilessly cleared away all idealistic systems and illusions, it has itself developed illusions which are no less questionable and unprovable than the earlier ones'.[19] His reservations centre upon communism's claim to be able to bring about a society in which antagonisms no longer exist, in which there is a unity, a collective consciousness. Psychoanalysis took the challenge to humanism one stage further. In proposing that human activity is governed in part by unconscious motives, Freud further problematised the Cartesian model, in which the critical determinant of being is rational, fully-conscious thought. According to Jacques Lacan, one of Freud's most compelling interpreters, and a figure to whom I will return, psychoanalysis requires that the words of Descartes be reformulated as follows: 'I think where I am not, therefore I am where I do not think.... I am not wherever I am the plaything of my thought; I think of what I am where I do not think to think'.[20]

The *Psychopathology of Everyday Life*, one of Freud's most accessible works, takes as its subject a wide range of events – slips of the tongue, the forgetting of names, lapses of memory – and proceeds to challenge the 'common-sense' explanation that such occurrences are mere aberrations, minor mistakes by an otherwise rational being. There is, Freud insists, 'a reason for every mistake',[21] including those made by the analyst himself:

> One evening, wishing to excuse myself for not having called for my wife at the theatre, I said: 'I was at the theatre at ten minutes after ten'. I was corrected: 'You meant to say before ten o'clock'. Naturally I wanted to say before ten. After ten would certainly be no excuse. I had been told that the theatre programme read, 'Finished before ten o'clock'. When I arrived at the theatre I found the foyer dark and the theatre empty. Evidently the performance was over earlier and my wife did not wait for me. When I looked at the clock it still wanted five minutes to ten. I determined to make my case more favourable at home, and say that it was ten minutes to ten. Unfortunately, the speech-blunder spoiled the intent and laid bare my dishonesty, in which I acknowledged more than there really was to confess.[22]

To read Freud is to witness the waning of humanism. Unmasked as a creature motivated by desires which escape the rule of consciousness, Man loses 'his' place at the centre of things. Precisely because it 'takes as its point of departure the impression ... that consciousness may be, not the most universal attribute of mental processes, but only a particular fraction of them',[23] psychoanalysis demands a rethinking of what it means to be human:

> In the course of centuries, the *naïve* self-love of men [sic] has had to submit to two major blows at the hands of science. The first was when they learnt that our earth was not the centre of the universe but only a tiny fragment of a cosmic system of scarcely imaginable vastness. This is associated in our minds with the name of Copernicus, though something similar had already been asserted by Alexandrian science. The second blow fell when biological research destroyed man's supposedly privileged place in creation and proved his descent from the animal kingdom and his ineradicable animal nature. This revaluation has been accomplished in our own days by Darwin, Wallace and their predecessors, though not without the most violent contemporary oppos-

ition. But human megalomania will have suffered its third and most wounding blow from the psychological research of the present time which seeks to prove to the ego that it is not even master in its own house, but must content itself with scanty information of what is going on unconsciously in its mind.[24]

The assault continued in the second half of the twentieth century when Jacques Lacan proposed a 'return to Freud' which would end the tendency of post-Freudian psychoanalysis – principally in the form of ego psychology – to regress towards humanism. This use of Freud to shore up the subject of consciousness was founded, Lacan argued, upon a fundamental misreading. I think that it is possible to interpret the whole of Lacan's work as a tirade against the subject of humanism. As early as 1954, in the first of his annual public seminars, he had clearly identified humanism as one of his principal targets, insisting that an interrogation of the transparent 'I' affirmed by figures like Descartes must lie at the heart of psychoanalytic enquiry: 'What is it to say *I*? ... One must start here'.[25] And this is also where the English translation of *Ecrits* begins, declaring on its opening page that the 'conception of the mirror stage ... is an experience that leads us to oppose any philosophy directly issuing from the *Cogito*'.[26] After Freud, Lacan went on to insist, 'the very centre of the human being was no longer to be found at the place assigned to it by a whole humanist tradition',[27] for the theory of the unconscious precipitated a 'Copernican revolution' in which the very understanding of what it means to be human 'change[d] perspective'.[28]

In the brief afterword to 'The Subversion of the Subject and the Dialectic of Desire in the Freudian Unconscious', Lacan wryly concurs with the accusation that his work is 'a-human' in approach.[29] It was not surprising, therefore, that he found himself – along with theorists like Louis Althusser and Michel Foucault – at the centre of the anti-humanist resistance movement which sought to issue, in the mid-twentieth century, 'a warrant for the death of Man'.[30] If, the anti-humanists argued, 'we' accept humanism's claim that 'we' are naturally inclined to think, organise and act in certain ways, it is difficult to believe that human society and behaviour could ever be other than they are now. Humanism was therefore to be opposed if radical change, the thinking of difference, was to become a possibility. The future would begin with the end of Man.

Meanwhile, in a galaxy far, far away, popular culture was also narrating the demise of humanism. Although a good deal more than geography separates the Left Bank from Los Angeles, it seems to me that the latter was not so distant in one respect, for while Lacan was holding court in Paris, productions such as *Invasion of the Body Snatchers, Them!, War of the Worlds,* and *The Blob* were emerging from

the Hollywood studios. In these science-fiction films – as in their literary counterparts – Man faced a threat from an inhuman other: 'his'
position at the centre of things was at risk. 'They' were ready to take
over, to subject 'us' to 'their' rule. Debate about the end of humanism,
in other words, was not the exclusive property of critical theory: it per-
vaded everyday life.

There was, of course, one fundamental difference between Paris and
Hollywood: whereas the intellectuals were celebrating the demise,
popular culture was committed to a defence of humanism (the aliens
were always defeated, frequently by a uniquely 'human' quality). Man,
the films insisted, would survive: this was destiny, the law of nature. In
making the end of humanism a central concern, however, these narratives tacitly suggested that something was awry. Why defend Man if 'his'
position at the centre of things is inevitable? What could possibly have
motivated such a compulsion? I want to suggest that, in obsessively
warding off an anxiety about the loss of human sovereignty, the films,
like poor Freud explaining himself to his wife, revealed considerably
more than they desired. Humanism was in trouble: Hollywood knew
this but took refuge in denial. To borrow a paradox from Jean-François
Lyotard, the cinema depicted Man dying in abundance, passing away
from prosperity, croaking from health.[31] And yet, although they shared a
common concern with the end of human sovereignty, theory and mass
culture were kept generically apart. When they eventually met, however,
posthumanism was born.

In a perceptive essay on the work of Donna Haraway and Jean
Baudrillard, both of whom are represented in this volume (essays
10 and 7), Istvan Csicsery-Ronay, Jr has noted that, although 'the
trends of their arguments differ greatly', both theorists have 'drawn
central concepts from the thesaurus of [science-fiction] imagery'.[32]
Haraway approaches the crisis in humanism through the cyborg, a
figure which, despite being popularised by science fiction, was originally the child of hard science (the neologism, a contraction of *cybernetic
organism*, was coined in 1960 by two scientists who saw the future of
extraterrestrial exploration in the technological modification of the
human body[33]). Baudrillard, meanwhile, proposes that life in a technological society transforms the autonomous Cartesian subject into a
figure resembling the Boy in the Bubble who depends upon machines
for everything, including survival. Reality has caught up with what
was once merely fantastic: futures past are here and now. The 'good
old imaginary of science fiction', as Baudrillard put it in another essay,
'is dead and ... something else is in the process of emerging (not only
in fiction but in theory as well)'.[34] 'We' have reached a point where, as
Csicsery-Ronay observes, the boundary between theory and fiction has
been breached beyond repair. The one space has invaded the other,

precipitating a change of style and mode of address. 'We' are witnessing the writing of what Maurice Blanchot has termed 'fictive theory'.[35] This is what it means to approach posthumanism. Of course, not all the posthumanist critics represented in this volume produce 'fictive theories'; there is, however, a general commitment to fiction (and I use the term in the broadest sense). This is no coincidence. What the contributors seem to recognise as they map posthumanism is that the crisis in humanism is happening *everywhere*. Although it continues to be debated by critical theorists, the reign of Man is simultaneously being called into question by literature, politics, cinema, anthropology, feminism, and technology.[36] These attacks are connected, part of the circuit of posthumanism.

In this respect, posthumanism inherits something of its 'post-' from poststructuralism, a philosophical movement that emerged in the 1960s with the work of Jacques Derrida. Although Derrida was writing at the same time and in the same city as Lacan, Foucault, and Althusser, his approach was somewhat different. While the anti-humanists were declaring a departure from the legacy of humanism, Derrida was patiently pointing out the difficulties of making such a break. Precisely because Western philosophy is steeped in humanist assumptions, he observed, the end of Man is bound to be written in the language of Man.[37] Each 'transgressive gesture re-encloses us'[38] because every such gesture will have been unconsciously choreographed by humanism. There is no pure outside to which 'we' can leap. To oppose humanism by claiming to have left it behind is to overlook the very way that opposition is articulated.

It does not follow, however, that poststructuralism is content to confirm the status quo, for Derrida's work repeatedly shows how systems are always self-contradictory, forever deconstructing themselves *from within*:

> The movements of deconstruction do not destroy structures from the outside. They are not possible and effective, nor can they take accurate aim, except by inhabiting those structures. Inhabiting them *in a certain way*, because one always inhabits, and all the more when one does not suspect it.[39]

Derrida's work permits a rethinking of the anti-humanist position. An approach informed by poststructuralism testifies to an endless opposition from within the traditional account of what it means to be human. Humanism never manages to constitute itself; it forever rewrites itself as posthumanism. This movement is always happening: humanism cannot escape its 'post-'. It seems to me that this is exactly what the posthumanist critics represented in the present volume realise. Wherever they look, they witness Man breathing 'himself' to death, raising himself to ruins. Posthumanism is out there, and *Posthumanism* announces this.

III

While this volume is intended to be an introduction to the subject of posthumanism, it does not claim to know once and for all what is at stake. Not all of the authors use the term to mean the same thing, if they use it at all. Something, however, links the writers represented here, and this is a refusal to take humanism for granted. It does not follow that the thirteen contributors form a happy family of posthumans. I have not selected texts with a view to a coherent and convenient (syn)thesis; my guiding principle was always to preserve difference, to leave the subject of posthumanism open both to question and to what is to come. The face and future of posthumanism are, as N. Katherine Hayles recognises, uncertain:[40] the prefix does not pre-fix. What matters, rather, is that thought keeps moving in the name of a beyond, in the shadow of the unknown, in the fault-lines of the 'post-'. A character in Douglas Coupland's collection of short stories, *Polaroids from the Dead*, sees this with perfect clarity:

We had a late dinner with my friend James, one of the smartest people I know. We discussed the notion of 'being real' with him – and of being 'hyper-real' and 'post-human' and I don't think we arrived at any definite answer, but it's important to know people who think about these things.[41]

2

The Great Family of Man

Roland Barthes

A big exhibition of photographs has been held in Paris, the aim of which was to show the universality of human actions in the daily life of all the countries of the world: birth, death, work, knowledge, play, always impose the same types of behaviour; there is a family of Man.

The Family of Man, such at any rate was the original title of the exhibition which came here from the United States. The French have translated it as: *The Great Family of Man*. So what could originally pass for a phrase belonging to zoology, keeping only the similarity in behaviour, the unity of a species, is here amply moralised and sentimentalised. We are at the outset directed to this ambiguous myth of the human 'community', which serves as an alibi to a large part of our humanism.

This myth functions in two stages: first the difference between human morphologies is asserted, exoticism is insistently stressed, the infinite variations of the species, the diversity in skins, skulls and customs are made manifest, the image of Babel is complacently projected over that of the world. Then, from this pluralism, a type of unity is magically produced: man is born, works, laughs and dies everywhere in the same way; and if there still remains in these actions some ethnic peculiarity, at least one hints that there is underlying each one an identical 'nature', that their diversity is only formal and does not belie the existence of a common mould. Of course this means postulating a human essence, and here is God re-introduced into our Exhibition: the diversity of men proclaims his power, his richness; the unity of their gestures demonstrates his will. This is what the introductory leaflet confides to us when it states, by the pen of M. André Chamson, that *'this look over the human condition must somewhat resemble the benevolent gaze of God on our absurd and sublime ant-hill'*. The pietistic intention is underlined by the quotations which accompany each chapter of the Exhibition: these quotations often are 'primitive' proverbs or verses from the Old Testament. They all define an eternal wisdom, a class of assertions which escape History: *'The Earth is a Mother who never dies, Eat bread and salt and speak the truth, etc.'* This is the reign of gnomic truths, the meeting of all the ages of humanity at the most neutral point of their nature, the point where the obviousness of the truism has no longer any value except in the realm of a purely

11

'poetic' language. Everything here, the content and appeal of the pictures, the discourse which justifies them, aims to suppress the determining weight of History: we are held back at the surface of an identity, prevented precisely by sentimentality from penetrating into this ulterior zone of human behaviour where historical alienation introduces some 'differences' which we shall here quite simply call 'injustices'.

This myth of the human 'condition' rests on a very old mystification, which always consists in placing Nature at the bottom of History. Any classic humanism postulates that in scratching the history of men a little, the relativity of their institutions or the superficial diversity of their skins (but why not ask the parents of Emmet Till, the young Negro assassinated by the Whites what *they* think of *The Great Family of Man*?), one very quickly reaches the solid rock of a universal human nature. Progressive humanism, on the contrary, must always remember to reverse the terms of this very old imposture, constantly to scour nature, its 'laws' and its 'limits' in order to discover History there, and at last to establish Nature itself as historical.

Examples? Here they are: those of our Exhibition. Birth, death? Yes, these are facts of nature, universal facts. But if one removes History from them, there is nothing more to be said about them; any comment about them becomes purely tautological. The failure of photography seems to me to be flagrant in this connection: to reproduce death or birth tells us, literally, nothing. For these natural facts to gain access to a true language, they must be inserted into a category of knowledge which means postulating that one can transform them, and precisely subject their naturalness to our human criticism. For however universal, they are the signs of an historical writing. True, children are *always* born: but in the whole mass of the human problem, what does the 'essence' of this process matter to us, compared to its modes which, as for them, are perfectly historical? Whether or not the child is born with ease or difficulty, whether or not his birth causes suffering to his mother, whether or not he is threatened by a high mortality rate, whether or not such and such a type of future is open to him: this is what your Exhibitions should be telling people, instead of an eternal lyricism of birth. The same goes for death: must we really celebrate its essence once more, and thus risk forgetting that there is still so much we can do to fight it? It is this very young, far too young power that we must exalt, and not the sterile identity of 'natural' death.

And what can be said about work, which the Exhibition places among great universal facts, putting it on the same plane as birth and death, as if it was quite evident that it belongs to the same order of fate? That work is an age-old fact does not in the least prevent it from remaining a perfectly historical fact. Firstly, and evidently, because of its modes, its motivations, its ends and its benefits, which matter to such an extent that it will never be fair to confuse in a purely gestural identity the colonial and the Western worker (let us also ask the North African workers of the Goutte d'Or district in Paris what they think of *The Great Family of Man*). Secondly, because of the very differences in its inevitability: we know very well that work is 'natural' just as long as it is 'profitable', and that in modifying the inevitability of the profit, we shall perhaps one day modify the inevitability of labour. It is this entirely historified work which we should be told about, instead of an eternal aesthetics of laborious gestures.

So that I rather fear that the final justification of all this Adamism is to give to the immobility of the world the alibi of a 'wisdom' and a 'lyricism' which only make the gestures of man look eternal the better to defuse them.

3
The Instinct
Rosalind Coward

For every form of sexual arrangement approved by this society, there's an explanation in terms of natural instincts. Women tend to look after children, so there's evidence of a maternal instinct. Heterosexuality is the dominant form of sexual behaviour; that's the natural bond because animals mate. The nuclear family is the approved social unit, and the pairing and parental bond between animals proves that's natural. Instinct is the knee-jerk reflex with which this society responds to any discussion of sexual arrangements. Instinct explains why we do what we do. Instinct also explains why we shouldn't do what some people do – an elastic concept.

Instinct is a term which seems to be particularly useful for explaining away conventional forms of 'male' and 'female' behaviour. Instinct explains male aggression and instinct explains female passivity and the desire to nurture others. One rationale of instinct dominates all these ideas about male and female behaviour, parenting and so on. This is the rationale of reproduction, and it runs thus: the central purpose of human life is to reproduce itself but men and women have different relations to this aim, and this explains the difference between male and female behaviour. Men would do it with whomever and whatever, strewing their seed around as widely as possible, in the hope that some will hit home. This makes men naturally promiscuous and naturally aggressive, competing as they do with other men. Women, however, are more fussy; women select their partners either as good providers or as good genetic stock, and then set about securing these partners. Once trapped in marriage, however, men acquire a taste for it, and especially a commitment to their offspring.

But when it comes to it, just how useful are these arguments about natural instincts – so prevalent, so plastic, so unexplained? At one level, such arguments are very comforting. After all, if the way you are living is 'natural', you can feel better about it. However difficult things may be in your life, you can explain it all away. 'It's natural. It can't be helped'. But however comforting, these ideas obscure more than they explain. Take the defence of male aggression, where the term instinct is used to explain the curious enmeshing of violence and sex which sometimes characterises some aspects of male sexuality in this society.

In 1977, Mr Nicholas Fairburn, who was then Solicitor General for Scotland, described rape as a 'crime which I have never been forced to commit'. He went on, 'MPs would do well to remember that rape involves an activity which is normal. It is part of the business of men and women that they hunt and be hunted and say 'yes' and 'no' and mean the opposite. If it is misinterpreted let a jury decide whether it was reasonable to misinterpret it' (quoted in the *Guardian*, 22 January 1982). Natural behaviour here is a world of male predators, aggressive animals who hunt the female of the species. The female is passive and coy; at first she will say no but secretly she may want the advances to continue – how else could she have her desires and stay 'modest'? So by this rationale rape is merely a normal pursuit of sex where sometimes the female signals are misread. Fairburn's definition of normal sex might well be rape with consent. The usual legal definition of rape is the opposite: rape is sex without consent. Both views share certain assumptions about sexual relations: men's role in sex is to initiate and (sometimes) to wait for permission to proceed. Women's role is to give the go-ahead or withhold it.

The idea that female sexuality works as a lure and a response to male predatory and probing sexuality is quite patently an ideology belonging to a particular historical epoch. The ideology has the effect of endorsing the mixture of violence and sex which characterises some aspects of masculine behaviour in contemporary society. And the ideology also endorses a definite view of female passivity: women's sexuality is limited to making a choice between yes and no. In some areas of the media we can see such views actively promoted. For instance, in some forms of tabloid journalism, it is customary to refer to women as 'birds' or sex kittens (usually a reference which goes beside a 'topless' picture). Men, however, accrue such epithets as 'the office wolf'. And those 'sex offenders', in whom such newspapers are excessively interested, are referred to as 'monsters' and 'fiends': 'A savage sex monster was being hunted last night after raping an eight-year-old girl inside her school' (*Sun*, 22 May 1981). Such language promotes a view of the sexes as two species; the strong species – dogs and wolves – pursue the weak – birds and kittens. When the customary limits are overstepped, men become monsters, gone too far in their natural pursuits.

There is in fact nothing in nature which permits a reading of male aggression as inevitable, female passivity and weakness as eternal. Certainly, animals mate, animals breed and animals sometimes fight (often male animals, but not always). But it is an illegitimate leap of thought to deduce that the same *meanings* can be derived from the same acts in both the human and animal worlds.

There can be no way in which aggression, dominance, mating and so on have the same place within human society as they do in animal

society. There are crucial differences between human and animal societies; in human societies divisions between the sexes and between groups
have enmeshed with specifically *human* history, where dominance and
power are closely associated with the control of resources and therefore
imply that other members of society are placed in 'subordinate' and
weak positions.

As far as can be deduced, animals have not yet instituted a division
of labour geared towards the production of surplus resources for the
future. As a result, there's no evidence that certain groups either create
or appropriate a surplus of resources and then control the distribution
of these resources for future profit. Indeed, as far as the evidence goes,
immediate survival is the name of the game. Complex societies,
complex ecologies exist, but food is consumed as it appears or at most
stored for the ensuring winter. As far as we know, when squirrels bury
acorns, they do not have in mind harvesting from the resulting trees in
twenty years' time, and selling acorns at vastly inflated prices to the
hedgehogs.

Some human societies, though not all, do just this.[1] Food and goods
are produced and accumulated not to ensure immediate survival but to
be used for exchange for other goods. And in some societies, this process
of exchange is linked to the creation of profit – profit from the control of
surplus goods and resources. In these societies, the creation of profit has
also developed linked to unequal distribution of the resources: one
group controls how the surplus is distributed, and in short has power
over other groups.

In animal society there's a startling absence of complex accumulation
and unequal distribution of resources. Of course, scientists, not to be
daunted by the shocking absence of bourgeois traits among animals,
have found what they regard as a solution. 'Genes', they say, are every
animal's natural property. Thus all mating, parenting and territorial
behaviour is seen as a sort of economic calculation for the future. Both
animals and humans share this common concern – to perpetuate their
genes.

Whatever animals are up to when they mate, it is ridiculous to establish a logical connection between the activities of the selfish gene and a
complex society where control of the surplus produces certain groups in
dominance and others in positions of inferiority.[2] Genes can go on
forever without a bean in their pocket. But in some human societies, the
activity of reproduction has been harnessed to the control of property. In
some hierarchical societies, property is appropriated and controlled, and
transmitted to the future via biological families, thus ensuring the reproduction of inequalities in the future. In such societies, women's reproductive capacities are linked to one particular family. Thus some
hierarchies are based on reproductive relationship (kinship relations or

what we call family relations); certain groups appropriate and control the surplus to their own advantage, and against the interests of other members of that society.

The history of this process of accumulation is none other than the specific history of *property* relations. In some cases, like our own, it has led to the capitalist mode of production. This history of property relations is not the same as territoriality, mating and male aggression. The history of property relations belongs to human history not as an inevitable aspect of humanity but as a chance by-product whose outcome has been the inequitable control of resources. Now in the animal world some animals do suffer or get destroyed – a harsh winter might wipe out the wren population; one species may find its access to a watering hole limited by the aggression of another; there may be a shortage of food due to natural failure. But as far as anyone can tell animals do not have an inequitable distribution of available resources within species, or a system of biological reproduction ensuring that the inequitable distribution as well as the genes continue in perpetuity.

Now the point of this argument is to demonstrate that aggression, dominance and power in our society do not occur as in nature. They occur in a society based on divisions and on divisions which have overwhelming consequences for what a person's position in that society will be. Among others, the division between men and women has fatal consequences for the *social* position of those sexes. For in the end, men and women do have an unequal relation to the distribution of resources. The issue has been horrendously confused because virtually all political arguments – from the left and the right alike – insist on seeing men and women as one. We are led to believe that because men and women marry, they therefore make up one family, with identical access to social resources. But the truth is that, whatever the class, men and women do have a different relation to social resources. Because of inequalities in the job market, because of how care for children and the elderly is arranged, and because of the way the state treats women, women rarely have the same relation to resources as men. And in a hierarchical society, this separation of groups from the control of resources is not a neutral event. Groups separated from the means of production are viewed as inferior by those in control. We're not in the same situation as animals. Male animals may fight; dominant males may sit on their dung heaps. But it is illegitimate to assume that the female of the species is therefore 'inferior', 'weaker', 'subordinate'. Indeed, this whole language of inferiority, weakness, subordination, dominance and power is a *human* language. It arises from certain societies where some groups have been disadvantaged to the benefit of others.

In human society, sexuality has become entangled in this separation
of groups into 'privileged', 'dominant' and 'disadvantaged' or 'weak'.
Because the relations between the sexes are unequal, sexual relations
are imbued with meanings about dominance and subordination. What
we encounter in rape, then, has nothing to do with the rituals of mating
according to seasonal patterns, as in the animal world. It may well be a
ritual but it is a ritual connected more with symbolic statements than
with seasonal activities. As far as the evidence goes, rape seems to be
tied up with the assertion of power – that's why it is always difficult to
draw a distinction between violence against women, sexual violence
and violently imposed sexual intercourse (rape). Quite often, they have
the same meanings – the humiliation of one group. When men feel
compelled to act aggressively towards women, they may well be driven
by the internal psychic expression of external circumstances. Ideologies
lead men to believe that women are inferior, yet that women are desirable. Ideologies also tell men (as they told Nicholas Fairburn) that
normal sex means men take the initiative. It isn't altogether surprising,
given the prevalence of such beliefs, that rape should appear in this
society as a way of satisfying both the desire to dominate and the
desire to have sex.

Far from being a natural expression of male and female sexual behaviour, male aggression is more likely to be the ritualistic enactment of cultural meanings about sex. And this is true of just about every
manifestation of sexual activity. Sex in human society is never instinctual; sex is always an activity wrapped in cultural meanings, cultural
prescriptions, and cultural constraints.

Even the 'normal' pairing of men and women – apparently the most
natural of human activities – is infused with cultural meanings. Of
course men and women have sex, but 'mating and reproduction' neither
exhausts the kinds of sexual activity which are possible and enjoyable,
nor does it tell us anything about the variety of meanings attached to
'doing it' by different cultures or indeed individuals. Indeed, only by dis-
torting or ignoring the evidence do some people assert the universality
and naturalness of the marriage bond. Mrs Thatcher's adviser on the
family concluded his book on the subject with a rhetorical flourish,
aimed at proving the naturalness of the married bond: 'Marriage and the
family make other experiences, both pleasant and unpleasant, seem a
little tame and bloodless. And it is difficult to resist the conclusion that a
way of living which is both so intense and so enduring must somehow
come naturally to us, that it is part of being human' (Ferdinand Mount,
The Subversive Family).

Such rhetorical appeals about the enduring bond of the natural family
are useful only as ways of avoiding serious scholarship on the subject of
sex and the family. They characterise the manipulation of the question of

sex and the family for political ends, where material is selected and distorted according to overall political aims. There are impressive distortions at work which can represent a narrow bond between men and women as the universal and natural, instinctual form.

To make this assertion rounds all humans up into one happy family, the animal family. But to do so shows a breathtaking disregard first for the diversity of family life within our own culture, and secondly for the different meanings attached to marriage in other cultures.[3]

Only in our culture, for instance, is the bond between a man and a woman expected to provide all emotional and material support. In other cultures, a marriage ceremony may well be far more important for the relationship which it creates between the kin of the man and woman rather than for the bond itself. The heterosexual bond tends to be the basis for the alliances between groups, presumably because this bond implies procreation and most societies are interested in this. But the implications of this bond are by no means the same from culture to culture, nor is the strictness with which it is enforced.

Even that biological act – reproduction – which seems so unavoidable, so enduring, is a biological act which may be interpreted differently according to cultures and different individuals. Women's natural instinct for reproduction, the maternal instinct, is supposed to be the base line of all her behaviour, her ultimate *raison d'être*. Indeed, arguments about the natural instinct seem to reach a climax around the designation of women as the reproductive sex, and therefore the caring and nurturing sex. It is clear that women's anatomy makes her the childbearing sex; it is clear also that most women experience extraordinarily powerful feelings towards their children. But it is also clear that the notion of the reproductive instinct has again acted as a barrier to understanding sexual relations, rather than as a source of illumination.

There seems to be an enormous problem about the conventional designation of women as the reproductive sex. The fact that women's bodies are geared up for reproduction is taken as the fundamental explanation for women's sexual behaviour. These natural phenomena are supposed to explain everything about women – why we stay at home, why we don't get promoted, why we don't get well paid, why we cook and clean. But when it comes to sexuality, which sex really is the reproductive sex? Men or women? When it comes to *sexuality*, men not women are the reproductive sex. There are only about four days in a month when sex with men might result in conception for women. For the rest of the time, women are capable of a multiple orgasmic sexuality which – in theory at least – produces nothing but pleasure. Even on a fertile day, women's orgasm is not tied to reproduction. A woman could conceive without orgasm; sexual pleasure is irrelevant to the reproductive function. Men's sexuality on the other hand is unavoidably reproductive. Men can't even masturbate without some visible evidence of their reproductive capacity. Orgasm and reproduction are truly synonymous for men.

I can't help but suspect a case of projection here. Women are labelled the reproductive sex and stigmatised thus by society. Designated the reproductive sex, we also become the sex which has to assume the full responsibility for reproduction. Women must take responsibility for contraception; women must also take primary responsibility for child care – all because of our reproductive sexuality. But the equation made between women's ability to give birth, women's sexual behaviour and women's responsibility for child care is not a necessary equation, derived from nature. The equation has emerged through the history of this society and has been projected on to nature.

Recent changes in the position of women have allowed the apparently indissoluble link between women and reproduction to become at least slightly attenuated. Widespread contraception is one change, but general shifts in attitude and sexual practice are probably more important. Both have allowed heterosexual women to be explicit about a sexuality autonomous from reproduction, an autonomy which previously was only possible for lesbians. For those with children, or wanting children, or for those who want to forgo the experience, it is now much easier to talk in terms of what children mean or will mean in their lives.

Instead of a blanket term – the maternal instinct – dumped over the whole area of childbirth, childbirth can now be explored as a biological event the meaning of which is very different from different individuals, and the consequences of which are enormous.

'Don't ever believe anyone if they say having children won't change your life. It does. I'm not saying I regretted having children but some of it is very difficult. It's the problem of having people totally dependent on you, who are always around, dying for you to be interested in them, involving you in their quarrels, following you to the toilet, never giving you a moment's peace. In some ways, I don't think I'm a very good mother in the conventional sense – my husband's a lot more maternal.' 'Having children is all the joy and the problems of suddenly having another person in your life, whose own survival depends on your every move.' 'I get on quite well with children but I just can't imagine having one of my own. I can't imagine disrupting my life like that.' 'It's been very difficult to combine a career with children, I've had to make sacrifices. Once you've been away from work for a bit, your man's career begins to take precedence. We had exactly the same qualifications from college – that's where we met. Now I'm moving where his job takes him and trying to fit in. In fact I haven't been able to find a job. There's not much work here and, you know, in spite of all they say, employers aren't keen on women with young children. I'm very happy with my children. I love them. In many ways, it's much more rewarding than paid work. But sometimes I despair. I feel as if I've lost touch with the world.' 'I just don't want children. I'm put off by what that relationship of dependency does to you. I've seen to many people screwed up by awful relationships with their parents – so much guilt and obligation. I want to have other kinds of loving relationships.'

Even the positive, overwhelming desire to have children isn't a uniform desire. There are so many different *reasons* why women want children:

'I had not longed for children, thought about the subject much or discussed it with my partner. A very indulged cat was the only evidence that the maternal instinct might be waiting to take the world by surprise. There is no doubt that some instinct took over and was sufficiently strong to overcome the grave doubts I had about life with children ... In retrospect I also wanted to repay my parents for all they gave me as a child – the only way to do this seemed to be to give to my own children in some way.' 'I still feel little natural attraction towards other people's children, but am obviously deeply involved with my own. I simply obeyed an instinct by having them, and they (not the lifestyle they have dictated!) have exceeded my expectation.'

That instinct or urge to have children seems to have so many different explanations: some speak of a sense that a child might fill up a feeling of loneliness, some of a sensual desire for a child's body close to their own, some of a desire just to have the experience, some of a desire for a 'normal' family, some of a sense that having children has just got to be better than being pushed around in rotten low-paid jobs, and some of the desire to have a particular person's child. All these different *meanings* are often referred to as an instinct. But the variety of reasons and consequences and the variety of circumstances in which a child could be born are a sure indication that the same anatomical events may have vastly different meanings in the lives of individuals. The differences between the desires and consequences surrounding pregnancy are like a microcosm of the differences between cultures. There are no simple, unilateral interpretations of biological acts.

People have bodies, anatomies, and certain anatomical capacities. But our bodies are not our destinies. Around the sensations of the body, the activities of reproduction and sex, are a whole series of complicated emotions and meanings. Some come from general cultural definitions of sexuality, but some come from our own personal histories. If humans are animals, it isn't stretching credibility to insist that humans are also natural, therefore anything they do is natural. Things are natural because they happen to us, but beyond that, there are drastic differences between how societies organise them, what they mean in our lives and how we feel about those events.

4

The Wretched of the Earth

Frantz Fanon

Come, then, comrades; it would be as well to decide at once to change our ways. We must shake off the heavy darkness in which we were plunged, and leave it behind. The new day which is already at hand must find us firm, prudent and resolute.

We must leave our dreams and abandon our old beliefs and friendships of the time before life began. Let us waste no time in sterile litanies and nauseating mimicry. Leave this Europe where they are never done talking of Man, yet murder men everywhere they find them, at the corner of every one of their own streets, in all the corners of the globe. For centuries they have stifled almost the whole of humanity in the name of a so-called spiritual experience. Look at them today swaying between atomic and spiritual disintegration.

And yet it may be said that Europe has been successful in as much as everything that she has attempted has succeeded.

Europe undertook the leadership of the world with ardour, cynicism and violence. Look at how the shadow of her palaces stretches out ever farther! Every one of her movements has burst the bounds of space and thought. Europe has declined all humility and all modesty; but she has also set her face against all solicitude and all tenderness.

She has only shown herself parsimonious and niggardly where men are concerned; it is only men that she has killed and devoured.

So, my brothers, how is it that we do not understand that we have better things to do than to follow that same Europe?

That same Europe where they were never done talking of Man, and where they never stopped proclaiming that they were only anxious for the welfare of Man: today we know with what sufferings humanity has paid for every one of their triumphs of the mind.

Come, then, comrades, the European game has finally ended; we must find something different. We today can do everything, so long as we do not imitate Europe, so long as we are not obsessed by the desire to catch up with Europe.

Europe now lives at such a mad, reckless pace that she has shaken off all guidance and all reason, and she is running headlong into the abyss; we would do well to avoid it with all possible speed.

Yet it is very true that we need a model, and that we want blueprints and examples. For many among us the European model is the most inspiring. We have therefore seen [...] to what mortifying set-backs such an imitation has led us. European achievements, European techniques and the European style ought no longer to tempt us and to throw us off our balance.

When I search for Man in the technique and the style of Europe, I see only a succession of negations of man, and an avalanche of murders.

The human condition, plans for mankind and collaboration between men in those tasks which increase the sum total of humanity are new problems, which demand true inventions.

Let us decide not to imitate Europe; let us combine our muscles and our brains in a new direction. Let us try to create the whole man, whom Europe has been incapable of bringing to triumphant birth.

Two centuries ago, a former European colony decided to catch up with Europe. It succeeded so well that the United States of America became a monster, in which the taints, the sickness and the inhumanity of Europe have grown to appalling dimensions.

Comrades, have we not other work to do than to create a third Europe? The West saw itself as a spiritual adventure. It is in the name of the spirit, in the name of the spirit of Europe, that Europe has made her encroachments, that she has justified her crimes and legitimised the slavery in which she holds four-fifths of humanity.

Yes, the European spirit has strange roots. All European thought has unfolded in places which were increasingly more deserted and more encircled by precipices; and thus it was that the custom grew up in those places of very seldom meeting man.

A permanent dialogue with oneself and an increasingly obscene narcissism never ceased to prepare the way for a half delirious state, where intellectual work became suffering and the reality was not at all that of a living man, working and creating himself, but rather words, different combinations of words, and the tensions springing from the meanings contained in words. Yet some Europeans were found to urge the European workers to shatter this narcissism and to break with this unreality.

But in general the workers of Europe have not replied to these calls; for the workers believe, too, that they are part of the prodigious adventure of the European spirit.

All the elements of a solution to the great problems of humanity have, at different times, existed in European thought. But Europeans have not carried out in practice the mission which fell to them, which consisted of bringing their whole weight to bear violently upon these elements, of modifying their arrangement and their nature, of changing them and, finally, of bringing the problem of mankind to an infinitely higher plane.

Today, we are present at the stasis of Europe. Comrades, let us flee from this motionless movement where gradually dialectic is changing into the logic of equilibrium. Let us reconsider the question of mankind. Let us reconsider the question of cerebral reality and of the cerebral mass of all humanity, whose connexions must be increased, whose channels must be diversified and whose messages must be re-humanised.

Come, brothers, we have far too much work to do for us to play the game of rear-guard. Europe has done what she set out to do and on the whole she has done it well; let us stop blaming her, but let us say to her firmly that she should not make such a song and dance about it. We have no more to fear; so let us stop envying her.

The Third World today faces Europe like a colossal mass whose aim should be to try to resolve the problems to which Europe has not been able to find the answers.

But let us be clear: what matters is to stop talking about output, and intensification, and the rhythm of work.

No, there is no question of a return to Nature. It is simply a very concrete question of not dragging men towards mutilation, of not imposing upon the brain rhythms which very quickly obliterate it and wreck it. The pretext of catching up must not be used to push man around, to tear him away from himself or from his privacy, to break and kill him.

No, we do not want to catch up with anyone. What we want to do is to go forward all the time, night and day, in the company of Man, in the company of all men. The caravan should not be stretched out, for in that case each line will hardly see those who precede it; and men who no longer recognise each other meet less and less together, and talk to each other less and less.

It is a question of the Third World starting a new history of Man, a history which will have regard to the sometimes prodigious theses which Europe has put forward, but which will also not forget Europe's crimes, of which the most horrible was committed in the heart of man, and consisted of the pathological tearing apart of his functions and the crumbling away of his unity. And in the framework of the collectivity there were the differentiations, the stratification and the bloodthirsty tensions fed by classes; and finally, on the immense scale of humanity, there were racial hatreds, slavery, exploitation and above all the bloodless genocide which consisted in the setting aside of fifteen thousand millions of men.

So, comrades, let us not pay tribute to Europe by creating states, institutions and societies which draw their inspiration from her.

Humanity is waiting for something other from us than such an imitation, which would be almost an obscene caricature.

If we want to turn Africa into a new Europe, and America into a new Europe, then let us leave the destiny of our countries to Europeans. They will know how to do it better than the most gifted among us.

But if we want humanity to advance a step farther, if we want to bring it up to a different level than that which Europe has shown it, then we must invent and we must make discoveries.

If we wish to live up to our peoples' expectations, we must seek the response elsewhere than in Europe.

Moreover, if we wish to reply to the expectations of the people of Europe, it is no good sending them back a reflection, even an ideal reflection, of their society and their thought with which from time to time they feel immeasurably sickened.

For Europe, for ourselves and for humanity, comrades, we must turn over a new leaf, we must work out new concepts, and try to set afoot a new man.

5

The Order of Things: An Archaeology of the Human Sciences

Michel Foucault

In our day, and once again Nietzsche indicated the turning-point from a long way off, it is not so much the absence or the death of God that is affirmed as the end of man (that narrow, imperceptible displacement, that recession in the form of identity, which are the reason why man's finitude has become his end); it becomes apparent, then, that the death of God and the last man are engaged in a contest with more than one round: is it not the last man who announces that he has killed God, thus situating his language, his thought, his laughter in the space of that already dead God, yet positing himself also as he who has killed God and whose existence includes the freedom and the decision of that murder? Thus, the last man is at the same time older and yet younger than the death of God; since he has killed God, it is he himself who must answer for his own finitude; but since it is in the death of God that he speaks, thinks, and exists, his murder itself is doomed to die; new gods, the same gods, are already swelling the future Ocean; man will disappear. Rather than the death of God – or, rather, in the wake of that death and in a profound correlation with it – what Nietzsche's thought heralds is the end of his murderer; it is the explosion of man's face in laughter, and the return of masks; it is the scattering of the profound stream of time by which he felt himself carried along and whose pressure he suspected in the very being of things; it is the identity of the Return of the Same with the absolute dispersion of man. Throughout the nineteenth century, the end of philosophy and the promise of an approaching culture were no doubt one and the same thing as the thought of finitude and the appearance of man in the field of knowledge; in our day, the fact that philosophy is still – and again – in the process of coming to an end, and the fact that in it perhaps, though even more outside and against it, in literature as well as in formal reflection, the question of language is being posed, prove no doubt that man is in the process of disappearing.

For the entire modern *episteme* – that which was formed towards the
end of the eighteenth century and still serves as the positive ground of
our knowledge, that which constituted man's particular mode of being
and the possibility of knowing him empirically – that entire *episteme* was
bound up with the disappearance of Discourse and its featureless reign,
with the shift of language towards objectivity, and with its reappearance
in multiple form. If this same language is now emerging with greater
and greater insistence in a unity that we ought to think but cannot as yet
do so, is this not the sign that the whole of this configuration is now
about to topple, and that man is in the process of perishing as the being
of language continues to shine ever brighter upon our horizon? Since
man was constituted at a time when language was doomed to dispersion, will he not be dispersed when language regains its unity? And if
that were true, would it not be an error – a profound error, since it could
hide from us what should now be thought – to interpret our actual experience as an application of the forms of language to the human order?
Ought we not rather to give up thinking of man, or, to be more strict, to
think of this disappearance of man – and the ground of possibility of all
the sciences of man – as closely as possible in correlation with our
concern with language? Ought we not to admit that, since language is
here once more, man will return to that serene non-existence in which he
was formerly maintained by the imperious unity of Discourse? Man had
been a figure occurring between two modes of language; or, rather, he
was constituted only when language, having been situated within representation and, as it were, dissolved in it, freed itself from that situation at the cost of its own fragmentation: man composed his own figure
in the interstices of that fragmented language. Of course, these are not
affirmations; they are at most questions to which it is not possible to
reply; they must be left in suspense, where they pose themselves, only
with the knowledge that the possibility of posing them may well open
the way to a future thought.

One thing in any case is certain: man is neither the oldest nor the most
constant problem that has been posed for human knowledge. Taking a
relatively short chronological sample within a restricted geographical
area – European culture since the sixteenth century – one can be certain
that man is a recent invention within it. It is not around him and his
secrets that knowledge prowled for so long in the darkness. In fact,
among all the mutations that have affected the knowledge of things and
their order, the knowledge of identities, differences, characters, equiva-
lences, words – in short, in the midst of all the episodes of that profound
history of the *Same* – only one, that which began a century and a half ago
and is now perhaps drawing to a close, has made it possible for the
figure of man to appear. And that appearance was not the liberation of

an old anxiety, the transition into luminous consciousness of an age-old concern, the entry into objectivity of something that had long remained trapped within beliefs and philosophies: it was the effect of a change in the fundamental arrangements of knowledge. As the archaeology of our thought easily shows, man is an invention of recent date. And one perhaps nearing its end.

If those arrangements were to disappear as they appeared, if some event of which we can at the moment do no more than sense the possibility – without knowing either what its form will be or what it promises – were to cause them to crumble, as the ground of Classical thought did, at the end of the eighteenth century, then one can certainly wager that man would be erased, like a face drawn in sand at the edge of the sea.

6

Marxism and Humanism

Louis Althusser

In 1845, Marx broke radically with every theory that based history and politics on an essence of man. This unique rupture contained three indissociable elements.

(1) The formation of a theory of history and politics based on radically new concepts: the concepts of social formation, productive forces, relations of production, superstructure, ideologies, determination in the last instance by the economy, specific determination of the other levels, etc.

(2) A radical critique of the *theoretical* pretensions of every philosophical humanism.

(3) The definition of humanism as an *ideology*.

This new conception is completely rigorous as well, but it is a new rigour: the essence criticised (2) is defined as an ideology (3), a category belonging to the new theory of society and history (1).

This rupture with every *philosophical* anthropology or humanism is no secondary detail; it is Marx's scientific discovery.

It means that Marx rejected the problematic of the earlier philosophy and adopted a new problematic in one and the same act. The earlier idealist ('bourgeois') philosophy depended in all its domains and arguments (its 'theory of knowledge', its conception of history, its political economy, its ethics, its aesthetics, etc.) on a problematic of *human nature* (or the essence of man). For centuries, this problematic had been transparency itself, and no one had thought of questioning it even in its internal modifications.

This problematic was neither vague nor loose; on the contrary, it was constituted by a coherent system of precise concepts tightly articulated together. When Marx confronted it, it implied the two complementary postulates he defined in the Sixth Thesis on Feuerbach:

(1) that there is a universal of man;

(2) that this essence is the attribute of *'each single individual'* who is its real subject.

These two postulates are complementary and indissociable. But their existence and their unity presuppose a whole empiricist-idealist world outlook. If the essence of man is to be a universal attribute, it is essential that *concrete subjects* exist as absolute givens; this implies an *empiricism of the subject*. If these empirical individuals are to be men, it is essential that each carries in himself the whole human essence, if not in fact, at least in principle; this implies an *idealism of the essence*. So empiricism of the subject implies idealism of the essence and vice versa. This relation can be inverted into its 'opposite' – empiricism of the concept/idealism of the subject. But the inversion respects the basic structure of the problematic, which remains fixed.

In this type-structure it is possible to recognise not only the principle of theories of society (from Hobbes to Rousseau), of political economy (from Petty to Ricardo), of ethics (from Descartes to Kant), but also the very principle of the (pre-Marxist) idealist and materialist 'theory of knowledge' (from Locke to Feuerbach, via Kant). The content of the human essence or of the empirical subjects may vary (as can be seen from Descartes to Feuerbach); the subject may change from empiricism to idealism (as can be seen from Locke to Kant): the terms presented and their relations only vary within the invariant type-structure which constitutes this very problematic: *an empiricism of the subject always corresponds to an idealism of the essence (or an empiricism of the essence to an idealism of the subject).*

By rejecting the essence of man as his theoretical basis, Marx rejected the whole of this organic system of postulates. He drove the philosophical categories of the *subject*, of *empiricism*, of the *ideal essence*, etc., from all the domains in which they had been supreme. Not only from political economy (rejection of the myth of *homo œconomicus*, that is, of the individual with definite faculties and needs as the *subject* of the classical economy); not just from history (rejection of social atomism and ethico-political idealism); not just from ethics (rejection of the Kantian ethical idea); but also from philosophy itself: for Marx's materialism excludes the empiricism of the subject (and its inverse: the transcendental subject) and the idealism of the concept (and its inverse: the empiricism of the concept).

This total theoretical revolution was only empowered to reject the old concepts because it replaced them by new concepts. In fact Marx established a new problematic, a new systematic way of asking questions of the world, new principles and a new method. This discovery is immediately contained in the theory of historical materialism, in which Marx did not only propose a new theory of the history of societies, but at the same time implicitly, but necessarily, a new 'philosophy', infinite in its implications. Thus, when Marx replaced the old couple individuals/human essence in the theory of history by new concepts (forces of production, relations of production, etc.), he was, in fact, simultaneously proposing a new conception of 'philosophy'. He replaced the old postulates (empiricism/idealism of the subject, empiricism/idealism of the essence) which were the basis not only for idealism but also for pre-Marxist materialism, by a historico-dialectical materialism of *praxis*: that is, by a theory of the different specific *levels* of *human practice* (economic practice, political practice, ideological practice, scientific practice) in their characteristic articulations, based on the specific articulations of the unity of human society. In a word, Marx substituted for the 'ideological' and universal concept of Feuerbachian 'practice' a concrete conception of the specific differences that enables us to situate each particular practice in the specific differences of the social structure.

So, to understand what was radically new in Marx's contribution, we must become aware not only of the novelty of the concepts of historical materialism, but also of the depth of the theoretical revolution they imply and inaugurate. On this condition it is possible to define humanism's status, and reject its *theoretical* pretensions while recognising its practical function as an ideology.

Strictly in respect to theory, therefore, one can and must speak openly of *Marx's theoretical anti-humanism*, and see in this *theoretical anti-humanism* the absolute (negative) precondition of the (positive) knowledge of the human world itself, and of its practical transformation. It is impossible to *know* anything about men except on the absolute precondition that the philosophical (theoretical) myth of man is reduced to ashes. So any thought that appeals to Marx for any kind of restoration of a theoretical anthropology or humanism is no more than ashes, *theoretically*. But in practice it could pile up a monument of pre-Marxist ideology that would weigh down on real history and threaten to lead it into blind alleys.

For the corollary of theoretical Marxist anti-humanism is the recognition and knowledge of humanism itself: as an *ideology*. Marx never fell into the idealist illusion of believing that the knowledge of an object might ultimately replace the object or dissipate its existence. Cartesians, knowing that the sun was two thousand leagues away, were astonished that this distance only looked like two hundred paces: they could not even find enough of God to fill in this gap. Marx never believed that a knowledge of the nature of *money* (a social relation) could destroy its *appearance*, its form of existence – a thing, for this appearance was its very being, as necessary as the existing mode of production.[1] Marx never believed that an ideology might be dissipated by a knowledge of it: for the knowledge of this ideology, as the knowledge of its conditions of possibility, of its structure, of its specific logic and of its practical role, within a given society, is simultaneously knowledge of the conditions of its necessity. So Marx's theoretical *anti-humanism* does not suppress anything in the historical *existence* of humanism. In the real world philoso-

phies of man are found after Marx as often as before, and today even
some Marxists are tempted to develop the themes of a new theoretical
humanism. Furthermore, Marx's theoretical anti-humanism, by relating
it to its conditions of existence, recognises a necessity for humanism as
an *ideology*, a conditional necessity. The recognition of this necessity is
not purely speculative. On it alone can Marxism base a policy in relation
to the existing ideological forms, of every kind: religion, ethics, art, philosophy, law – and in the very front rank, humanism. When (eventually)
a Marxist policy of humanist ideology, that is, a political attitude to
humanism, is achieved – a policy which may be either a rejection or a critique, or a use, or a support, or a development, or a humanist renewal of
contemporary forms of ideology in the *ethico-political* domain – this
policy will only have been possible on the absolute condition that it is
based on Marxist philosophy, and a precondition for this is theoretical
anti-humanism.

7

Prophylaxis and Virulence

Jean Baudrillard

The growing cerebrality of machines must logically be expected to occasion a technological purification of bodies. Inasmuch as bodies are less and less able to count on their own antibodies, they are more and more in need of protection from outside. An artificial sterilisation of all environments must compensate for faltering internal immunological defences. And if these are indeed faltering, it is because the irreversible process often referred to as progress tends to strip the human body and mind of their systems of initiative and defence, reassigning these functions to technical artifacts. Once dispossessed of their defences, human beings become eminently vulnerable to science and technology; dispossessed of their passions, they likewise become eminently vulnerable to psychology and its attendant therapies; similarly, too, once relieved of emotions and illnesses, they become eminently vulnerable to medicine.

Consider the 'Boy in the Bubble', surrounded, in his NASA-donated tent, by an atmospheric distillate of medical knowledge, protected from any conceivable infection by an artificial immune system, 'cuddled' by his mother through the glass, laughing and growing up in an extraterrestrial ambiance under the vigilant eye of science. Here we have the experimental version of the wolf-child, the 'wild child' raised by wolves. The parenting in this case, however, is done by computers.

The Boy in the Bubble is a prefiguration of the future – of that total asepsis, that total extirpation of germs, which is the biological form of transparency. He epitomises the kind of vacuum-sealed existence hitherto reserved for bacteria and particles in laboratories but now destined for us as, more and more, we are vacuum-pressed like records, vacuum-packed like deep-frozen foods and vacuum-enclosed for death as victims of fanatical therapeutic measures. That we think and reflect in a vacuum is demonstrated by the ubiquitousness of artificial intelligence.

It is not absurd to suppose that the extermination of man begins with the extermination of man's germs. One has only to consider the human being himself, complete with his emotions, his passions, his laughter, his sex and his secretions, to conclude that man is nothing but a dirty little germ – an irrational virus marring a universe of transparency. Once he has been purged, once everything has been cleaned up and all infection –

whether of a social or a bacillary kind – has been driven out, then only the virus of sadness will remain in a mortally clean and mortally sophisticated world.

Thought, itself a sort of network of antibodies and natural immune defences, is also highly vulnerable. It is in acute danger of being conveniently replaced by an electronic cerebrospinal bubble from which any animal or metaphysical reflex has been expunged. Even without all the technological advantages of the Boy in the Bubble, we are already living in the bubble ourselves – already, like those characters in Bosch paintings, enclosed in a crystal sphere: a transparent envelope in which we have taken refuge and where we remain, bereft of everything yet overprotected, doomed to artificial immunity, continual transfusions and, at the slightest contact with the world outside, instant death.

This is why we are all losing our defences – why we are all potentially immunodeficient.

All integrated and hyperintegrated systems – the technological system, the social system, even thought itself in artificial intelligence and its derivatives – tend towards the extreme constituted by immunodeficiency. Seeking to eliminate all external aggression, they secrete their own internal virulence, their own malignant reversibility. When a certain saturation point is reached, such systems effect this reversal and undergo this alteration willy-nilly – and thus tend to self-destruct. Their very transparency becomes a threat to them, and the crystal has its revenge.

In a hyperprotected space the body loses all its defences. So sterile are operating rooms that no germ or bacterium can survive there. Yet this is the very place where mysterious, anomalous viral diseases make their appearance. The fact is that viruses proliferate as soon as they find a free space. A world purged of the old forms of infection, a world 'ideal' from the clinical point of view, offers a perfect field of operations for the impalpable and implacable pathology which arises from the sterilisation itself.

This is a third-level pathology. Just as our societies are confronting a new kind of violence, born of the paradoxical fact that they are simultaneously both permissive and pacified, so too we face new illnesses, those illnesses which beset bodies overprotected by their artificial, medical or computer-generated shield. This pathology is produced not by accident, nor by anomie, but rather by *anomaly*. The very same thing happens with the social body, where the same causes bring about the same perverse effects, the same unforeseeable dysfunctions – a situation comparable to the genetic disorder that occurs at the cellular level, again occasioned by overprotection, overcoding, overmanagement. The social system, just like the biological body, loses its natural defences in precise proportion to the growing sophistication of its prostheses. Moreover, this unprecedented pathology is unlikely to be effectively conjured away by medicine, because medicine is itself part of the system of overprotection, and contributes to the fanatical protective and preventive measures lavished upon the body. Just as there seems to be no political solution to the problem of terrorism, so there seems to be no biological solution at present to the problems of AIDS and cancer. Indeed, the causes are identical: anomalous symptoms generated at the most fundamental level by the system itself represent a reactive virulence designed to counter, in the first case, a political overmanagement of the social body, and in the second case, a biological overmanagement of the body *tout court*.

At an early stage the evil genie of otherness takes the forms of accident, breakdown, failure. Only later does the viral, epidemic form make its appearance: a virulence that ravages the entire system, and against which the system is defenceless precisely because its very integrity paradoxically engenders this alteration.

Virulence takes hold of a body, a network or other system when that system rejects all its negative components and resolves itself into a combinatorial system of simple elements. It is because a circuit or a network has thus become a *virtual* being, a non-body, that viruses can run riot within it; hence too the much greater vulnerability of 'immaterial' machines as compared with traditional mechanical devices. Virtual and viral go hand in hand. It is because the body itself has become a non-body, a virtual machine, that viruses are taking it over.

It is logical that AIDS (and cancer) should have become the prototypes of our modern pathology, as of all lethal viral onslaughts. Saddling the body with replacement parts and abandoning it to genetic whims inevitably dislocates its systems of defence. A fractal body whose external functions are fated to multiply is, by the same token, fated to suffer internal proliferation at the cellular level. Metastasis occurs – and internal and biological metastases are paralleled by the external metastases constituted by prostheses, networks and ramiform systems.

Under the reign of the virus you are destroyed by your own antibodies. This is the leukaemia of an organism devouring its own defences, precisely because all threat, all adversity, has disappeared. Total prophylaxis is lethal. This is what medicine has failed to grasp: it treats cancer or AIDS as if they were conventional illnesses, when in fact they are illnesses generated by the very success of prophylaxis and medicine, illnesses bred of the disappearance of illnesses, of the elimination of pathogenic forms. We are confronted by a third-level pathology, one that is inaccessible to the pharmacopoeia of an earlier period (characterised by visible causes and mechanically produced effects). Suddenly all afflictions seem to originate in immunodeficiency – rather as all violence now seems to have its roots in terrorism. The onslaught of viruses and their strategies have in a sense taken over the work of the unconscious.

Just as human beings, conceived of as digital machines, have become the preferred field of operations of viral illnesses, so have software networks become the preferred field of operations of electronic viruses. Here too there is no effective prevention or cure: metastasis affects entire networks, and desymbolised machine languages offer no more resistance to viral infection than do desymbolised bodies. The familiar breakdowns and mechanical accidents of earlier times responded to good old-fashioned reparative medicine, but for these sudden weakenings, sudden anomalies, sudden 'stabs in the back' by antibodies, we have no remedy. We knew how to cure illnesses of forms; against pathologies of formulas we are without defences. Having everywhere sacrificed the natural balance of forms in favour of an artificial concordance between code and formula, we have unleashed the threat of a far graver disorder, of a destabilisation without precedent. Having turned the body and language into artificial systems in thrall to artificial intelligence, we have abandoned them not only to artificial stupidity but also to all the viral aberrations generated by this irreversible artificiality.

Viral attack is the pathology of the closed circuit, of the integrated circuit, of promiscuity and of the chain reaction – in a broad and metaphorical sense, a pathology of incest. He who lives by the same shall die by the same. The absence of otherness secretes another, intangible otherness: the absolute other of the virus.

That AIDS should have struck homosexuals and drug-users first is a reflection of the incestuousness of groups which function as closed circuits. We had known for a long time that haemophilia was linked to consanguine marriages and predominantly endogamous social systems. Even the strange sickness that affected cypress trees for so long turned out to be a sort of virus attributable to a lessening of the temperature difference between winter and summer – to a promiscuity, so to speak, of the seasons. The spectre of the Same had struck again. In every compulsion to resemblance, every extradition of difference, in all contiguity of things and their own image, all conflation of beings and their own code, lies the threat of an incestuous virulence, a diabolical otherness boding the breakdown of all this humming machinery. This is the reappearance of the principle of Evil in a new guise. No morality or guilt is implied, however: the principle of Evil is simply synonymous with the principle of reversal, with the turns of fate. In systems undergoing total positivisation – and hence desymbolisation – evil is equivalent, in all its forms, to the fundamental rule of reversibility.

Still, there is an ambiguity in this very virulence. AIDS serves to justify a new prohibition on sex – no longer a moral prohibition but a functional one, one directed not at sex *per se* but merely at its unhindered circulation. The current is to be interrupted, the flow stopped. But this runs counter to all the commandments of modernity, according to which sex, money and information must circulate freely. Everything is supposed to be fluid, everything should accelerate inexorably. The placing of strictures upon sexuality on grounds of viral risk seems as absurd as halting foreign-exchange dealings because they foster speculation or wild fluctuations in the value of the dollar. Unthinkable! And yet, all of a sudden, there it is: no more sex. Is there a contradiction in the system here?

Could it be that this suspension has a paradoxical aim, one bound up with the equally paradoxical aim of sexual liberation? We are acquainted with that spontaneous self-regulation of systems whereby they themselves produce accidents or slowdowns in order to survive. No society can live without in a sense opposing its own value system: it has to have such a system, yet it must at the same time define itself in contradistinction to it. At present we live according to at least two principles: that of sexual liberation and that of communication and information. And everything suggests that the species itself, via the threat of AIDS, is generating an antidote to its principle of sexual liberation; that by means of cancer, which is a breakdown of the genetic code, it is setting up a resistance to the all-powerful principle of cybernetic control; and that the viral onslaught in general signals its sabotaging of the universal principle of communication.

What if all this betokened a refusal of the obligatory flows of sperm, sex and words, a refusal of forced communication, programmed information and sexual promiscuity? What if it heralded a vital resistance to the spread of flows, circuits and networks – at the cost, it is true, of a new and lethal pathology, but one, nevertheless, that would protect us from something even worse? If so, then AIDS and cancer would be the price we are paying for our own system: an attempt to cure its *banal* virulence by recourse to a *fatal* form. Nobody can predict the effectiveness of such an exorcism, but the question has to be asked: What is cancer a resistance to, what even worse eventuality is it saving us from? (Could it be the total hegemony of genetic coding?) What is AIDS a resistance to, what even worse eventuality is it saving us from? (Could it be a sexual epidemic, a sort of total promiscuity?) The same goes for drugs: all melodramatics aside, what exactly do they protect us from, from what even worse scourge do they offer us an avenue of escape? (Could it be the brutalising effects of rationality, normative socialisation and universal conditioning?) As for terrorism, does not its secondary, reactive violence shield us from an epidemic of consensus, from an ever-increasing political leukaemia and degeneration and from the imperceptible transparency of the State? All things are ambiguous and reversible. After all, it is neurosis that offers human beings their most effective protection against madness. AIDS may thus be seen not as a divine punishment, but as quite the opposite – as a defensive abreaction on the part of the species against the danger of a total promiscuity, a total loss of identity through the proliferation and speed-up of networks.

The high degree to which AIDS, terrorism, crack cocaine or computer viruses mobilise the popular imagination should tell us that they are more than anecdotal occurrences in an irrational world. The fact is that they contain within them the whole logic of our system: these events are merely the spectacular expression of that system. They all hew to the same agenda of virulence and radiation, an agenda whose very power over the imagination is of a viral character: a single terrorist act obliges a reconsideration of politics as a whole in the light of terrorism's claims; an outbreak of AIDS, even a statistically insignificant one, forces us to view the whole spectrum of disease in the light of the immunodeficiency thesis; and the mildest of computer viruses, whether it vitiates the Pentagon's memory banks or merely erases a shower of on-line Christmas messages, has the potential to destabilise all data contained in information systems.

Whence the special status of such extreme phenomena – and of catastrophe in general, understood as an anomalous turn of events. The secret order of catastrophe resides in the affinity between all these processes, as in their homology with the system as a whole. Order within disorder: all extreme phenomena are consistent both with respect to each other and with respect to the whole that they constitute. This means that it is useless to appeal to some supposed rationality of the system against that system's outgrowths. The vanity of seeking to abolish these extreme phenomena is absolute. Moreover, they are destined to become more extreme still as our systems grow more sophisticated. And this is in fact a good thing – for they are the leading edge of therapy here. In these transparent, homeostatic or homeofluid systems there is no longer any such thing as a strategy of Good against Evil, there is only the pitting of Evil against Evil – a strategy of last resort. Indeed, we really have no choice in the matter: we simply watch as the lesser evil – homeopathic virulence – deploys its forces. AIDS, crack and computer viruses are merely outcroppings of the catastrophe; nine-tenths of it remain buried in the virtual. The full-blown, the absolute catastrophe would be a true omnipresence of all networks, a total transparency of all data – something from which, for now, computer viruses preserve us. Thanks to them, we shall not be going straight to the culminating point of the development of information and communications, which is to say: death. These viruses are both the first sign of this lethal transparency and its alarm signal. One is put in mind of a fluid travelling at increasing speed, forming eddies and anomalous countercurrents which arrest or dissipate its flow. Chaos imposes a limit upon what would otherwise hurtle into an absolute void. The secret

disorder of extreme phenomena, then, plays a prophylactic role by
opposing its chaos to any escalation of order and transparency to their
extremes. But these phenomena notwithstanding, we are already
witness to the beginning of the end of a certain way of thinking.
Similarly, in the case of sexual liberation, we are already witness to the
beginning of the end of a certain type of gratification. If total sexual
promiscuity were ever achieved, however, sex itself would self-destruct
in the resulting asexual flood. Much the same may be said of economic
exchange. Financial speculation, as turbulence, makes the boundless
extension of real transactions impossible. By precipitating an instanta-
neous circulation of value – by, as it were, electrocuting the economic
model – it also short-circuits the catastrophe of a free and universal com-
mutability – such a total liberation being the true catastrophic tendency
of value.

In the face of the threats of a total weightlessness, an unbearable light-
ness of being, a universal promiscuity and a linearity of processes liable
to plunge us into the void, the sudden whirlpools that we dub
catastrophes are really the thing that saves us from catastrophe.
Anomalies and aberrations of this kind re-create zones of gravity and
density that counter dispersion. It may be hazarded that this is how our
societies secrete their own peculiar version of an accursed share, much
after the fashion of those tribal peoples who used to dispose of their
surplus population by means of an oceanic suicide: the homeopathic
suicide of a few serving to maintain the homeostatic balance of the
group.

So the actual catastrophe may turn out to be a carefully modulated
strategy of our species – or, more precisely, our viruses, our extreme
phenomena, which are most definitively real, albeit localised, may be
what allow us to preserve the energy of that *virtual* catastrophe which is
the motor of all our processes, whether economic or political, artistic or
historical.

To epidemic, contagion, chain reactions and proliferation we owe at once
the worst and the best. The worst is metastasis in cancer, fanaticism in
politics, virulence in the biological sphere and rumour in the sphere of
information. Fundamentally, though, all these also partake of the best,
for the process of chain reaction is an immoral process, beyond good and
evil, and hence reversible. It must be said, moreover, that we greet both
worst and best with the same fascination.

That it should be possible for certain processes – economic, political,
linguistic, cultural, sexual, even theoretical and scientific – to set aside
the limitations of meaning and proceed by immediate contagion, according to the laws of the pure reciprocal immanencies of things among
themselves rather than the laws of their transcendence or their referen-

tiality – that this is possible poses an enigma to reason while offering a marvellous alternative to the imagination.

One has but to consider the phenomenon of fashion, which has never been satisfactorily explained. Fashion is the despair of sociology and aesthetics: a prodigious contagion of forms in which chain reactions struggle for supremacy over the logic of distinctions. The pleasure of fashion is undeniably cultural in origin, but does it not stem even more clearly from a flaring, unmediated consensus generated by the interplay of signs? Moreover, fashions fade away like epidemics once they have ravaged the imagination, once the virus has run its course. The price to be paid in terms of waste is always exorbitant, yet everyone consents. The marvellous in our societies resides in this ultra-rapid circulation of signs at a surface level (as opposed to the ultra-slow circulation of meanings). We love being contaminated by this process, and not having to think about it. This is a viral onslaught as noxious as the plague, yet no moral sociology, no philosophical reason, will ever extirpate it. Fashion is an irreducible phenomenon because it partakes of a crazy, viral, mediationless form of communication which operates so fast for the sole reason that it never passes via the mediation of meaning.

Anything that bypasses mediation is a source of pleasure. In seduction there is a movement from the one to the other which does not pass via the same. (In cloning, it is the opposite: the movement is from the same to the same without passage via the other; and cloning holds great fascination for us.) In metamorphosis, the shift is from one form to another without passing via meaning. In poetry, from one sign to another without passing via the reference. The collapsing of distances, of intervening spaces, always produces a kind of intoxication. What does speed itself mean to us if not the fact of going from one place to another without traversing time, from one moment to another without passing via duration and movement? Speed is marvellous: time alone is wearisome.

8

Soft Fictions and Intimate Documents: Can Feminism Be Posthuman?

Paula Rabinowitz

Question no. 1: Do posthuman bodies have histories, genders, or sexualities? In posing this question the editors of *Posthuman Bodies* challenge conventional relations between the human and gender, the human and history, the human and sexuality. A simplistic reading of the posthuman might see it as beyond and before time and type, and outside the boundaries – chronological and spatial and generic – that have held humanity and humanism. While obviously the posthuman cannot claim for itself such a utopic space, still the question also fixes a certain stability onto the constructs of history and gender and sex – as if we know precisely what these highly fluid, contested and malleable forms actually are or have been before we 'posted' them. It was not so long ago – as Virginia Woolf noted in her search through the British Museum's archive – that learned men could ask of women: Do you have history, gender, sex – are you human? Does that make women posthuman or prehuman? Does the term human have any meaning for women? As many feminist scholars have noted, following Foucault, the rise of the human sciences comes fast on the heels of the rise of feminine self-fashioning.[1] But in claiming space for the posthuman are we erasing yet again women's lives and stories? I am not arguing for making women human. Who needs it? Rather I want to suggest that women's stories circulate apart from human knowledge.

Question no. 2: Can the posthuman speak? And if so, what's there to say? When Gayatri Spivak asked her provocative question – can the subaltern speak? – she exposed the politics within posthumanist critiques of the subject.[2] Speaking is always already something done to us or for us by others whose presence as antecedents, as authorities, as interpreters, overpowers ours, even when one inhabits the most privileged of positions – that of the Western, educated, middle-class professional, like myself. How can the stories of others far outside the circulation of narrative, capital, goods, and so forth be heard? Their voices only accessible through vast networks of mediation prone to recuperation and misinterpretation at best, more likely imperial silence and violation. Poised between action and representation, posthuman bodies – voguing queens, PWAs – are bodies living outside national, sexual, economic borders. They exceed and override borders by turning bodies into acts and actions into representations. Eliminating the distinction between action and articulation, deed and word, the posthuman body is still saturated with the stories of humanity that circulate around it; it speaks through a language straddling the borders between health/sickness, male/female, real/imaginary. It tells its stories, however, through those already told; it rips off the past to refuse the future. And so the posthuman, alien and marginal like the subaltern, probably cannot speak because it is always spoken through the stories that someone else already told.

Question no. 3: Is there a posthuman woman? When women began 'speaking bitterness' in the consciousness-raising groups of the 1960s and 1970s, women's humanity was still up for debate. Feminists sought to document women's struggle to be heard politically, historically, sexually, through the immediacy and realism of testimony in film, women's studies courses, poetry, and c–r groups. These groups, modelled on the Chinese and Vietnamese practices of criticism/self-criticism which cultivated anger and hatred within peasants and cadres where none existed – hatred being to some degree the luxury of an individualistic and mobile culture; not one based on familial, filial, ancestral ties to the land – channelled (mostly) middle-class white women's anger into political action and theory. Basic to the c–r groups was the unspoken assumption that each woman told the truth. Her story, her secret, her fury, her memory, perhaps her fantasy became the evidence from which to fashion a theory of women's oppression. But what if she were lying, or if not lying, then embroidering, weaving a fabulous story from odd encounters with the world? Feminism required sincerity for women to claim their experiences as authentically human. Perhaps a posthuman feminism develops from the evasion of truth – from fantasy, exaggeration and lies. In this essay, I want to explore this possibility (and suggest some answers to the questions asked) by examining a little-known film by California film-maker, Chick Strand.

Chick Strand's *Soft Fiction* reveals secrets. This film signals realness and truth through various cinematic devices to allow women to voice their fantasies. However, the film's re-enactments, restagings, retellings of gang rape, addiction, incest, seduction, into tales of power and control undermine and betray the feminist-humanist project of truth-telling. As in Bette Gordon's *Variety* the fantasy and power of genre conspire to alter sexual histories. *Variety*'s heroine, who sells tickets at a 42nd Street porn theatre, begins watching the films; gradually they inhabit her, but she ultimately inhabits them as she retells their plots as if recalling the day's events. Has she been made over by the images she watches, or have they provided her with new ways to speak about herself? Is she in them, or are they in her? The borders between words and deeds are permeable; acts and images dwell in the same room.

This room may be the safe space of a friend's home, where one is free to expose oneself because the thick vegetation surrounding the yard shades the interiors, because a friend will never betray a secret even though a camera is fixed on you and at some point everyone will see you, hear you. When you tell a secret after all, you expect it to get around; it becomes the substance of gossip. The exchange of secrets is fundamental to friendship, but also to power – johns tell prostitutes state secrets, informants tell ethnographers local secrets – the exchange gives away something but gets something in return: Control of the story. The mundane secrets of middle-class girlhood are divulged over kitchen sinks, across telephone wires, in private female spaces. But what if the rooms are bugged, what if a camera is there, too? Are the secrets still secret? Do the stories ring true, sound real? Hardly. And yet laden with meaning as they are we still want to believe them. More so perhaps because we know them not to be secrets anymore.

From its inception, feminism has engendered radical scepticism; once the lid was blown off and culture revealed to be hopelessly male-dominated, who could take anything seriously? Even women's authentic voices. By 'speaking truth to power', women called into question both truth and power. But the joke was on those sincere believers, acting like naïve ethnographers in the field soaking up authentic culture, who found women's voices pure. The fact is that posthuman bodies have been around a long time. They do have histories and these histories will be found in what has been left out of the official accounts of the marginal. Posthumans always lie. Can posthuman women speak? Of course. Will they speak to us? Not likely. Orthodoxies get established very quickly, and those out of bounds are made to disappear, kept silent, even by those of us whose job it is to listen. Feminists talk, theorise, act, but in whose (human) interest?

As I perform my role as posthuman feminist film critic, I want to suggest that this process is itself cinematic, that is, it is both a spectacle and speculative. The idea of critique as cultural performance, as posthuman activity, can perhaps point a way out of the political impasses that both identity politics and psychoanalytic theory construct for feminism. A sense of the dynamic intersubjectivity of the performance of cinema – of the bodies on screen enacting conscious performances and of the bodies in the audience taking up and remaking these performances (un)consciously and collectively – might open film to posthuman acts.[3] Something different happens in a movie theatre from a dream or fantasy. Other people surround you – coughing, laughing, eating, kissing – who have also travelled to the theatre, paid money, and expect affective results. In short, the performance of cinema – on screen and in the audience – defies the boundaries of individuals and their psyches by recasting them into mass formations, posthuman assortments.

Chick Strand's *Soft Fiction* recirculates many of the clichés about women's erotic and sexual fantasies within its visual and sound tracks. Bringing to focus questions about the range of female sexuality and fantasy, the modes of female address, the genre(s) of women's stories, the form of the female body as visual spectacle and narrative subject, *Soft Fiction* dwells between the borders of ethnography, documentary, pornography, avant-garde and feminist counter-cinema.[4] Its title evocative of soft core, true romance, hard fact, Strand herself describes her beautifully shot, black-and-white film as an 'ethnography of women'.[5] In doing so, she places it directly within the realm of anthropological filmmaking, where she began her career. Strand invokes, yet resists, the 'exotic' cultural Other that forms the subject of much ethnography.

One of Strand's earliest films, *Mosori Monika* (1971), investigates the impact of a Spanish Mission on the Warao Indians of central Venezuela through the differing narratives of a young Spanish nun and an elderly Warao woman. This film exposes the missionary project as an essentially imperialist one that teaches the Indians 'how to live a human life. ... The life of a man', while demonstrating that the Warao cagily employ a form of resistance to the colonial presence of the Mission despite their apparent willingness to be clothed, fed, and feted by the nuns. Strand's narrow focus – on the stories of these two women – and her evocative close-ups of the bodies of men and women working, resting, eating, playing, break many of the conventions of the anthropological documentary by refusing to present the 'whole' picture of the body or the culture. In her justification of that film, 'Notes on Ethnographic Film by a Film Artist', she challenges the conventions of 'wholeness' which Karl Heider had established as the mark of well-wrought ethnographic cinema.[6] Arguing for the use of extreme close-ups, fragmented movements and the 'small talk' of daily life, she seeks to 'get a microscopic view of one of the threads that makes up the tapestry of the whole culture'. Locating the partial and the conditional, her films 'evolve in the field' into 'works of art' rather than scientific 'textbooks'.[7]

Since the mid-1960s Strand has been filming the life story of her friend Anselmo, an Indian from Northern Mexico who makes his living as a street musician. Because each film involves a level of 'performance' that is self-consciously rendered to alter the 'purity' of ethnographic forms, she describes the films variously as 'experimental documentary', 'expressive documentary', or 'intimate documentary'. Her first film, *Anselmo* (1967) is a 'symbolic re-enactment of a real event' in which Strand tried to fulfil Anselmo's wish for a 'double E flat tuba'. She failed to find one, but managed to locate a brass wrap-around tuba which she smuggled into Mexico and presented to him. Later, they reproduced the transaction for the camera. In *Cosas de mi Vida* (1976), Strand traces ten years in Anselmo's life as he struggles to endure poverty. The film is narrated by Anselmo in English although he does not speak the language. Strand translated the Spanish narration Anselmo provided and then taught him how to say it for the film. Again, Anselmo 'performs' himself as a subject for these (inauthentic) ethnographies. Her most celebrated film, *Mujeres de Milfuegos* (1976), presents a 'fake' ethnography about the 'women who wear black from the age of 15 and spend their entire lives giving birth, preparing food and tending to household and farm responsibilities', by depicting 'their daily repetitive tasks as a form of obsessive ritual'.[8]

The idea of transforming the ethnographic film from an observational tool, one which records daily life and/or ritual as data, into an expressive, intimate, experimental documentary requires a sense of cinematic address as performative. It also presumes that cultural identities and ideas of the individual subject are constructed as performances – for the self, for others, for the camera – within various cultural arenas. Performing everyday activities as rituals for the camera undermines the concept of ritual as well as the concept of cinema. It suggests that the images on the screen respond to the capacities of the 'actors' to take up one position, leave it and take up another in a stylised fashion. Perhaps this same sense of mobility – of moving in and out of a performance – occurs as well for the spectator, who, rather than being locked into a unified, or even split gaze, is always calling up various performative aspects of identity which echo, refuse, confront or merge with the screen performances. To give another example, toward the end of Trinh T. Minh-ha's film about Senegalese women, *Reassemblage* (1982), the film-maker remarks:

> I come with the idea that I would seize the unusual by catching the person unawares. There are better ways to steal. With the other's consent. After seeing me labouring with the camera, women invite me to their place and ask me to film them. ... What I see is life looking at me/I am looking through a circle in a circle of looks/115° Fahrenheit. I put on a hat while laughter bursts behind me. I haven't seen any woman wearing a hat.

The film-maker takes up her position among the women she has been filming and responds to their responses to her. They are happy to be filmed but the filming must be by invitation. The village women engage the film-making process as an exchange of looks, as a gesture and recognition of differences and so perform the daily lives for Trinh who herself becomes a spectacle for her subjects.

Recent feminist and gay studies theories of performance stress the constructedness and historically contingent nature of gender and sexual identities. Judith Butler, for instance, argues that 'gender is an identity tenuously constituted in time, instituted on exterior space through a *stylised repetition of acts*'.[9] Denise Riley suggests that the condition of 'women' is as contested and historically indeterminant as the mythical category of 'woman'. Neither term – women, woman – she declares, can sufficiently pin down the multivalent claims and strategies (as Butler calls them) entailed in constituting a subject. I believe feminist politics must take its cue from queer and AIDS politics and become self-conscious of its contingent aspect – of itself as a performance responding to its own cultural space and historical period.

Likewise, I would argue that feminist film theory needs to embrace its performative quality – both as it speaks of an object productive of and produced by performances, and as it becomes another form of cinematic performance. The over-valuation of the psychoanalytic model, which reads the effects of the cinematic apparatus through the subject's unconscious responses to the imaginary, forgets just how constructed and how performative even that primal scene is. After all, the 'scene' to which cinematic voyeurism supposedly refers is rarely seen – it is an imaginative reconstruction, a symbolic performance, of desire. For all its critique of narrative realism as oppressive and of critical reflectionism as vulgar, feminist psycho-semiotic film theory has perhaps unconsciously reinstated a reflectionist aesthetics by declaring the cinematic apparatus to be a map of the unconscious. Rather than describe films' contents as reflective of sociological formations (like gender roles), cinesemiotics represents cinematic form as a mirror of imaginary constructions (like sexual difference). By prying film away from its historical references – to performers, film-makers, critics, and audiences – psychoanalytic feminist film theorists veer close to the analyses of cultural feminists.

Strand's manufacture of 'ritual' performances, her reconstructions of real events, her rephrased translations, indicate to me that the ethnographic scene, as much as the psychoanalytic, is also a performance that depends on the film-maker's desire for the encounter and the informant's willingness to act it out for an audience.[10] Films like hers and Trinh's depict the historicity of cinematic engagement by calling attention to the performances of documentary film's subjects and objects. Strand describes a recent film, *Artificial Paradise* (1986), as an 'Aztec romance and the dream of love. The anthropologist's most human desire, the ultimate contact with the informant.' A romance *and* a dream: a cultural construction and a psychic re-enactment. Thus, as an 'ethnography of women' – which is just a group of Strand's friends who visit her home in Tujunga Canyon between 1976 and 1979 to tell their stories – Strand's film challenges the notions of the 'exotic' and the 'whole' and of the 'informant' and the 'scientist' but also insists on social relations of cinematic address. 'The erotic content and style' of *Soft Fiction* suggests the malleability and the pornographic, i.e., mythic (in Angela Carter's sense), quality of all fictions, including ethnographies, and the fictionality of all oral and visual testimonies, especially those of feminine desire.[11]

The film begins with a sequence of train sounds and horizontally moving patterns of light and dark. It takes a few minutes to orient oneself to the sound and image which finally resolve into a close-up of a woman's face against a window. She departs the train and like Maya Deren in *Meshes of the Afternoon* (1943), to which *Soft Fiction* pays homage, walks in the late afternoon Southern California sun through some greenery to a locked house. She remains outside, but the camera enters the room and surveys it voyeuristically: checking the kitchen, bathroom, bedroom – recreating the dizzying descent of the staircase in *Meshes* – grazing the shadow of the film-maker herself to discover a woman sitting in an armchair near a window calmly smoking as a woman's voice-over exhorts us to 'move, first one way then the other – gathering, lifting, squeezing, releasing, just so it feels good'. This reference to counter-cultural California sensuality also nods to a female avant-garde film history.

Beginning with Germaine Dulac's *La Souriante Mme Beudet* (1922) and continuing through Deren's *Meshes* and Menken's *Glimpses in a Garden*, much women's avant-garde cinema develops as an exploration and exposure of interiors. Deren's and Strand's cameras scrutinise the empty houses they enter, but these houses are their own, turning the voyeuristic gaze into an exhibitionist display of its objects. However, where Deren multiplied her own body to display the terrors and desires of the female subject, Strand includes the voices of many women to demonstrate the multiplicity and resistance of women's fantasies. Like Carmelita, the Warao woman, whose incorporation into the mission can be read as victimisation but whose own rendering of it challenges us to read resistance in her very acceptance of the nun's offerings, the women tell stories of incest, addiction and Nazis which are potent tropes for women's victimisation. Yet the women's voices, the images they construct to accompany their tales and the sequencing of these images counter preconceptions of female powerlessness by substituting in its place the power of acting. The challenge to politically correct feminism has a forgotten history. Long before Camille Paglia and Katie Roiphe were condemning feminism's embrace of female victimisation, Strand and her 'informants' were exploring, even celebrating, their politically incorrect desires, fantasies and experiences.

As the seated woman begins her story, initiated by rubbing the curving banister of the Pasadena Art Museum, her desire to 'become this railing – become this piece', invites us to question the very terms of representation that objectify women's bodies. That the play on the word 'piece' is deliberate, we hear in her slow, precise language. We see her lips, nose and eyes peering directly into the camera; cinematic convention tells us she is revealing truth. The camera leaves her as she asks, 'Haven't you ever wanted to live within black fur?' The tactile transvestism of this woman's desire – to inhabit curved alloyed metals, black fur, to turn her body into an object of touch – destroys the sensation of inside/outside for us as it extends the body into new spaces, new desires. It also transgresses both cultural feminism's and psychoanalytic feminism's rigid resistance to (yet ironic insistence upon) woman's objectification. The speaking subject of this sequence desires objecthood.

Another woman appears intently studying a piece of paper with a magnifying glass before she begins to read a letter addressed to Strand recounting the story of a photographer whose escapade at a rodeo she had gone to shoot ends with her giving a series of blow jobs to anonymous cowboys in a dark dormitory room. The incidents seem 'inevitable' to the letter writer; her loss of control at the rodeo becomes visible to the letter reader in her handwriting – she fails to capitalise her 'I's. Already mediated on several levels (the woman's story appears as a letter written to Chick but read by a giggling woman through a magnifying glass to the camera), her story is deeply ambivalent. Has she been coerced? Is this a case of gang rape? Or is it a staging of a fantasy which oscillates between her power – as voyeur, as photographer – and theirs – as exhibitionists, as sexual cowboys? After she and her camera escape unharmed from this encounter, she picks up yet another cowboy to shoot. He takes her to a stable where she photographs him naked except for his belt, hat and boots – the regalia of s/m scenes – and where again she gives him a blow job while his buddies watch. Her fear is countered by her excitement, which is mediated further by his final remarks of comfort: 'It will make a good story to tell your grandchildren.' In a bizarre re-ordering of the female oral tradition, sexual pleasure exists for the man in his fellated orgasm, but for the woman, who never quite gets off herself, it is deferred, available only in the verbal recreation of desire through memory, narrative, and performance.[12]

In this story, Strand and her informant manipulate one of the privileged scenes of hard-core porn, the blow job, evoking visceral reactions from audience members about the woman's status as a 'victim'.[13] Linda Williams has argued that the growing popularity during the 1970s of feature-length porn films, such as *Deep Throat*, *The Devil in Miss Jones* (Damiano, 1972), *Behind the Green Door* (Mitchell, 1972), signalled that there was an audience for the visible evidence of desire as a fetishised commodity and that mass media could produce it. These films invoked women's demands for more and better sex through fantasies that

fulfilled male desire, thus resisting the threat of feminism by constructing women's desire as a turn-on for men. Like the radical feminist Anne
Koedt, *Deep Throat* rejects 'the myth of the vaginal orgasm', but, as it
orchestrates its 'sexual numbers' around the ejaculation of fellated
penises into Linda Lovelace's ecstatic face, its ultimate audience is
male.[14] Still, the narrative appeal to a broader audience (one that presumably included heterosexual women) refracted the messages of soft-
core melodramas, such as *Looking for Mr Goodbar* (Brooks, 1977), which
also assumed women's independent desires for sexual adventure, but
provided cautionary tales about the dangers of arousing male sexual
aggression for their largely female audiences.[15] The soft-core films
looked back to the 1940s woman's film genre, and to the popular
woman's romances found in *True Confessions*, where transgressive sexuality in a woman always resulted in shame and punishment.[16]

But in *Soft Fiction*, the photographer returns to her pleasure and her
power. In her ironic reply to us, not to her handsome cowboy, she
asserts, 'Well, photography is a power to be reckoned with', revealing
that after she prints his photo she discovers his name on his belt, tracks
him down, obsessively follows him home, and declares 'I know where he
lives now'. As Strand says of all her 'informants', they take 'responsibility for having had the experience. It's not that they take responsibility for
the experience happening but for "having had" it'.[17] The claim of
'responsibility' challenges women's victimisation in/by narrative by
asserting that their stories are conscious re-enactments. The process
occurs as a translation – a refashioning of the experience into a narrative
and visual sequence. This recurs at various times throughout the film
which continues to switch codes between the expressionistic frame of the
woman's quest (for pleasure?) and the concrete documentary-like stories
women tell about the real and fantasised causes and effects of these
quests – stories of pain, violation, and desire.

The next shot reveals a sun-drenched kitchen. We watch a nude
woman enter, her body strong; she is unself-conscious of it as she flips
on the radio before she starts preparing a hearty breakfast of juice, coffee,
eggs, buttered toast. The show, *Grand Central Station*, begins with the
sounds of a train over which the narrator intones 'this is a love story',
reminding us that 'the door to the great white way is usually through the
back alley'. At this point, we hear a voice-over as a woman describes a
sensuous memory of swimming in a pond as a child – diving 'in and up
and down' – until tired she ran to her grandfather waiting with a towel.
She describes walking back to their cabin watching the drops of water
splashing in the dust. Then, matter-of-factly, states, 'I was young, only
seven. We would make love on the couch, the red couch, I trusted
grampa – even fell into enjoying it.' She describes how he kissed her and
undressed her, noting that only once did she see his penis ... 'like a

snake, a pink velvet snake ... he used it on my clitoris ... he wanted to teach me how to make love ... how to be sensual'. By this time, she is eating. The camera no longer displays her whole body, but again is extremely close-up. Cutting into the egg yolk with the side of her spoon and smearing it over the whites, she remembers how 'it scared me – it was too close and too strong. ... I just wouldn't allow myself to be alone with him – jump out of bed, feign sleep, all the typical tactics of female avoidance – I learned them young – now I'm a master. Pursued and cap-tured, really captured cause there's no way out', she declares as she exhales her after-breakfast cigarette.

Again, ambivalence is crucial to the performance of this scene. Hers is the only body we see whole, performing a whole act, her story distanced by the off-screen narrator. Her voice is strong, ironical, yet vulnerable. She is angry, but the circumstances she has constructed to disclose her secret imply that she has power over them. Hers is certainly 'Not a Love Story' and the 'responsibility' is certainly not hers, yet her image and her story – its disembodied narration running over her real time act – unpacks the cinematic baggage this story of female powerlessness holds for us and perhaps her.

The film now cuts to a clichéd image of feminine eroticism as a nude woman dances to Sidney Bechet's rendition of 'Petit Fleur', and we see the play of light and dark as her body and hair break the sun's rays. This diversion momentarily breaks the tension of captivity encoded in the woman-in-the-kitchen's story and in the previous use of the extreme close-up in the woman-at-the-museum's and rodeo's stories. But the next woman tells about being 'really hooked'. Again, lips, eyes, brow are prominent in extreme close-up, as the woman chain-smokes, drinks wine and describes her 'plan', her 'programme', to become hooked first on a man, then on the pain he caused, then on heroin to escape the pain. Ultimately, she kicks, despite wondering why: 'It was so good, so clear, so real, so spacious. But I did it – that was the plan and I exorcised him.' The exorcism extends into the film-making process. Strand claims that 'the most incredible part of making the film was my relationship to the women when they were talking and being on camera, and doing it knowing the result, knowing that they would be on this big screen and a lot of people, strangers, would see them ... them telling it on camera acted as an exorcism. ... '[18] In other words, the informants became self-styled performers for an audience who was both distant from, yet inti-mate with, the 'connections' in these stories.

The complicity between storyteller, film-maker, and audience in the production of a voyeuristic fantasy continues as we watch a dog arrang-ing itself into a comfortable position on an armchair. The sound track is of loud voices – a train station perhaps, no, an audience at a performance who breaks into applause when the dog stands, revealing that it has only

three legs. Then a white face and white hands emerge from the black-
ness, the woman begins singing Schubert's 'Death and the Maiden',
whose lyrics evoke the longing for 'dreams', for 'sleep'. In calling forth
the romantic vision of desire as death, the conventional reading of
women's masochism is reinserted as a commentary on the women's
stories so far. Yet, by doing so through a soprano's rendition of the *lieder*,
the female body as a performative tool is reasserted. Although each story
has been painful – we see their faces contort, hear their voices crack as
they speak – they have all been humorous as well. Each woman has
restaged her 'tragedy' into a story of power and pleasure by the styles of
their telling and the compositions of their images. Still, these tropes of
captivity are the stuff of female masochism, their 'true confessions', the
stories of surrender and desire that fuelled my politically incorrect pre-
adolescence. As if to confirm our secret complicity with the mechanisms
of pornographic surrender, after the *lieder*, we find the travelling woman
again. Watching her depart the house, her suitcase opens exposing yards
of cloth and a sequined teddy.

The final segment frames a tight, nervous face: 'Okay', she says, 'this is
going to be a little bit difficult.' Her story is set during the war in the
Poland of her childhood, when she says 'it was demanded of me that I
stay quiet … people were after you'. It is not clear whether her family
was hiding Jews or were themselves Jews in hiding, but after a neigh-
bour informs on them the Gestapo visits her home. She 'remember[s]
being put on a Gestapo officer's lap to divert his attention – I understood
that – what my job was. … I remember flirting with him.' Her faltering
voice continues with a memory of being awakened by her mother when
she was $3\frac{1}{2}$ and walking at night for miles:

> It was necessary for me to be very brave. I remember that I liked that
> and I remember that I like that now – that I was brave then. And I
> remember a hill with fire and explosions of all sorts. I remember how
> frightened everyone was and my father carrying the bird cage with the
> kittens. And I remember feeling proud that I didn't want to be carried.
> And I remember that hill and there was something very bad going on
> on the other side, and then there's a blank.

Unlike the preceding stories of sexual adventure and surrender, which
emerge as coherent, well-plotted narratives – the stuff of conventional
melodrama – these memories of historical necessity are fractured, disrupted, and lack clarity. Yet, even here, the sensation is of control, of the
power this young girl experienced despite, or rather because of, knowing
she was an object of exchange in a larger transaction.

The last images of the film return to more clichéd images from soft-
core porn – a woman's abandon as a shower of clear water washes over

her, a woman walking barefoot along the shore, two naked women frolicking on horseback. These also are the clichés of California independent film-making of the 1960s – the sensuous display of the body at play in nature. Like the Schubert *Lieder*, the train journey, or the solo dance, they recontain the stories of female transgression and pleasure in the face of masculine power within the limits of conventionalised depictions of female desire. Yet the stories undercut this containment, violating boundaries, just as the excesses of the extreme close-ups explode the documentary conventions of the talking head by overvaluing the partial elements of the face – lips, brows, nostrils – and body – hands, legs, feet. These fragmented, cut-up icons of femininity that appear commodified in advertisements have been recharged by the speakers. By allowing movement in and out of frame, the stationary camera enables the speakers to take control of and produce their images.

The stories in *Soft Fiction* flow out of each other – the way one might reveal secrets to a stranger on a train. They are intensely private and personal, yet by orchestrating them within the compositions of avant-garde cinematography, documentary address, ethnographic film-making and soft-core porn, Strand wants us to begin questioning how female pleasures are experienced and represented in patriarchal culture. The film's ethnographic inquiry seems to ask, what are the narrative and visual components of white middle-class women's (hetero)sexualities? How are they represented and performed in bourgeois culture? The stories acquire their meanings through a complex interplay of image, sequence, and sound. The tight framing of faces restricts women's bodies as cinematic spectacle, yet we also participate in a voyeuristic invasion of private space and conventionalised modes of displaying female desire as well as listen in on some juicy secrets. The stories seem private, yet their performances enter public spaces. In the process, the tropes of the victim are recast through the process of storytelling into a grand panorama leading from narcissistic joy to genocidal horror. As they invoke a history of genres – melodrama, case study, gossip, romance – all too familiar in their containments of women's desires and their commodifications of women's pleasure and pain, these stories ask us to step outside of conventional narratives and images put forth by hard and soft core porn, and by their anti-porn feminist critics, to allow for the possibility that the 'story is a sexual fantasy lived out'.[19] In their development of women's powers of performance – powers depending upon cultural contradictions that recognise both the Oedipal narrative's power over, but also its ancillary status for women – this film also challenges the psychoanalytic model of spectatorship. In so doing, the verbal and visual performances of desire present what Adena Rosmarin calls 'the power of genre' as a put-on, because here the genre's power is put on and displayed through its clichés.[20]

Strand's limited ethnography provides a partial view of the culture of heterosexual practices that are both oppressive and pleasurable to women. Her picture of white, middle-class women's culture owes much to the boy-crazy girls' gossip sessions I remember from junior high school slumber parties in which secrets, fantasies, and homoerotic desires merged with popular cultural renderings of woman's surrender. However this fantasy depends upon and fuels the racism and class division that produces the fantasy of women's culture in the first place (for instance, the only black woman on screen is seen dancing nude to Bechet – jazz and the black woman's body being icons for white dreams of sexual escape). In short, the film becomes retrograde in its obsessive explorations of white, middle-class heterosexuality.[21] Thus, to a certain extent, *Soft Fiction* participates in the anti-porn feminist (and American New Right) hysteria that elides women's victimisation by male sexuality with genocidal practices of fascism as it moves from the private fantasy experienced outside political contexts to the intrusion of military force into the domestic space. In addition, the straightforward presentation of women's voices, coupled with the ecstatic images of female sensuality appear as 'unsophisticated' representations of desire.[22] These distortions reveal the fault lines of, because they stem from, Strand's investment in a universalised vision of women's culture.

Moreover, Strand is caught in a serious dilemma when she embraces (albeit critically) ethnographic cinema. On the one hand, ethnography as a historical practice in which white people look at and (through cinema) display people of colour maintains imperialist relations of domination. On the other hand, by turning the lens on her own culture – that of white middle-class film artists – Strand's ethnography of women would seem to rectify the colonial relationship of ethnographer to informant. But by removing her lens to her own backyard, *Soft Fiction* places the third world under complete erasure. In either case, as sympathetic yet still colonising spectator of the other, or as empathetic exhibitor of the self, Strand's films, by invoking ethnography, despite problematising subject and object, inevitably fall victim to their own tensions.

Nevertheless, her films depend on the performances of their informants' memories appearing simultaneously authentic and constructed, human and posthuman. As restagings, the artifice involved in the deliberate diction and the claustrophobic framing of *Soft Fiction* constructs speaking subjects who eventually call into question the possibility of a 'culture' of women about whom one could make an ethnography. The stories indicate the ways in which culture as a human practice may be irrelevant. Posthuman feminists perform the competing collective strategies of story-telling and acting we carry out in all their contradictory modes every day. That may be woman's culture, thereby calling forth an ethnography, but maybe it's something else instead.

I'm not seeking to rehabilitate *Soft Fiction* by inserting it into an existing canon of films. I would hope that my discussion of the film has pointed up some of the polarised positions within feminisms – anti-porn/pro-sex, cultural/psychoanalytic – that verge in their drive toward purity and truth on the aestheticisation of politics that Walter Benjamin called fascism. I believe we need to rethink the categories governing our political and cultural theorising in order to begin the posthuman project of (re)politicising art. Second-wave feminism in the United States, like its predecessors, has relied on cultural performances – from the Miss America Pageant demonstration through the Women's Pentagon Action to the Guerilla Girls' recent billboards – to foreground politics. Theory also might best be considered as a performance – a collective playing out of cultural codes in public spaces that are socially and historically constructed and reconstructed in response to political challenges. Strand's film and the many other expressions that step out of bounds demand that we constantly inspect the ways, in the name of political correctness or theoretical sophistication, we police the borders of feminism.

9

Skinflick: Posthuman Gender in Jonathan Demme's *The Silence of the Lambs*

Judith Halberstam

The monster, as we know it, died in 1963 when Hannah Arendt published her 'Report on the Banality of Evil' entitled *Eichmann in Jerusalem*. Adolf Eichmann, as the representative of a system of unspeakable horror, stood trial for 'Crimes Committed Against Humanity'. Arendt refused, in her report, to grant the power of horror to the ordinary looking man who stood trial. While the press commented on the monster who hides behind the banal appearance, Arendt turned the equation around and recognised the banality of a monstrosity that functions as a bureaucracy. She writes:

> [The prosecutor] wanted to try the most abnormal monster the world had ever seen ... [The Judges] knew, of course, that it would have been very comforting indeed to believe that Eichmann was a monster, even though if he had been Israel's case against him would have collapsed. ... The trouble with Eichmann was precisely that so many were like him, and that the many were neither perverted nor sadistic, that they were, and still are, terribly and terrifyingly normal.[1]

Arendt's relegation of Eichmann from monster dripping with the blood of a people to the conformist clerk who does his job and does not ask questions suggests that crime and corrupt politics and murder all demand complicit and silent observers. Eichmann's crime was that he was no monster, no aberration from the norm.

What exactly is the comfort of making Eichmann or others like him into monsters? Monsters confirm that evil resides in specific bodies, particular psyches. Monstrosity as the bodily manifestation of evil makes evil into a local effect, not generalisable across a society or culture. But modernity has eliminated the comfort of monsters because we have seen, in Nazi Germany and elsewhere, that evil works often as a system, it works through institutions and it works as a *banal* (meaning 'common to all') mechanism. In other words evil stretches across cultural and political productions as complicity and collaboration.

Modernity makes monstrosity a function of consent and a result of habit. Monsters of the nineteenth century – like Frankenstein, like Dracula – certainly still scare and chill but they scare us from a distance. We wear modern monsters like skin, they are us, they are on us and in us. Monstrosity no longer coagulates into a specific body, a single face, a unique feature, it is replaced with a banality that fractures resistance because the enemy becomes harder and harder to locate, and looks more and more like the hero. What were monsters are now facets of identity; the sexual other and the racial other cannot be separated from self. But still, we keep our monsters ready.

Horror lies just beneath the surface, it lurks in dark alleys, it hides behind a rational science, it buries itself in respectable bodies, so the story goes. In a postmodern horror movie, *The Silence of the Lambs* (1991) by Jonathan Demme, fear no longer assumes a depth/surface model; after this movie (but perhaps all along) horror resides at the level of skin itself. Skin is at once the most fragile of boundaries and the most stable of signifiers; it is the site of entry for the vampire, the signifier of race for the nineteenth-century monster; skin is precisely what does not fit, Frankenstein sutures his monster's ugly flesh together by binding it in a yellow skin, too tight and too thick. When, in the modern horror movie, terror rises to the surface, the surface itself becomes a complex web of pleasure and danger; the surface rises to the surface, the surface becomes Leatherface, becomes Demme's Buffalo Bill, and everything that rises must converge.

Demme's film weaves its horror and its pleasure around the remains of other horror films and literature. It quotes from Alfred Hitchcock's *Psycho*, from Brian De Palma's *Dressed To Kill*, from William Wyler's *The Collector* and it features a reincarnation of Bram Stoker's insane Renfield, the murderous idiot savant of *Dracula*. This film, indeed, has cannibalised its genre, consumed it bones and all and reproduced it in a slick and glossy representation of representations of violence, murder, mutilation, matricide and the perverse consequences of gender confusion. *The Silence of the Lambs* is precisely never silent, it hums with past voices, other stories; it holds the murmur of vampires, the outrage of the monster's articulations, the whispers of the beasts who were told but never got to tell. The viewer is now a listener, a listener to the narrative of the monster.

But, in *The Silence of the Lambs*, the monster is everywhere and everyone and the monster's story is not distinguishable from other textual productions validated within the film. *The Silence of the Lambs* skilfully pits Jodie Foster as FBI agent Clarice Starling against the charismatic intellect of ex-psychiatrist and serial murderer Dr Hannibal 'the Cannibal' Lecter played by Anthony Hopkins. Starling goes to visit Lecter in his maximum security cell in order to engage his help in tracking down a serial killer. The murderer has been nicknamed Buffalo Bill because he skins his female victims after murdering them. Starling is no match for Lecter and he manipulates her by insisting upon 'quid pro quo' or an equal exchange of information. In return for information about Buffalo Bill, Lecter demands that Starling tell him her nightmares, her most awful memories of childhood, her darkest fears. As she reveals her stories to Lecter's scrutiny, Starling is forced to relinquish the authority invested in her position as detective. Suddenly, with only the glass separating the two, Starling seems no more free than Lecter; both are incarcerated by knowledge or lack of, by memory, by power structures, by violence, by the unnameable menace of Lecter the Intellecter.

Dr Hannibal Lecter is considered an unusual threat to society not simply because he murders people and consumes them, but because as a psychiatrist he has access to minds. He is someone 'you don't want inside your head', Starling's boss warns her; of course you don't want him inside your body either and you certainly don't want to let him put you inside his! Boundaries between people (detective and criminal, men and women, murderers and victims) are all mixed up in this film until they disappear altogether, becoming as transparent as the glass that (barely) divides Lecter and Starling. Lecter illustrates to perfection the spooky and uncanny effect of confusing boundaries, inside and outside, consuming and being consumed, watching and being watched. He specialises in getting under one's skin, into one's thoughts and he makes little of the classic body/mind split as he eats bodies and sucks minds dry.

The subplot in *The Silence of the Lambs* involves the tracking of murderer-mutilator Buffalo Bill. Buffalo Bill, we find out, skins his victims because he suffers a kind of gender dysphoria that he thinks can be solved by covering himself in female skin; in fact, he is making himself a female body suit, or 'a woman suit' as Starling puts it, and he murders simply to gather the necessary fabric. Buffalo Bill, of course, is no Lecter, no thinker, he is all body, but the wrong body. Lecter points out that Buffalo Bill hates identity, he is simply at odds with any identity whatsoever; no body, no gender will do and so he has to sit at home with his skins and fashion a completely new one. What he constructs is a posthuman gender; a gender beyond the body, beyond human, a carnage of identity.

Buffalo Bill symbolises the problem of a kind of literal skin dis-ease but all the other characters in the film are similarly, although not necessarily pathologically, discomforted. Skin, in this movie, creeps and crawls, it is the most fragile of covers and also the most sticky. Skin becomes a metaphor for surface, for the external; it is the place of pleasure and the site of pain, it is the thin sheet that masks bloody horror. But skin is also the movie screen, the destination of the gaze, the place that glows in the dark, the violated site of visual pleasure.

In a by now very influential article, Laura Mulvey writes 'sadism demands a story'. 'Visual Pleasure and Narrative Cinema', of course, attempts to develop a theory of spectatorship that addresses itself to questions of who finds what pleasurable.[2] Such questions become all too pertinent when we consider that audiences change through history even as monsters do. Women were once the willing audience of the literature of horror, Gothic indeed was written for female consumers, but now women watch horror films, with reluctance and with fear, reluctant to engage with their everyday nightmares of rape and violation, fearful that the screen is only a mirror and that the monster may be sitting next to them as they watch. Films that feature sadistic murderers stalking un-suspecting female victims simply confirm a certain justified paranoia which means that women aren't crazy to be paranoid about rape and murder but rather they are crazy not to be.

For the female spectator of the horror movie, pleasure has to do with identification. Do we identify, in other words, with the detective or the victim, with the murderer persecuted by his gender markings or with the disembodied intellect of the imprisoned psychiatrist? This film allows us the pleasure of many different identifications and refuses to reduce female to a mess of mutilated flesh. The woman detective or female dick alters traditional power relations and changes completely the usual trajectory of the horror narrative. So does Dr Hannibal Lecter when he refuses to answer Starling's questions until she has answered his. His story requires her story, and hers depends upon his. Each role in this narrative is now fraught with violence, with criminality, with text-uality; no role is innocent, no mind is pure, no body impenetrable. Each role demands and produces a narrative, a text, about violence and evil, about the painful things people do to each other. Like the skin that Buffalo Bill attempts to suture into identity, stories in *The Silence of the Lambs* cover the nakedness of fear and fashion it into horror. The camera glances at mutilation and then frames it within more stories, more sadism, more silence. The silence of the lambs of course is no silence at all but rather a babble of voices fighting to be heard.

I resist, then, the temptation to submit Demme's film to a feminist analysis that would identify the danger of showing mass audiences an aestheticised version of the serial killing of women. I resist the tempta-tion to brand the film as homophobic because gender confusion becomes the guilty secret of the mad man in the basement. I resist indeed the readings that want to puncture the surface and enter the misogynist and homophobic unconscious of Buffalo Bill, Hannibal the Cannibal and Clarice Starling. The film indeed demands that we stay at the surface

and look for places where the surface stretches too thin. We cannot look
to the ruptures to reveal the truth of pleasure or the pleasure of truth but
we can look to the places where skin becomes transparent and see that
nothing is hidden. Gender trouble, indeed, is not the movie's secret, it is
a confession that both Starling and Buffalo Bill are all too willing to
make.

And yet, the gender trouble that Buffalo Bill represents, as he prances
around in a wig and plays with a poodle called Precious, cannot be
simply dismissed. It seems to me that *The Silence of the Lambs* emphasises
that we are at a peculiar time in history, a time when it is becoming
impossible to tell the difference between prejudice and its representations, between, then, homophobia and representations of homophobia.
In the example of *The Silence of the Lambs*, I would agree with Hannibal
Lecter's pronouncement that Buffalo Bill is not reducible to 'homosexual', or 'transsexual'. He is indeed a man at odds with gender identity or
sexual identity and his self-presentation is a confused mosaic of
signifiers. In the basement scene he resembles a heavy metal rocker as
much as a drag queen and that is precisely the point. He is a man imitat-
ing gender, exaggerating gender and finally attempting to shed his
gender in favour of a new skin. Buffalo Bill is prey to the most virulent
conditioning heterosexist culture has to offer. He believes that anatomy
is destiny.

A film like *The Silence of the Lambs* creates disagreement not just
between those who see it as homophobic and those who don't, but
between the lesbian and heterosexual feminists who were thrilled to see
a woman cast as a tough detective character, and the gay men who felt
offended by Buffalo Bill. It also divides sentiment along gender lines: I
think *The Silence of the Lambs* is a horror film that, for once, is not
designed to scare women, it scares men instead with the image of a fragmented and fragile masculinity, a male body disowning the penis.

Buffalo Bill, we may recall, uses female skin to cover his pathological
gender dysphoria. He is a seamstress, a collector of textiles and fabrics
and an artist who fashions death into new life and in so doing he
divorces sex from murder. This is a new kind of killer. Buffalo Bill is not
interested in getting in women, he never rapes them, he simply wants to
get them out of a skin that he perceives as the essence of female. Buffalo
Bill reads his desire against his body and realises that he has the wrong
body, at least externally. He is a woman trapped in a man's skin but no
transsexual. Hannibal's remark to Starling that this man is not a transsexual and not a homosexual suggests that if he were the first, Buffalo
Bill would be simply confused about his genitals; if he were the second,
he would be confused about an object choice. Neither is the case.

The 'case' is precisely the problem and Buffalo Bill's case becomes
Starling's as she tracks him to his sewing room. Buffalo Bill thinks he is

not in the wrong body, but the wrong skin, an incorrect casing. He is not interested in what lies beneath the skin for skin is gender for the murderer just as skin, or outward appearance, becomes the fetishised signifier of gender for a heterosexist culture. Buffalo Bill's sewing machine treats gender as an outfit made of natural fibres. Skin becomes the material which can be transformed by the right pattern into a seamless suit. But the violent harvest that precedes Buffalo Bill's domestic enterprise suggests that always behind the making of gender is a bloodied female body cut and measured to the right proportions.

And the case is also Hannibal the Cannibal's for he knows Buffalo Bill as a former case history and he knows what he is doing and why. Hannibal was once Buffalo Bill's psychiatrist, Buffalo Bill was once his case. Hannibal, however, created a monster as an inverted model of his own pathology. Inversion in this film depends upon two terms always and neither one can function as a norm. If homosexuality is an inversion of heterosexuality, this assumes that heterosexuality is the desired term. But in *The Silence of the Lambs* inversion reduces norm and pathology, inside and outside to meaningless categories: there is only pathology and varying degrees of it, only an outside in various forms. Buffalo Bill is an inversion of Hannibal the Cannibal, and Hannibal inverts his patient's desire because what Hannibal wants to put inside of himself, Buffalo Bill wants to dress in.

Buffalo Bill is Starling's case and when a new body is found in Clay County, West Virginia, Starling's home state, she flies home with her boss to conduct the autopsy. The corpse laid out on the table, of course, is a double for Starling, the image of what she might have become had she not left home, as Lecter points out, and aspired to greater things. This scene, in many ways, represents a premature climax of the horror in the movie. We see laid out for us exactly what it is that Buffalo Bill does to his victims. Prior to the autopsy, the camera has protected the viewer from close-ups of photographs taken of victims' bodies. Similarly, when Starling is being taken to Lecter, she is shown a photographic image of what Lecter did to a nurse. He attempted to bite her face off but the image of that hideous unmasking is kept hidden from the viewer. In the autopsy scene, the camera reveals all that it had promised to spare us: it lingers on the green and red flesh, the decayed body with two regular diamonds of flesh cut from its back.

The autopsy scene, indeed, resolves the drama of identification for the female spectator who found herself torn between detective and victim. After this scene the gaze is most definitely Starling's. The narrative has seemed to implicate Starling with the victim by identifying the two women in relation to their backgrounds and ages, and so there is some tension as Starling enters the morgue to begin the examination of the body. But Starling quickly establishes the difference between herself and the body in the body bag by setting herself up as an authority. She begins her visual analysis of the corpse and at first, as her voice trembles and her hands shake, as her body gives her away, the camera watches her from a position below the corpse – the spectator is positioned with the victim on the table. 'What do you see, Starling?' asks Crawford. 'She's not local', she replies, 'her ears are pierced three times and there's glitter nail polish. Looks like town to me.' Unlike Starling, then, the victim is not a hometown girl. The camera moves now to a position above the body and the gaze of the camera abruptly becomes Starling's gaze as we look down upon a mottled arm rotting and covered with dead leaves and other traces of the river she was hauled out of. Starling's examination of the corpse becomes more sure and the tension of identification between detective and victim is relieved for the moment.

Starling, like the viewer, seemed inclined to look away from the corpse, horrified perhaps by the nakedness of violence so plainly detailed before her. But, the corpse finally becomes object, thing, post-human when Starling looks at a photograph of its teeth and sees something in the throat. Before the photograph, her gaze, like our gaze, begins to linger. Turning back to the corpse moments later, Starling surveys the undignified flesh and speaking into a tape recorder, she begins to piece the body together, rebuild the mutilated body, and learn what the body has to tell.

The camera itself has done a kind of violence to whatever humanity remained upon or within the body – this is no longer a body framing an inner life, the body is merely surface, a picture. The camera has framed the victim in much the same way as Buffalo Bill does as he prepares his lambs for the slaughter. Keeping his victim naked in an old well shaft, he addresses her as 'it' when he must talk to her. And the camera also enables Starling to turn the corpse into a case, a case that she must solve even as the victim has become a case that Buffalo Bill will wear. This hideous wake, then, foreshadows the scenes in Buffalo Bill's basement gender factory and the autopsy becomes a site of trauma in terms of the film's narrative about gender – the corpse is no woman, it has been degendered, it is postgender, skinned and fleshed, it has been reified, turned at last into a fiction of the body.

We know from what happened to Buffalo Bill that Hannibal's patients go on to lead illustrious careers and so it is an ominous finale in the movie when Starling, Lecter's fledgling patient and the FBI's fledgling agent, steps up to accept her graduation certificate from the FBI: different degree, same profession – crime. As a camera captures her moment of graduation, the flash bulb is reminiscent of that earlier moment, that prior photograph of the victim's teeth in the autopsy lab. As she becomes a 'real' agent, Starling is framed as victim, as a lamb in wolf's clothing. As if to capitalise on the decline of Starling's authority, a phone call interrupts her graduation celebration. It is from the now escaped Hannibal; he tells her not to worry, he will not pursue her. Hannibal and Starling are both loose, both free, both out and about. The scene shows Hannibal on a Caribbean isle watching his psychiatrist from his prison days. Hannibal tells Starling, 'I'm having an old friend for dinner', and he adjusts his clothes elegantly. Hannibal is dressed to kill. Buffalo Bill, of course, kills to dress and only one costume will do.

Hannibal Lecter feeds upon both flesh and fiction. He needs Starling's stories as much as he needs to track down his next victim. 'Quid pro quo', he tells Starling; he wants a fair rate of exchange. Hannibal demands that no one be innocent and Starling must have a story to match the story he will sell her. Starling's story is a fiction of her power that is revealed in the process as no power at all but only the difference between two sides of the glass. Hannibal determines the limits of a carceral system. He is not disciplined by his imprisonment nor punished because as long as there are people around him he can cannibalise their stories. The ever hungry mind, Hannibal analyses people to death. He whispers all night to the man in the cell next to him and by morning the man, Multiple Miggs, has swallowed his own tongue; Hannibal enacts murders through bars and cages, through minds. Prisons come in all shapes and sizes and while Hannibal's is a restricted area equipped with a screen playing a TV evangelist at high volume, Starling is stuck inside her head, her body and the disturbing memories that Hannibal insists are not buried far beneath the power suit but quite present at the surface, on the top, visible and readable.

Starling's narrative of her childhood flight from her aunt and uncle's house becomes as terrifying as any other aspect of the horror narrative. The pieces of her past cohere slowly as Hannibal extracts each one surgically and then confronts her with it. The secret of her past that threatened all along to be some nasty story of incest or rape is precisely not sexual. Clarice Starling is the girl who wanted to save the lambs from the slaughter, who could only carry one at a time and who finally could not support the weight. Clarice Starling is the girl who freed the lambs from the pen and then watched in horror as they refused to leave it. Starling saves others in order to save her own skin.

Hannibal stays imprisoned until there is no longer a story to hear. The instalments that Starling gave him of her life maintained his interest just as each new killing maintains the FBI's interest in Buffalo Bill. The serial killing, indeed, like the psychoanalytic session, promises interminable chapters, promises to serialise, to keep one waiting for an ever deferred conclusion. Serial murders have something of a literary quality to them: they happen regularly over time and each new one creates an expectation; they involve a plot, a consummate villain and an absolutely pure (because randomly picked) victim; they demand explanation; they demand that a pattern be forced onto what appears to be 'desperately random' (as Hannibal Lecter tells Starling). 'Sadism demands a story', I noted earlier, quoting Mulvey. And, the story that sadism demands is the Gothic story embedded in the heart of a consumer culture *and* the realistic story embedded deep within Gothic culture. Lecter's Gothic sadism demands Starling's benign story, and Starling's innocence demands the Gothic tale that she as much as Lecter chooses to tell about a series of 'desperately random' killings.

Serial killings, like chapters in a periodical, stand in need of interpretation and interpreters (like the police, the tabloids, the public, the detective, the psychologist, the critic) produce the story that the bodies cannot tell. Starling and the FBI insist that there be a reason, a concrete explanation for the skinning of women, and Lecter complies but only as long as Starling recognises that she also is complicit in the narrative, she too must tell and be told. Telling does not mean finding a story in the unconscious that fits, it means inventing the unconscious and inventing the unconscious so that it can lie well enough to keep up with the fiction of everyday life.

Like some monstrous parody of nineteenth-century Gothic, these two characters mimic the vampire and Frankenstein's monster. Franco Moretti describes Shelley's monster and Stoker's vampire as 'dynamic, *totalising,* monsters' who 'threaten to live forever, and to conquer the world'.[3] Buffalo Bill and Hannibal are also totalising and each consumes other lives in order to prolong his own. Buffalo Bill combines in one both Frankenstein and the monster; he is the scientist, the creator and he is the body being formed and sculpted, stitched and fitted. Like Frankenstein, Buffalo Bill must search abroad for the body parts he needs and bring them back to the laboratory. The 'filthy workshop of creation' is now a basement sweatshop and new material is stored in a well in the form of a woman who Buffalo Bill is starving out of her skin. Buffalo Bill, however, is pickier than his predecessor; he demands particular human remains, size 14 to be precise, no one size fits all.

'Is he a vampire?', a policeman asks Starling as she is on her way to pay Hannibal a final visit. 'There's no word for what he is', she replies. Of course, he is a vampire, and a cannibal, a murderer and a psychopath. He is also a psychiatrist who drains minds before he starts on the bodies and perhaps he makes no distinction between the two. Hannibal is, Starling might have answered, a psychoanalyst, a doctor in the most uncanny of sciences. Freud predicted Hannibal when he noted in 'The Uncanny': 'Indeed, I should not be surprised to hear that psycho-analysis, which is concerned with laying bare these hidden forces, has itself become uncanny to many people. ...'[4] Hannibal and Buffalo Bill play out the doctor/patient dynamic that has precisely become uncanny, homoerotic (heimoerotic), transferential in the most literal way. Buffalo Bill leaves Hannibal his first victim, an ex-lover, in the form of a severed head. This is totem or taboo or something more than oedipal/edible. Not exactly father and son, certainly not a professional relationship, the two 'monsters' bond in the business of death and divorce death once and for all from sexuality. Murder is no romance in *The Silence of the Lambs*, it is a lesson in home economics – eating and sewing.

Hannibal the Cannibal and Buffalo Bill are Dr Jekyll and Mr Hyde as much as they are Dracula and Frankenstein. Jekyll, of course, produced Hyde from within his own psyche and he cannibalises him when the pressure is on. Hyde is an incredibly close relative to Buffalo Bill – he too is 'hide-bound', trapped in his skin, hidden by his hide, hiding from the law.[5] Like Buffalo Bill, Hyde performs his ritualistic crimes for his other half; he murders for Jekyll, he carouses for Jekyll, he indulges perverse desire for Jekyll. The homoerotic dyad bound to one body, hiding one self in the other, allows one self to feed off the others' strengths and weaknesses. No longer homosexuals, they are simply victims of modern science: psychiatry, a mind fuck.

Criticism has psychologised horror, made it a universal sign of humanity or depravity: horror, supposedly, is what we *all* fear in our oedipal unconscious. It is archetypal and yet individual, a condition of language or separation from the mother, a fragmentation or unspeakable desire. Now, in *The Silence of the Lambs*, horror is psychology, a bad therapeutic relationship, a fine romance between the one who knows and the one who eats, the one who eats and the one who grows skins; the one who castrates and the one who enacts a parody of circumcision. Psychology is no longer an explanation for horror, it generates horror, it founds its most basic fantasies and demands their enactment in the name of transference and truth.

It is no surprise that psychoanalysis and cinema have replaced fiction as the privileged locus of the horror/pleasure thrill. Psychoanalysis, writes Foucault, is 'both a theory of the essential relatedness of the law and desire, and a technique for relieving the effects of the taboo where its rigour makes it pathenogenic'.[6] Psychoanalysis uncovers and prohibits and in its prohibition lies the seeds of a desire. The moment of uncovering, of course, the moment when the skin is drawn back, the secrets of the flesh exposed, that moment is cinematic in its linking of seeing and knowing, vision and pleasure, power and punishment. The making visible of bodies, sex, power and desire provokes a new monstrosity and dares the body to continue its striptease down to the bone. Hannibal Lecter elicits Starling's poor little flashbacks only to demonstrate that stripping the mind is no less a violation than stripping the body and that mind and body are no longer split: Starling's memories are peeled back even as Buffalo Bill prepares his next lamb for the slaughter; and the raw nerve of Starling's memory is as exposed as the corpse that she dissected.

As a curious trademark, Buffalo Bill leaves a cocoon of the Death Head Moth in his victims' throats after he has killed them. Starling first finds one of the cocoons during the postmortem when she notices something is lodged in the corpse's throat. Later, we discover that Buffalo Bill collects butterflies and hatches moth cocoons. While the skull and crossbones markings on the moth are an obvious standard of the horror genre, the cocoon and the moth symbolise Buffalo Bill's particular pathology. Buffalo Bill and his victims are both cocoon and moth, larva and imago. Buffalo Bill is the cocoon holed up in a basement waiting for his skin to grow, for his beautiful metamorphosis to take place, and he is the moth that lives and breeds in clothes. Lecter calls Buffalo Bill's crime 'transformation' – he knows that Buffalo Bill is waiting in the dark for his beautiful gender suit to grow.

Buffalo Bill's victims are also cocoon and moth, they must shed their skins and fly on to death. Or, they are the moths, the producers of material. By placing the cocoon in his victims' throats, Buffalo Bill marks the difference between moth and larvae, outside and inside as no difference at all. The cocoon is inside the victims and the victims have shed their cocoons, the covering is internal and outside there is nothing but raw flesh. The blocked throat, of course, symbolises the silence of the lambs to the slaughter. A woman who has been reduced to a size 14 skin has no voice, no noise coming from inside to be heard outside. The voice, 'the grain of the voice', is the last signifier of something internal to the body.

But Hannibal too attempts a transformation. In order to escape from his prison cell, Hannibal murders two policemen. He cuts the face off one of them and covers himself with it and dresses in his clothes. When help arrives, Hannibal is taken out of the facility on a stretcher. By draping the bloody face over his own, Hannibal tears a leaf out of Buffalo Bill's casebook. Identity again proves to be only skin deep, and freedom depends upon appropriate dress. But even when he was in the cage, Hannibal was not bound by his chains, indeed he seemed only to be there because he wanted to be, because he wanted to hear the end of Starling's story. Sitting calmly behind the bars, his hands on his knees, his mouth open, the story of Starling's personal horror issuing from his lips, Hannibal resembles a Francis Bacon 'Face'. His features are blurred, his flesh resembles meat and his mouth, open to tell, forms the image of a scream that is felt not heard. But another Bacon painting also provides a fitting backdrop to this baconesque film. His 'Figure with Meat' blurs human flesh into animal flesh and makes the slaughterhouse a central image of human cruelty. The abattoir, of course, was at the centre of Starling's childhood nightmare and it becomes the setting for Buffalo Bill's sartorial activities. The figure with meat, in this narrative, is Starling but also Lecter and Buffalo Bill. The horrific human figure sits framed by the dripping flesh of what he will eat, a skinned animal with a recyclable hide, a carcass no longer worth saving.

Like the mythical moth that flutters too close to the flame, Buffalo Bill both covets and fears light. He keeps himself entrapped in the darkness and stalks his victims by night using infrared glasses. Like Buffalo Bill, the viewer of *The Silence of the Lambs* can also see in the dark. In the climactic hunting scene towards the end of the film, when Buffalo Bill plays hide and seek with Clarice Starling, the spectator watches through Buffalo Bill's eyes. Clarice's clarity deserts her and again, as she was in relation to Hannibal Lecter, Clarice is reduced to a listener. We see Clarice stumbling around through the infrared of Buffalo Bill's bloody vision. But even as we see with Buffalo Bill, it would not be accurate to say we, as spectators, are simply identified with his murderous gaze. We are in fact divided between the gaze of the camera that frames its object (here it is Starling) into still life or thingness and Starling's blindness that manages to direct a gun straight at the camera. Starling has been framed and blinded – but blindness (like silence) has a power all its own. To be blind is to avoid being trapped by appearance, it confers the freedom to look back.[7] Her shot in the dark hits Buffalo Bill and blows out a window, letting the light in. Starling has not only returned the gaze, she has destroyed it and remade it.

As a final point of contact with posthuman gender and the cinematic gaze, I want to examine one more manifestation of transformation in the film. Starling traces her clues to the house of the first murder victim and she goes into the victim's bedroom that has been kept exactly as Frederika left it. The camera looks over Starling's shoulder as she picks over the dead woman's belongings – a jewellery box, a romance novel called *Silken Threads*, a diet book. The room is decorated with butterfly wallpaper, a tailor's dummy and in the closet hangs material with paper diamonds pinned to it, ready to cut out. In Frederika's room, Starling finally realises Buffalo Bill's sartorial pathology. Later, in Buffalo Bill's basement, the camera again lingers upon the signifiers of the crime – textiles, threads, needles, cocoons, a sewing machine and tailor's dummies. The two rooms are collapsed into one momentarily as the next victim's screams bleed through from the cellar. Buffalo Bill, of course, has become Frederika just as Frederika has become Buffalo Bill – he wears her, she is upon him, he is inside her. Victim and murderer are folded into each other as Starling enters gun in hand to attempt to fix boundaries once and for all.

Buffalo Bill's misidentity forced him to assume what we might call a posthuman gender. He divorces once and for all sex and gender or nature and gender and remakes the human condition as a posthuman body suit. Buffalo Bill kills for his clothes and emblematises the ways in which gender is always posthuman, always a sewing job which stitches identity into a body bag. Skin, in this film, is identity itself rather than the surface of an interior identity. Buffalo Bill, in other words, is a limit

case for gender, for identity, for humanness. He does not understand
gender as inherent, innate; he reads it only as a surface effect, a
representation, an external attribute engineered into identity. Buffalo Bill
is at odds with identity because he is willing to kill to get one, he
commits violent acts in order to stabilise his condition. While we are
repelled by Buffalo Bill for what he does to women, while the female
spectator must ultimately look away from his experimentation, nonetheless Buffalo Bill represents a subtle change in the representation of
gender. Not simply murderer-monster, Buffalo Bill challenges the heterosexist and misogynist constructions of the humanness, the naturalness, the interiority of gender even as he is victimised by them. He rips
gender apart and remakes it as a mask, a suit, a costume. Gender identity
for Buffalo Bill is not the transcendent signifier of humanity, it is its most
efficient technology.

Hannibal Lecter, with his own masks and dissemblings, is the image of
a violence that cannot be kept in a cage; he is not evil incarnate, but a
representation of the evil that spreads across discourse, sound and sense;
across people, bodies and minds; across behaviours, actions and passiv-
ities; across systems, bureaucracies and institutions. Monstrosity in *The
Silence of the Lambs* in fact is an effect of the surface, a ripple across fields
of criminality, surveillance and discipline. Monstrosity, in this film,
cannot be limited to a body, even a body that kills in order to clothe
itself, or a body that cannibalises in order to feed. Monstrosity is now a
disembodied and disembodying force, reduced to silence, to blindness,
to surface.

Horror is the relation between carcass and history, between flesh and
fiction. The destruction of the boundary between inside and outside that
I have traced here marks a historical shift. *The Silence of the Lambs* equates
history with cannibalism; aesthetic production with a sacralised meal,
Gothic horror with the abject form of that cannibalism leaving the body.
The Silence of the Lambs has cannibalised nineteenth-century Gothic, eaten
its monsters alive and thrown them up onto the screen. The undead, the
monsters who threaten to live forever, find eternal life in the circularity
of consumption and production that characterises Hollywood cinema.

10

A Cyborg Manifesto: Science, Technology, and Socialist-Feminism in the Late Twentieth Century

Donna J. Haraway

AN IRONIC DREAM OF A COMMON LANGUAGE FOR WOMEN
IN THE INTEGRATED CIRCUIT

This essay[1] is an effort to build an ironic political myth faithful to feminism, socialism, and materialism. Perhaps more faithful as blasphemy is faithful, than as reverent worship and identification. Blasphemy has always seemed to require taking things very seriously. I know no better stance to adopt from within the secular-religious, evangelical traditions of United States politics, including the politics of socialist feminism. Blasphemy protects one from the moral majority within, while still insisting on the need for community. Blasphemy is not apostasy. Irony is about contradictions that do not resolve into larger wholes, even dialectically, about the tension of holding incompatible things together because both or all are necessary and true. Irony is about humour and serious play. It is also a rhetorical strategy and a political method, one I would like to see more honoured within socialist-feminism. At the centre of my ironic faith, my blasphemy, is the image of the cyborg.

A cyborg is a cybernetic organism, a hybrid of machine and organism, a creature of social reality as well as a creature of fiction. Social reality is lived social relations, our most important political construction, a world-changing fiction. The international women's movements have constructed 'women's experience', as well as uncovered or discovered this crucial collective object. This experience is a fiction and fact of the most crucial, political kind. Liberation rests on the construction of the consciousness, the imaginative apprehension, of oppression, and so of possibility. The cyborg is a matter of fiction and lived experience that changes what counts as women's experience in the late twentieth century. This is a struggle over life and death, but the boundary between science fiction and social reality is an optical illusion.

Contemporary science fiction is full of cyborgs – creatures simultaneously animal and machine, who populate worlds ambiguously natural and crafted. Modern medicine is also full of cyborgs, of couplings between organism and machine, each conceived as coded devices, in an intimacy and with a power that was not generated in the history of sexuality. Cyborg 'sex' restores some of the lovely replicative baroque of ferns and invertebrates (such nice organic prophylactics against heterosexism). Cyborg replication is uncoupled from organic reproduction. Modern production seems like a dream of cyborg colonisation work, a dream that makes the nightmare of Taylorism seem idyllic. And modern war is a cyborg orgy, coded by C^3I, command-control-communication-intelligence, an $84 billion item in 1984's US defence budget. I am making an argument for the cyborg as a fiction mapping our social and bodily reality and as an imaginative resource suggesting some very fruitful couplings. Michel Foucault's biopolitics is a flaccid premonition of cyborg politics, a very open field.

By the late twentieth century, our time, a mythic time, we are all chimeras, theorised and fabricated hybrids of machine and organism; in short, we are cyborgs. The cyborg is our ontology; it gives us our politics. The cyborg is a condensed image of both imagination and material reality, the two joined centres structuring any possibility of historical transformation. In the traditions of 'Western' science and politics – the tradition of racist, male-dominant capitalism; the tradition of progress; the tradition of the appropriation of nature as resource for the productions of culture; the tradition of reproduction of the self from the reflections of the other – the relation between organism and machine has been a border war. The stakes in the border war have been the territories of production, reproduction, and imagination. This essay is an argument for *pleasure* in the confusion of boundaries and for *responsibility* in their construction. It is also an effort to contribute to socialist-feminist culture and theory in a postmodernist, non-naturalist mode and in the utopian tradition of imagining a world without gender, which is perhaps a world without genesis, but maybe also a world without end. The cyborg incarnation is outside salvation history. Nor does it mark time on an oedipal calendar, attempting to heal the terrible cleavages of gender in an oral symbiotic utopia or post-oedipal apocalypse. As Zoe Sofoulis argues in her unpublished manuscript on Jacques Lacan, Melanie Klein, and nuclear culture, *Lacklein*, the most terrible and perhaps the most promising monsters in cyborg worlds are embodied in non-oedipal narratives with a different logic of repression, which we need to understand for our survival.

The cyborg is a creature in a post-gender world; it has no truck with bisexuality, pre-oedipal symbiosis, unalienated labour, or other seduct-ions to organic wholeness through a final appropriation of all the powers of the parts into a higher unity. In a sense, the cyborg has no origin story in the Western sense – a 'final' irony since the cyborg is also the awful apocalyptic *telos* of the 'West's' escalating dominations of abstract indi-viduation, an ultimate self untied at last from all dependency, a man in space. An origin story in the 'Western', humanist sense depends on the myth of original unity, fullness, bliss and terror, represented by the phallic mother from whom all humans must separate, the task of indi-vidual development and of history, the twin potent myths inscribed most powerfully for us in psychoanalysis and Marxism. Hilary Klein has argued that both Marxism and psychoanalysis, in their concepts of labour and of individuation and gender formation, depend on the plot of original unity out of which difference must be produced and enlisted in a drama of escalating domination of woman/nature. The cyborg skips the step of original unity, of identification with nature in the Western sense. This is its illegitimate promise that might lead to subversion of its teleology as star wars.

The cyborg is resolutely committed to partiality, irony, intimacy, and perversity. It is oppositional, utopian, and completely without innocence. No longer structured by the polarity of public and private, the cyborg defines a technological polis based partly on a revolution of social relations in the *oikos*, the household. Nature and culture are reworked; the one can no longer be the resource for appropriation or incorporation by the other. The relationships for forming wholes from parts, including those of polarity and hierarchical domination, are at issue in the cyborg world. Unlike the hopes of Frankenstein's monster, the cyborg does not expect its father to save it through a restoration of the garden; that is, through the fabrication of a heterosexual mate, through its completion in a finished whole, a city and cosmos. The cyborg does not dream of community on the model of the organic family, this time without the oedipal project. The cyborg would not recognise the Garden of Eden; it is not made of mud and cannot dream of returning to dust. Perhaps that is why I want to see if cyborgs can subvert the apocalypse of returning to nuclear dust in the manic com-pulsion to name the Enemy. Cyborgs are not reverent; they do not re-member the cosmos. They are wary of holism, but needy for connection – they seem to have a natural feel for united front politics, but without the vanguard party. The main trouble with cyborgs, of course, is that they are the illegitimate offspring of militarism and patriarchal capitalism, not to mention state socialism. But illegitimate offspring are often exceedingly unfaithful to their origins. Their fathers, after all, are inessential. [...]

By the late twentieth century in United States scientific culture, the boundary between human and animal is thoroughly breached. The last beachheads of uniqueness have been polluted if not turned into amusement parks – language, tool use, social behaviour, mental events, nothing really convincingly settles the separation of human and animal. And many people no longer feel the need for such a separation; indeed, many branches of feminist culture affirm the pleasure of connection of human and other living creatures. Movements for animal rights are not irrational denials of human uniqueness; they are a clear-sighted recognition of connection across the discredited breach of nature and culture. Biology and evolutionary theory over the last two centuries have simultaneously produced modern organisms as objects of knowledge and reduced the line between humans and animals to a faint trace re-etched in ideological struggle or professional disputes between life and social science. Within this framework, teaching modern Christian creationism should be fought as a form of child abuse.

Biological-determinist ideology is only one position opened up in scientific culture for arguing the meanings of human animality. There is much room for radical political people to contest the meanings of the breached boundary.[2] The cyborg appears in myth precisely where the boundary between human and animal is transgressed. Far from signalling a walling off of people from other living beings, cyborgs signal disturbingly and pleasurably tight coupling. Bestiality has a new status in this cycle of marriage exchange.

The second leaky distinction is between animal-human (organism) and machine. Pre-cybernetic machines could be haunted; there was always the spectre of the ghost in the machine. This dualism structured the dialogue between materialism and idealism that was settled by a dialectical progeny called spirit or history, according to taste. But basically machines were not self-moving, self-designing, autonomous. They could not achieve man's dream, only mock it. They were not man, an author to himself, but only a caricature of that masculinist reproductive dream. To think they were otherwise was paranoid. Now we are not so sure. Late twentieth-century machines have made thoroughly ambiguous the difference between natural and artificial, mind and body, self-developing and externally designed, and many other distinctions that used to apply to organisms and machines. Our machines are disturbingly lively, and we ourselves frighteningly inert.

Technological determination is only one ideological space opened up by the reconceptions of machine and organism as coded texts through which we engage in the play of writing and reading the world.[3] 'Textualisation' of everything in poststructuralist, postmodernist theory has been damned by Marxists and socialist feminists for its utopian disregard for the lived relations of domination that ground the 'play' of arbitrary reading.[4] It is certainly true that postmodernist strategies, like my cyborg myth, subvert myriad organic wholes (for example, the poem, the primitive culture, the biological organism). In short, the certainty of what counts as nature – a source of insight and promise of innocence – is undermined, probably fatally. The transcendent authorisation of inter-pretation is lost, and with it the ontology grounding 'Western' episte-mology. But the alternative is not cynicism or faithlessness, that is, some version of abstract existence, like the accounts of technological determin-ism destroying 'man' by the 'machine' or 'meaningful political action' by the 'text'. Who cyborgs will be is a radical question; the answers are a matter of survival. Both chimpanzees and artefacts have politics, so why shouldn't we (de Waal, 1982; Winner, 1980)?

The third distinction is a subset of the second: the boundary between physical and non-physical is very imprecise for us. Pop physics books on the consequences of quantum theory and the indeterminacy principle are a kind of popular scientific equivalent to Harlequin romances[5] as a marker of radical change in American white heterosexuality: they get it wrong, but they are on the right subject. Modern machines are quintessentially microelectronic devices: they are everywhere and they are invisible. Modern machinery is an irreverent upstart god, mocking the Father's ubiquity and spirituality. The silicon chip is a surface for writing; it is etched in molecular scales disturbed only by atomic noise, the ultimate interference for nuclear scores. Writing, power, and technology are old partners in Western stories of the origin of civilisation, but miniaturisation has changed our experience of mechanism. Miniaturisation has turned out to be about power; small is not so much beautiful as pre-eminently dan-gerous, as in cruise missiles. Contrast the TV sets of the 1950s or the news cameras of the 1970s with the TV wrist bands or hand-sized video cameras now advertised. Our best machines are made of sunshine; they are all light and clean because they are nothing but signals, electromagnetic waves, a section of a spectrum, and these machines are eminently portable, mobile – a matter of immense human pain in Detroit and Singapore. People are nowhere near so fluid, being both material and opaque. Cyborgs are ether, quintessence.

The ubiquity and invisibility of cyborgs is precisely why these sun-shine-belt machines are so deadly. They are as hard to see politically as materially. They are about consciousness – or its simulation.[6] They are floating signifiers moving in pickup trucks across Europe, blocked more effectively by the witch-weavings of the displaced and so unnatural Greenham women, who read the cyborg webs of power so very well, than by the militant labour of older masculinist politics, whose natural constituency needs defence jobs. Ultimately the 'hardest' science is about the realm of greatest boundary confusion, the realm of pure number, pure spirit, C^3I, cryptography, and the preservation of potent secrets. The new machines are so clean and light. Their engineers are sun-worshippers mediating a new scientific revolution associated with the night dream of post-industrial society. The diseases evoked by these clean machines are 'no more' than the minuscule coding changes of an antigen in the immune system, 'no more' than the experience of stress. The nimble fingers of 'Oriental' women, the old fascination of little Anglo-Saxon Victorian girls with doll's houses, women's enforced attention to the small take on quite new dimensions in this world. There might be a cyborg Alice taking account of these new dimensions. Ironically, it might be the unnatural cyborg women making chips in Asia and spiral dancing in Santa Rita jail[7] whose constructed unities will guide effective oppositional strategies.

So my cyborg myth is about transgressed boundaries, potent fusions, and dangerous possibilities which progressive people might explore as one part of needed political work. One of my premises is that most American socialists and feminists see deepened dualisms of mind and body, animal and machine, idealism and materialism in the social practices, symbolic formulations, and physical artefacts associated with 'high technology' and scientific culture. [...] Another of my premises is that the need for unity of people trying to resist world-wide intensification of domination has never been more acute. But a slightly perverse shift of perspective might better enable us to contest for meanings, as well as for other forms of power and pleasure in technologically mediated societies.

From one perspective, a cyborg world is about the final imposition of a grid of control on the planet, about the final abstraction embodied in a Star Wars apocalypse waged in the name of defence, about the final appropriation of women's bodies in a masculinist orgy of war (Sofia, 1984). From another perspective, a cyborg world might be about lived social and bodily realities in which people are not afraid of their joint kinship with animals and machines, not afraid of permanently partial identities and contradictory standpoints. The political struggle is to see from both perspectives at once because each reveals both dominations and possibilities unimaginable from the other vantage point. Single vision produces worse illusions than double vision or many-headed monsters. Cyborg unities are monstrous and illegitimate; in our present political circumstances, we could hardly hope for more potent myths for resistance and recoupling. [...]

FRACTURED IDENTITIES

It has become difficult to name one's feminism by a single adjective – or even to insist in every circumstance upon the noun. Consciousness of exclusion through naming is acute. Identities seem contradictory, partial, and strategic. With the hard-won recognition of their social and historical constitution, gender, race, and class cannot provide the basis for belief in 'essential' unity. There is nothing about being 'female' that naturally binds women. There is not even such a state as 'being' female, itself a highly complex category constructed in contested sexual scientific discourses and other social practices. Gender, race, or class consciousness is an achievement forced on us by the terrible historical experience of the contradictory social realities of patriarchy, colonialism, and capitalism. And who counts as 'us' in my own rhetoric? Which identities are available to ground such a potent political myth called 'us', and what could motivate enlistment in this collectivity? Painful fragmentation among feminists (not to mention among women) along every possible fault line has made the concept of *woman* elusive, an excuse for the matrix of women's dominations of each other. For me – and for many who share a similar historical location in white, professional middle-class, female, radical, North American, mid-adult bodies – the sources of a crisis in political identity are legion. The recent history for much of the US left and US feminism has been a response to this kind of crisis by endless splitting and searches for a new essential unity. But there has also been a growing recognition of another response through coalition – affinity, not identity.[8]

Chela Sandoval (n.d., 1984), from a consideration of specific historical moments in the formation of the new political voice called women of colour, has theorised a hopeful model of political identity called 'oppositional consciousness', born of the skills for reading webs of power by those refused stable membership in the social categories of race, sex, or class. 'Women of color', a name contested in its origins by those whom it would incorporate, as well as a historical consciousness marking systematic breakdown of all the signs of Man in 'Western' traditions, constructs a kind of postmodernist identity out of otherness, difference, and specificity. This postmodernist identity is fully political, whatever might be said about other possible postmodernisms. Sandoval's oppositional consciousness is about contradictory locations and heterochronic calendars, not about relativisms and pluralisms.

Sandoval emphasises the lack of any essential criterion for identifying who is a woman of colour. She notes that the definition of the group has been by conscious appropriation of negation. For example, a Chicana or US black woman has not been able to speak as a woman or as a black person or as a Chicano. Thus, she was at the bottom of a cascade of negative identities, left out of even the privileged oppressed authorial categories called 'women and blacks', who claimed to make the important revolutions. The category 'woman' negated all non-white women; 'black' negated all non-black people, as well as all black women. But there was also no 'she', no singularity, but a sea of differences among US women who have affirmed their historical identity as US women of colour. This identity marks out a self-consciously constructed space that cannot affirm the capacity to act on the basis of natural identification, but only on the basis of conscious coalition, of affinity, of political kinship.[9] Unlike the 'woman' of some streams of the white women's movement in the United States, there is no naturalisation of the matrix, or at least this is what Sandoval argues is uniquely available through the power of oppositional consciousness.

Sandoval's argument has to be seen as one potent formulation for feminists out of the world-wide development of anti-colonialist discourse; that is to say, discourse dissolving the 'West' and its highest product – the one who is not animal, barbarian, or woman; man, that is, the author of a cosmos called history. As orientalism is deconstructed politically and semiotically, the identities of the occident destabilise, including those of feminists.[10] Sandoval argues that 'women of colour' have a chance to build an effective unity that does not replicate the imperialising, totalising revolutionary subjects of previous Marxisms and feminisms which had not faced the consequences of the disorderly polyphony emerging from decolonisation.

[...]

The theoretical and practical struggle against unity-through-domination or unity-through-incorporation ironically not only undermines the justifications for patriarchy, colonialism, humanism, positivism, essentialism, scientism, and other unlamented -isms, but *all* claims for an organic or natural standpoint. I think that radical and socialist/Marxist-feminisms have also undermined their/our own epistemological strategies and that this is a crucially valuable step in imagining possible unities. It remains to be seen whether all 'epistemologies' as Western political people have known them fail us in the task to build effective affinities.

It is important to note that the effort to construct revolutionary standpoints, epistemologies as achievements of people committed to changing the world, has been part of the process showing the limits of identification. The acid tools of postmodernist theory and the constructive tools of ontological discourse about revolutionary subjects might be seen as ironic allies in dissolving Western selves in the interests of survival. We are excruciatingly conscious of what it means to have a historically constituted body. But with the loss of innocence in our origin, there is no expulsion from the Garden either. Our politics lose the indulgence of guilt with the *naïveté* of innocence. But what would another political myth for socialist-feminism look like? What kind of politics could embrace partial, contradictory, permanently unclosed constructions of personal and collective selves and still be faithful, effective – and, ironically, socialist-feminist?

I do not know of any other time in history when there was greater need for political unity to confront effectively the dominations of 'race', 'gender', 'sexuality', and 'class'. I also do not know of any other time when the kind of unity we might help build could have been possible. None of 'us' have any longer the symbolic or material capacity of dictating the shape of reality to any of 'them'. Or at least 'we' cannot claim innocence from practising such dominations. White women, including socialist feminists, discovered (that is, were forced kicking and screaming to notice) the non-innocence of the category 'woman'. That consciousness changes the geography of all previous categories; it denatures them as heat denatures a fragile protein. Cyborg feminists have to argue that 'we' do not want any more natural matrix of unity and that no construction is whole. Innocence, and the corollary insistence on victimhood as the only ground for insight, has done enough damage. But the constructed revolutionary subject must give late-twentieth-century people pause as well. In the fraying of identities and in the reflexive strategies for constructing them, the possibility opens up for weaving something other than a shroud for the day after the apocalypse that so prophetically ends salvation history.

[...]

THE INFORMATICS OF DOMINATION

In this attempt at an epistemological and political position, I would like to sketch a picture of possible unity, a picture indebted to socialist and feminist principles of design. The frame for my sketch is set by the extent and importance of rearrangements in world-wide social relations tied to science and technology. I argue for a politics rooted in claims about fundamental changes in the nature of class, race, and gender in an emerging system of world order analogous in its novelty and scope to that created by industrial capitalism; we are living through a movement from an organic, industrial society to a polymorphous, information system – from all work to all play, a deadly game. Simultaneously material and ideological, the dichotomies may be expressed in the following chart of transitions from the comfortable old hierarchical dominations to the scary new networks I have called the informatics of domination:

Representation	Simulation
Bourgeois novel, realism	Science fiction, postmodernism
Organism	Biotic component
Depth, integrity	Surface, boundary
Heat	Noise
Biology as clinical practice	Biology as inscription
Physiology	Communications engineering

Small group	Subsystem
Perfection	Optimisation
Eugenics	Population Control
Decadence, *Magic Mountain*	Obsolescence, *Future Shock*
Hygiene	Stress Management
Microbiology, tuberculosis	Immunology, AIDS
Organic division of labour	Ergonomics / cybernetics of labour
Functional specialisation	Modular construction
Reproduction	Replication
Organic sex role specialisation	Optimal genetic strategies
Biological determinism	Evolutionary inertia, constraints
Community ecology	Ecosystem
Racial chain of being	Neo-imperialism, United Nations humanism
Scientific management in home / factory	Global factory / Electronic cottage
Family / Market / Factory	Women in the Integrated Circuit
Family wage	Comparable worth
Public / Private	Cyborg citizenship
Nature / Culture	Fields of difference
Co-operation	Communications enhancement
Freud	Lacan
Sex	Genetic engineering
Labour	Robotics
Mind	Artificial Intelligence
Second World War	Star Wars
White Capitalist Patriarchy	Informatics of Domination

This list suggests several interesting things.[11] First, the objects on the right-hand side cannot be coded as 'natural', a realisation that subverts naturalistic coding for the left-hand side as well. We cannot go back ideologically or materially. It's not just that 'god' is dead; so is the 'goddess'. Or both are revivified in the worlds charged with microelectronic and biotechnological politics. In relation to objects like biotic components, one must think not in terms of essential properties, but in terms of design, boundary constraints, rates of flows, systems logics, costs of lowering constraints. Sexual reproduction is one kind of reproductive strategy among many, with costs and benefits as a function of the system environment. Ideologies of sexual reproduction can no longer reasonably call on notions of sex and sex role as organic aspects in natural objects like organisms and families. Such reasoning will be unmasked as irrational, and ironically corporate executives reading *Playboy* and anti-porn radical feminists will make strange bedfellows in jointly unmasking the irrationalism.

Likewise for race, ideologies about human diversity have to be formulated in terms of frequencies of parameters, like blood groups or intelligence scores. It is 'irrational' to invoke concepts like primitive and civilised. For liberals and radicals, the search for integrated social systems gives way to a new practice called 'experimental ethnography' in which an organic object dissipates in attention to the play of writing. At the level of ideology, we see translations of racism and colonialism into languages of development and under-development, rates and constraints of modernisation. Any objects or persons can be reasonably thought of in terms of disassembly and reassembly; no 'natural' architectures constrain system design. The financial districts in all the world's cities, as well as the export-processing and free-trade zones, proclaim this elementary fact of 'late capitalism'. The entire universe of objects that can be known scientifically must be formulated as problems in communications engineering (for the managers) or theories of the text (for those who would resist). Both are cyborg semiologies.

One should expect control strategies to concentrate on boundary conditions and interfaces, on rates of flow across boundaries – and not on the integrity of natural objects. 'Integrity' or 'sincerity' of the Western self gives way to decision procedures and expert systems. For example, control strategies applied to women's capacities to give birth to new human beings will be developed in the languages of population control and maximisation of goal achievement for individual decision-makers. Control strategies will be formulated in terms of rates, costs of constraints, degrees of freedom. Human beings, like any other component or subsystem, must be localised in a system architecture whose basic modes of operation are probabilistic, statistical. No objects, spaces, or bodies are sacred in themselves; any component can be interfaced with any other if the proper standard, the proper code, can be constructed for processing signals in a common language. Exchange in this world transcends the universal translation effected by capitalist markets that Marx analysed so well. The privileged pathology affecting all kinds of components in this universe is stress – communications breakdown (Hogness, 1983). The cyborg is not subject to Foucault's biopolitics; the cyborg simulates politics, a much more potent field of operations.

[...] The cyborg is a kind of disassembled and reassembled, postmodern collective and personal self. This is the self feminists must code.

[...] The only way to characterise the informatics of domination is as a massive intensification of insecurity and cultural impoverishment, with common failure of subsistence networks for the most vulnerable. Since much of this picture interweaves with the social relations of science and technology, the urgency of a socialist-feminist politics addressed to science and technology is plain. There is much now being done, and the grounds for political work are rich. For example, the efforts to develop forms of collective struggle for women in paid work, like SEIU's District 925,[12] should be a high priority for all of us. These efforts are profoundly tied to technical restructuring of labour processes and reformations of working classes. These efforts also are providing understanding of a more comprehensive kind of labour organisation, involving community, sexuality, and family issues never privileged in the largely white male industrial unions.

The structural rearrangements related to the social relations of science and technology evoke strong ambivalence. But it is not necessary to be ultimately depressed by the implications of late twentieth-century women's relation to all aspects of work, culture, production of knowledge, sexuality, and reproduction. For excellent reasons, most Marxisms see domination best and have trouble understanding what can only look like false consciousness and people's complicity in their own domination in late capitalism. It is crucial to remember that what is lost, perhaps especially from women's points of view, is often virulent forms of oppression, nostalgically naturalised in the face of current violation. Ambivalence towards the disrupted unities mediated by high-tech culture requires not sorting consciousness into categories of 'clear-sighted critique grounding a solid political epistemology' versus 'manipulated false consciousness', but subtle understanding of emerging pleasures, experiences, and powers with serious potential for changing the rules of the game.

There are grounds for hope in the emerging bases for new kinds of unity across race, gender, and class, as these elementary units of social-ist-feminist analysis themselves suffer protean transformations. Intensifications of hardship experienced world-wide in connection with the social relations of science and technology are severe. But what people are experiencing is not transparently clear, and we lack sufficiently subtle connections for collectively building effective theories of experience. Present efforts – Marxist, psychoanalytic, feminist, anthropological – to clarify even 'our' experience are rudimentary.

I am conscious of the odd perspective provided by my historical position – a PhD in biology for an Irish Catholic girl was made possible by Sputnik's impact on US national science-education policy. I have a body and mind as much constructed by the post-Second World War arms race and cold war as by the women's movements. There are more grounds for hope in focusing on the contradictory effects of politics designed to produce loyal American technocrats, which also produced large numbers of dissidents, than in focusing on the present defeats.

The permanent partiality of feminist points of view has consequences for our expectations of forms of political organisation and participation. We do not need a totality in order to work well. The feminist dream of a common language, like all dreams for a perfectly true language, of perfectly faithful naming of experience, is a totalising and imperialist one. In that sense, dialectics too is a dream language, longing to resolve contradiction. Perhaps, ironically, we can learn from our fusions with animals and machines how not to be Man, the embodiment of Western logos. From the point of view of pleasure in these potent and taboo fusions, made inevitable by the social relations of science and technology, there might indeed be a feminist science.

CYBORGS: A MYTH OF POLITICAL IDENTITY

[...] Writing is pre-eminently the technology of cyborgs, etched surfaces of the late twentieth century. Cyborg politics is the struggle for language and the struggle against perfect communication, against the one code that translates all meaning perfectly, the central dogma of phallogocentrism. That is why cyborg politics insist on noise and advocate pollution, rejoicing in the illegitimate fusions of animal and machine. These are the couplings which make Man and Woman so problematic, subverting the structure of desire, the force imagined to generate language and gender, and so subverting the structure and modes of reproduction of 'Western' identity, of nature and culture, of mirror and eye, slave and master, body and mind. 'We' did not originally choose to be cyborgs, but choice grounds a liberal politics and epistemology that imagines the reproduction of individuals before the wider replications of 'texts'.

From the perspective of cyborgs, freed of the need to ground politics in 'our' privileged position of the oppression that incorporates all other dominations, the innocence of the merely violated, the ground of those closer to nature, we can see powerful possibilities. Feminisms and Marxisms have run aground on Western epistemological imperatives to construct a revolutionary subject from the perspective of a hierarchy of oppressions and/or a latent position of moral superiority, innocence, and greater closeness to nature. With no available original dream of a common language or original symbiosis promising protection from hostile 'masculine' separation, but written into the play of a text that has no finally privileged reading or salvation history, to recognise 'oneself' as fully implicated in the world, frees us of the need to root politics in identification, vanguard parties, purity, and mothering. Stripped of identity, the bastard race teaches about the power of the margins and the importance of a mother like Malinche. Women of colour have transformed her from the evil mother of masculinist fear into the originally literate mother who teaches survival.

This is not just literary deconstruction, but liminal transformation. Every story that begins with original innocence and privileges the return to wholeness imagines the drama of life to be individuation, separation, the birth of the self, the tragedy of autonomy, the fall into writing, alienation; that is, war, tempered by imaginary respite in the bosom of the Other. These plots are ruled by a reproductive politics – rebirth without flaw, perfection, abstraction. In this plot women are imagined either better or worse off, but all agree they have less self-hood, weaker individuation, more fusion to the oral, to Mother, less at stake in masculine autonomy. But there is another route to having less at stake in masculine autonomy, a route that does not pass through Woman, Primitive, Zero, the Mirror Stage and its imaginary. It passes through women and other present-tense, illegitimate cyborgs, not of Woman born, who refuse the ideological resources of victimisation so as to have a real life. These cyborgs are the people who refuse to dis-appear on cue, no matter how many times a 'Western' commentator remarks on the sad passing of another primitive, another organic group done in by 'Western' technology, by writing.[13] These real-life cyborgs (for example, the Southeast Asian village women workers in Japanese and US electronics firms described by Aihwa Ong) are actively rewrit-ing the texts of their bodies and societies. Survival is the stakes in this play of readings.

To recapitulate, certain dualisms have been persistent in Western tra-ditions; they have all been systemic to the logics and practices of dom-ination of women, people of colour, nature, workers, animals – in short, domination of all constituted as others, whose task is to mirror the self. Chief among these troubling dualisms are self/other, mind/body, culture/nature, male/female, civilised/primitive, reality/appearance, whole/part, agent/resource, maker/made, active/passive, right/wrong, truth/illusion, total/partial, God/man. The self is the One who is not dominated, who knows that by the service of the other, the other is the one who holds the future, who knows that by the experience of domina-tion, which gives the lie to the autonomy of the self. To be One is to be autonomous, to be powerful, to be God; but to be One is to be an illusion, and so to be involved in a dialectic of apocalypse with the other. Yet to be other is to be multiple, without clear boundary, frayed, insubstantial. One is too few, but two are too many.

High-tech culture challenges these dualisms in intriguing ways. It is not clear who makes and who is made in the relation between human and machine. It is not clear what is mind and what body in machines that resolve into coding practices. In so far as we know ourselves in both formal discourse (for example, biology) and in daily practice (for example, the homework economy in the integrated circuit), we find our-selves to be cyborgs, hybrids, mosaics, chimeras. Biological organisms have become biotic systems, communication devices like others. There is no fundamental, ontological separation in our formal knowledge of machine and organism, of technical and organic. The replicant Rachel in the Ridley Scott film *Blade Runner* stands as the image of a cyborg culture's fear, love, and confusion.

[...]

There are several consequences to taking seriously the imagery of cyborgs as other than our enemies. Our bodies, ourselves; bodies are maps of power and identity. Cyborgs are no exception. A cyborg body is not innocent; it was not born in a garden; it does not seek unitary identity and so generate antagonistic dualisms without end (or until the world ends); it takes irony for granted. One is too few, and two is only one possibility. Intense pleasure in skill, machine skill, ceases to be a sin, but an aspect of embodiment. The machine is not an *it* to be animated, worshipped, and dominated. The machine is us, our processes, an aspect of our embodiment. We can be responsible for machines; *they* do not dominate or threaten us. We are responsible for boundaries; we are they. Up till now (once upon a time), female embodiment seemed to be given, organic, necessary; and female embodiment seemed to mean skill in mothering and its metaphoric extensions. Only by being out of place could we take intense pleasure in machines, and then with excuses that this was organic activity after all, appropriate to females. Cyborgs might consider more seriously the partial, fluid, sometimes aspect of sex and sexual embodiment. Gender might not be global identity after all, even if it has profound historical breadth and depth.

The ideologically charged question of what counts as daily activity, as experience, can be approached by exploiting the cyborg image. Feminists have recently claimed that women are given to dailiness, that women more than men somehow sustain daily life, and so have a privileged epistemological position potentially. There is a compelling aspect to this claim, one that makes visible unvalued female activity and names it as the ground of life. But *the* ground of life? What about all the ignorance of women, all the exclusions and failures of knowledge and skill? What about men's access to daily competence, to knowing how to build things, to take them apart, to play? What about other embodiments? Cyborg gender is a local possibility taking a global vengeance. Race, gender, and capital require a cyborg theory of wholes and parts. There is no drive in cyborgs to produce total theory, but there is an intimate experience of boundaries, their construction and deconstruction. There is a myth system waiting to become a political language to ground one way of looking at science and technology and challenging the informatics of domination – in order to act potently.

One last image: organisms and organismic, holistic politics depend on metaphors of rebirth and invariably call on the resources of reproductive sex. I would suggest that cyborgs have more to do with regeneration and are suspicious of the reproductive matrix and of most birthing. For salamanders, regeneration after injury, such as the loss of a limb, involves regrowth of structure and restoration of function with the constant possibility of twinning or other odd topographical productions at the site of former injury. The regrown limb can be monstrous, duplicated, potent. We have all been injured, profoundly. We require regeneration, not rebirth, and the possibilities for our reconstitution include the utopian dream of the hope for a monstrous world without gender.

Cyborg imagery can help express two crucial arguments in this essay: first, the production of universal, totalising theory is a major mistake that misses most of reality, probably always, but certainly now; and second, taking responsibility for the social relations of science and technology means refusing an anti-science metaphysics, a demonology of technology, and so means embracing the skilful task of reconstructing the boundaries of daily life, in partial connection with others, in communication with all of our parts. It is not just that science and technology are possible means of great human satisfaction, as well as a matrix of complex dominations. Cyborg imagery can suggest a way out of the maze of dualisms in which we have explained our bodies and our tools to ourselves. This is a dream not of a common language, but of a powerful infidel heteroglossia. It is an imagination of a feminist speaking in tongues to strike fear into the circuits of the supersavers of the new right. It means both building and destroying machines, identities, categories, relationships, space stories. Though both are bound in the spiral dance, I would rather be a cyborg than a goddess.

11

Posthumanist (Com)Promises: Diffracting Donna Haraway's Cyborg Through Marge Piercy's *Body of Glass*

Neil Badmington

'Going as much with the river as not'
> Van Morrison, 'You Don't Pull No Punches, but You Don't
> Push the River'

I

In the mid-1970s, a sign at the entrance to a castle near my hometown in the Welsh borderlands asked parents to caution their children about the dangers of jumping from the battlements. This was perfectly understandable. More unusual, perhaps, was the suggestion that the young be reminded that they were not bionic. I had just started school at the time and clearly remember the immense popularity of *The Six Million Dollar Man* (being the televisual adventures of an American test-pilot who had been reconstructed as a cyborg following a horrific accident). Many of 'us' – girls too, for *The Bionic Woman* followed soon after, providing a suitably 'feminised' counterpart to imitate – did not merely own the merchandise relating to the series. 'Our' devotion went deeper. 'We' wanted to *be* cyborgs, to leap, run, see, and hear with superhuman prowess. 'We' would run bionically around the school yard, singing the theme music, re-enacting favourite scenes from recent episodes.

A quarter of a century later, the cyborg is once again an object of desire. A viewer glancing over the current theoretical landscape might be tempted to agree with Allucquere Rosanne Stone's claim that many, particularly those interested in posthumanism, are suffering from something called *cyborg envy*.[1] The cyborg seems to be the answer, the messiah who will lead 'us' to a promised land where humanism is a thing of the past. This belief is the subject of my essay. Are the faithful correct? Does the cyborg terminate humanism? Is it the coming of pure posthumanism? Simply because it 'put cyborgs on the map of cultural criticism',[2] I will take Donna Haraway's 'Cyborg Manifesto' as my point of departure,[3] turning in time to Marge Piercy's novel, *Body of Glass*, in order to rethink what I see as some of the manifesto's more problematic features.[4] I cannot claim to be forging an entirely original link between these two texts, for Piercy openly acknowledges the influence of the manifesto.[5] What concerns me, rather, is the fidelity of this connection.

Haraway's cyborg is truly a creature of the 'post-': post-gender, post-humanist, post-modern, post-familial, post-natural. That the appearance of the cyborg should mark a clean break from the established order of things is evident from the 'chart of transitions' which maps the movement 'from the comfortable *old* hierarchical dominations to the scary *new* networks... .'[6] A series of oppositions is constructed, in which the terms occupying the right-hand column 'cannot be coded as "natural"'[7] because they refer to the posthumanism of the cyborg. When Haraway proposes that '[w]e cannot go back ideologically or materially',[8] the implication is that 'we' have progressed beyond the state of affairs signified by the left-hand column. The beyond is truly an *outside*, for the cyborg 'can suggest *a way out* of the maze of dualisms in which we have explained our bodies and our tools to ourselves'.[9] That was then, this is now: there has been an exodus from the space of humanism.

Jacques Derrida has consistently problematised such faith in pure ex-teriority. In 'Cogito and the History of Madness', for instance, he turns his attention to Michel Foucault's desire, in *Folie et déraison: Histoire de la folie à l'âge classique*,[10] to let 'madness speak for itself',[11] in a voice other than that of humanism. Foucault's claim to be working outside the legacy of reason is, Derrida declares, 'the *maddest* aspect of his project',[12] for the exit is itself articulated in the very language and conceptual appa-ratus of humanism: *Folie et déraison* has an order, establishes an argu-ment, and constructs a historical narrative; it is, in short, thoroughly *reasonable*. Foucault's 'revolution against reason can be made only within it': the outside is invaded by the inside.[13] It does not follow, however, that 'we' are condemned to dwell unproblematically within humanism. If 'we' cannot simply step outside tradition – one foot forever drags in the past – 'we' can, nonetheless, expose the incoherence of humanism from within, a strategy which Derrida calls, in another context, 'the necessity of lodging oneself within traditional conceptuality in order to destroy it'.[14] Where Foucault turns his back, Derrida turns back. This re-turn is not undertaken in the name of preservation; on the contrary, Derrida's work repeats things '*in a certain way*',[15] pushing internal contra-dictions to the point where the argument argues against itself.

These blindspots frequently occupy the margins of the text. The attack upon Foucault, for instance, centres upon three apparently inconsequential pages of *Folie et déraison* – a book which runs to almost 700 pages – devoted to Descartes. 'My point of departure might appear slight and artificial',[16] Derrida writes, but it soon becomes clear that when the implications of the margins are pursued back into the main body of the text, Foucault's revolution returns to humanism. A more recent work, *Of Spirit*, goes one step further, circling around what happens quite literally between the lines of Heidegger's philosophy. The quotation marks around the term 'spirit', Derrida notes, come and go: sometimes they 'stand guard',[17] holding the signifier at a critical distance; on other occasions, Heidegger relieves them from duty, allowing spirit *itself* to step forward.

A similar event occurs within the 'Cyborg Manifesto'. For most of the essay, Haraway chooses not to encase the signifier 'we' in quotation marks. On several occasions, however, 'we' encounter '"we"'. I want to suggest that this inconsistency announces the impossibility of Haraway's faith in exteriority, in a 'post-' that is truly 'post-'. As Bill Readings points out in his contribution to this volume, the term 'we' resounds with humanism: it should, therefore, be handled with care, picked up pincerlike with quotation marks.[18] Donna Haraway, however, is able to work – for most of the time, at least – without these marks because she insists that 'we' are no longer in a space where humanism has a voice: the quotation marks can stand down because there is no longer anything to guard against. It is, therefore, perfectly acceptable to write: 'By the late twentieth century, *our* time, a mythic time, *we* are all chimeras, theorised and fabricated hybrids of machine and organism; in short, *we* are cyborgs. The cyborg is *our* ontology; it gives *us our* politics',[19] for this is not the 'we' of 'absolute knowledge and anthropology, of God and man, of onto-theo-teleology and humanism'.[20]

And yet, the marks are called back to duty, for the manifesto contains sentences such as: '"We" did not originally choose to be cyborgs, but choice grounds a liberal politics and epistemology that imagines the reproduction of individuals before the wider replications of "texts"' and 'Cyborg feminists have to argue that "we" do not want any more natural matrix of unity and that no construction is whole'.[21] This throws Haraway's exteriority into crisis, for it implies that the term in question continues to be problematic (why else would it require such treatment?). If 'we' really had stepped completely outside humanism, the signifier 'we' would no longer need to be held at a distance. When Haraway handles the word with 'pincers', she unwittingly acknowledges that she is writing – however critically – from *within* the space of humanism. Her outside sides with the inside.

My mapping of the way in which Haraway's promises become compromises should not be read as pure blasphemy, for what follows is an attempt to keep the faith by rereading the manifesto through Marge Piercy's *Body of Glass*.[22] I characterise this not as a reading of Haraway *with* Piercy, or vice versa, but as a *diffraction* of the one through the other. 'Diffraction', Haraway writes, 'does not produce "the same" displaced, as reflection and refraction do. Diffraction is a mapping of interference, not of replication, reflection, or reproduction.'[23] I will not describe how one work reflects upon another, or reflect upon one in light of the other; I will, rather, map how the texts *interfere* with each other, throwing different shapes, changing 'our' view of the cyborg.

II

At the heart of *Body of Glass* lies an opposition. The opening chapter introduces the reader to the Yakamura-Stichen enclave, a dome in Nebraska owned by one of the capitalist corporations which dominate the global economy. Life in Yakamura-Stichen is technological, hierarchical, uniform, and, above all, patriarchal. There is, however, an alternative in the form of the 'free town' of Tikva (the Hebrew word for 'hope'[24]). The opposition between the two communities is marked in several ways. First, there is a temporal distinction: Tikva lies in a different time zone, one hour ahead of Nebraska. Second, whereas Yakamura-Stichen uses space 'to oppress and intimidate',[25] the protagonist, Shira, notices that the architecture of Tikva encourages openness and eclecticism:

> The buildings [in Tikva] were all different, although none could be higher than four storeys here. Some houses were made of wood, some of brick, some of the new resins, some of polymers, some of stone. She was tickled by the consonances and dissonances – little Spanish haciendas, stern Greek Revival houses, shingled saltboxes, an imitation of Fernandez' famous dancing house on its pedestal, jostled shoulders on the same block. After the uniformity of the Y-S enclave, the colours, the textures, the sounds and smells provoked her into a state of ecstasy. ...[26]

The most telling difference, however, is political, for Yakamura-Stichen's capitalist mode of production is opposed by Tikva's sense of non-patriarchal, non-competitive community:

> [T]he foundation of Tikva was libertarian socialism with a strong admixture of anarcho-feminism, reconstructionist Judaism (although there were six temples, each representing a different Jewishness) and greeners ...

Y-S was a hierarchy with a head. Tikva was a town meeting, a full and active democracy. They were accustomed to deciding every detail of town policy and budget openly and at whatever length it took to reach agreement.[27]

But Tikva's politics, like those of Donna Haraway, are not grounded in a resistance to technology. This is a town where robots roam the streets, and where 'every child [is] raised to be able to access directly, taught to project into the worldwide Net, into the local Base'.[28] Technology, in fact, becomes the locus of a struggle between Yakamura-Stichen and Tikva, a struggle over meaning and politics which occupies a significant part of the narrative. Having learned of Avram's experiments in artificial intelligence, the corporation begins to attack Tikva, eager to steal what it sees as a desirable commodity. To defend the free town, Avram – a Rabbi Loew for the digital age – constructs Yod. Because the law forbids the manufacture of robots which are either anthropomorphic or of an intelligence equal to human beings, Yod is created as a cyborg (while this does not make him legal, it does allow him to pass for human).

But if *Body of Glass* concurs with Haraway's refusal to divorce technology from oppositional politics, its approach to the cyborg establishes a significant distance between the two texts. At the risk of seeming reductively schematic, I want to propose that there are two principal points of divergence: the first of these concerns gender, true love and happy families, and the second centres upon the question of agency.

While Haraway's cyborg is a post-gender being, Yod is most definitely gendered: '"Avram made him male – entirely so"', remarks Malkah, Shira's grandmother. '"[He] thought that was the ideal: pure reason, pure logic, pure violence"'.[29] With gender, however, comes trouble. One of Yod's predecessors, Chet (the eighth letter of the Hebrew alphabet, as Yod is the tenth), pursues his logical programming to its logical conclusion: murder. To prevent further mishaps, Malkah supplements Yod with '"a gentler side, starting with emphasising his love for knowledge and extending it to emotional and personal knowledge, a need for connections... ."'[30] This need leads to Yod's passionate involvement with Shira, a narrative development which carries the novel away from Haraway's manifesto, towards both *Frankenstein* and popular romantic fiction. Like Mary Shelley's monster, Yod wants a mate; he ends up, however, not in a frozen wasteland but between the sheets with Shira. Here, he proves to be a dream lover, better than a 'real' man. Not only is he sexually inexhaustible, but Malkah's programming leads him to be more concerned with giving than taking pleasure. This is probably not what Donna Haraway had in mind when she suggested that she would 'rather go to bed with a cyborg than a sensitive man...'[31] Indeed, when it comes to romance, Marge Piercy cannot quite remain faithful to Donna Haraway, whose cyborg repudiates the longing for 'a heterosexual mate'.[32] Yod, quite simply, believes in love.

If *Body of Glass* is an affair to remember, it is also a family affair, and this constitutes a further infidelity to Haraway. Although the narrative begins with the legal dissolution of Shira's family, she soon begins to imagine a life of domestic bliss with Ari (her son) and the cyborg:

> And why not? Would Yod be a worse father than most? Than Josh? He would never abuse Ari. He has no temper. He has infinite patience. He would never confuse Ari with his own ego or become infuriated or disappointed because he felt Ari failed him. Ari would be even more a child of the age of information, because he would be raised by one human and one computer.[33]

Yod, denied a culture to call his own, shares this dream: '"Given loneliness"', he tells Malkah, '"a family is a rational construct for any conscious being"'.[34] Its hero may have been built in a laboratory, but *Body of Glass* is, in many ways, an old-fashioned tale of boy (borg?) meets girl.

Reflecting upon the manifesto six years after its original publication, Donna Haraway remarked: 'We need a concept of agency that opens up possibilities for figuring relationality within social worlds where actors fit oddly, at best, into previous *taxa* of the human, the natural, or the constructed.'[35] The question of agency, I want to propose, is the point at which the distance between Haraway and Piercy appears to be at its greatest. Written between the lines of the manifesto is a dismissal of Isaac Asimov's theory of human/machine relations, proposed in his famous Three Laws of Robotics:

(1) A robot may not injure a human being, or, through inaction, allow a human being to come to harm;
(2) A robot must obey the orders given it by human beings except where such orders would conflict with the First Law;
(3) A robot must protect its own existence as long as such protection does not conflict with the First or Second Laws.[36]

What Asimov implies – and what much subsequent science fiction has reiterated – is that robots and other machines can be amiable, useful, perhaps even 'cute', as long as their subservience is guaranteed by some variation of the distinctly humanist Three Laws. Haraway never mentions Asimov by name, but his approach epitomises the humanism ceaselessly called into question by the manifesto.

At first glance it would appear that Yod evades the Laws. Each tenet is violated at some stage in the text: Josh is murdered; Shira learns from

Avram's notes that Yod is not always obedient; and, towards the end of the novel, the cyborg terminates his own existence. There is, however, a definite retreat from Haraway's posthumanism, for reference is repeatedly made to the fact that Avram retains ultimate control over Yod. This is described precisely as a desire for mastery:

> Yod was Avram's finest creation; Avram could not view lightly any weakening of possession or control ... In her most recent onslaught on Avram's log, [Shira] had discovered that every cyborg since Dalet had had an abort mechanism built in: they could be deactivated by one code; destroyed by another; a further capacity, to cause a much larger explosion, was built in. Avram indeed retained the power of life and death over Yod. The codes were not given in the notes.[37]

Although his presence is intended to ensure that Tikva remains a free town, Yod is forever denied personal liberty: '"Freedom is a concept I'm not sure I comprehend..."', he remarks at one point, '"Perhaps because I've never been free"'.[38] As the narrative develops, this contradiction becomes increasingly acute, culminating in Avram's decision to use the cyborg as a bomb in the struggle against Yakamura-Stichen. When Yod learns of this, he detonates himself, deliberately destroying his creator and the laboratory in the process.

It might appear, therefore, that *Body of Glass* invokes the manifesto only to drift back into the space of humanism. Where Haraway turns her back, it would seem that the novel turns back, stripping posthumanism of its prefix. But what if things are not what they seem? What if *Body of Glass* is far from transparent? I want to suggest that the novel actually stages an impasse which exposes the contradictions of humanism. What happens, it asks, when a machine (which ought to remain under human control) reaches a point at which it is thoroughly 'human'? How can humanism grant liberty and rights to a machine it deems inhuman? This is not to say that the text is content merely to write itself into a corner; on the contrary, it seems to me that it offers a way to think beyond the impasse precipitated by Yod.

According to Peter Fitting, Avram's creation deviates further from Haraway's model than I have suggested. For him, Piercy's decision to use the term 'cyborg' is confusing:

> For most science fiction readers, Yod would be called an 'android', a humanoid robot rather than a cyborg ... A cyborg is the physical bonding of human and machine – a human who has in some way been augmented or enhanced. A robot or android on the other hand, is a new entity, built or grown from organic and/or non-organic materials.[39]

In *Body of Glass*, he concludes, 'the true cyborg is Nili'. A footnote reveals that Fitting's understanding of cyborgs derives from Brian Stableford's somewhat outdated entry in the *Encyclopedia of Science Fiction*,[40] which accords with the classical paradigm formulated by Clynes and Kline, fixing the point of origin in the human being.[41] Because he does not conform to this decidedly limited model, Yod cannot, for Fitting, be termed a cyborg.[42]

And yet, although I disagree with Fitting's reason for refocusing attention on Nili, I concur with the strategy itself. At one point in the novel, a meeting of Tikva's council is called to discuss whether or not Yod is entitled to full citizenship of the town. This is, perhaps, a reference to 'The Bicentennial Man',[43] Asimov's tale of a robot – Andrew Martin – who wishes, like Yod, for autonomy. When Andrew convinces a tribunal that he understands the concept of freedom, he is granted nominal liberty (although his conduct remains governed by the Three Laws of Robotics, Andrew takes comfort from the observation that human existence is similarly regulated). As the robot's behaviour becomes increasingly 'human', the narrative negotiates a series of ethical dilemmas, culminating in Andrew's demand for complete recognition as a human being. When this is refused (his inorganic, immortal brain is cited as the insurmountable obstacle), Andrew decides to end his life by reconfiguring his brain so that it decays. On the bicentennial anniversary of his creation, Andrew is finally declared to be a man. He dies shortly after, happy to have been human.

Body of Glass differs from Asimov's story because the official apparatus never reaches a decision. Although the council agrees to debate the matter until a verdict is reached, Yod commits suicide before this moment comes. The legal process is inaugurated, but the result – and hence the criterion for telling the difference between the human and the inhuman – is withheld. Shortly before Yod's death, Malkah makes a remark which captures the attention of Peter Fitting, prompting him to deem Nili (the lover of Shira's mother) the true cyborg:

'Yod was a mistake. You're the right path, Nili. It's better to make people into partial machines than to create machines that feel and yet are still controlled like cleaning robots. The creation of a conscious being as any kind of tool – supposed to exist only to fill our needs – is a disaster.'[44]

When Nili enters the narrative, she is immediately likened to Yod, thus establishing a pattern which is repeated throughout the text.[45] I want to modify Fitting's thesis regarding Nili to read her *alongside* Yod as a cyborg. I resist labelling either character 'the true cyborg', for this would imply that there is a false counterpart.

It seems to me that Yod's function within the narrative is not unlike that of the Hitchcockian *MacGuffin*. As the director himself once explained,

> Well, [the MacGuffin is] the device, the gimmick, if you will, or the papers the spies are after. I'll tell you about it. Most of Kipling's stories, as you know, were set in India, and they dealt with the fighting between the natives and the British forces on the Afghanistan border. Many of them were spy stories, and they were concerned with the efforts to steal the secret plans out of a fortress. The theft of secret documents was the original MacGuffin. So the MacGuffin is the term we use to cover all that sort of thing: to steal plans or documents, or discover a secret, it doesn't matter what it is. And the logicians are wrong in trying to figure out the truth of a MacGuffin, since it's beside the point. The only thing that really matters is that ... the plans, documents, or secrets must seem to be of vital importance to the characters ... So you see that a MacGuffin is actually nothing at all.[46]

The analogy is not entirely applicable, however, for I am not implying that Yod is ultimately irrelevant. Nonetheless, although he is the figure around whom the main narrative appears to orbit, the moment at which Malkah deems Yod a 'mistake' and Nili the 'right path' calls, as Peter Fitting recognises, for a shift of focus.

Shortly after Shira's mother, Riva, arrives in Tikva with her lover, Shira asks if Nili is a human or a cyborg, to which Riva replies: '"That's a matter of definition. ... . Where do you draw the line?"'[47] If *Body of Glass*, as I have already suggested, draws parallels between Yod and Nili, it nonetheless draws a line between the two – Nili is human, Yod is a cyborg – and, in doing so, draws away from the 'Cyborg Manifesto'. Where Haraway envisions a new set of signifiers for a new cultural condition, *Body of Glass* constructs a world in which terms such as 'artificial' and 'real' continue to circulate. The exit from 'the maze of dualisms in which we have explained our bodies and our tools to ourselves' proposed by Haraway has not occurred: a binary opposition between the human and the inhuman remains. I want to suggest, however, that the novel actually deconstructs this opposition, rewriting as posthumanism the humanism it appears to write. This is the effect of a calculated approach to meaning.

In her desire to know the truth about Nili, Shira invokes the familiar criterion of birth (as distinguished from construction). Because she has a mother, Nili is deemed authentically human, but Riva subsequently reveals that Shira herself was conceived through artificial insemination. Asked if this knowledge is unsettling, Shira replies: '"Oh, come on. Half the kids in this town are born from petri dishes or test tubes.

At Y-S they used to say every baby has three parents nowadays – the mother, the father and the doctor who does all the chemistry. And there Y-S is the fourth parent.'"[48] Although her words imply that 'natural' reproduction is always already implicated in technological (which is to say, cultural) practices, Shira nonetheless clings to a belief that giving birth '"the ancient way"'[49] creates a unique bond between mother and child. Although I think that June Deery is right to suggest that *Body of Glass* is more ambiguous than Piercy's earlier novel, *Woman on the Edge of Time*, when it comes to the politics of reproduction, [50] I do not believe that the former text restores humanism in this domain.

First, reference is made on several occasions to the severe ecological damage that has rendered a significant proportion of the world's human population incapable of producing children.[51] Second, and more significantly, Shira's belief in a natural bond between mother and child is quite clearly contradicted by her relationship with Riva – her 'biological' mother – for what the novel actually shows is a *lack* of innate connection between the two characters. Shortly after Riva's arrival, the reader is informed that 'Shira spent the next day with the visitors, but she did not find it easy to feel close to her biological mother'.[52] Not only does she have a greater intimacy with Yod – a cyborg – than Riva, but she finds it difficult to mourn the apparent death of the latter (her reaction to Yod's suicide, by comparison, is one of profound grief). When it transpires that Riva's 'death' was faked, Shira, in a moment of anger, describes her mother as an '"alien"', 'a woman who felt *artificially* rather than *naturally* important to her'. It is Malkah, in fact, whom she feels to be her '"real mother"'.[53]

I have suggested that Yod drifts away from Haraway's custody when he willingly takes up a position within a family. There is, however, a sense in which the novel clearly refuses to understand the family as a natural, biologically-bound entity; what is described, rather, is a *construct* that is forever open to revision, to arrangements to come. Although the traditional nuclear family is represented, from the opening page, as a site of pain, trauma and oppression, the 'weird but fulfilling family'[54] consisting of Shira, Yod, Malkah, Riva, Nili, Ari and Avram becomes a formidable mode of resistance to Yakamura-Stichen. The meaning of the term 'family' is, in other words, thrown open to contingency. There is no necessary connection between the signifier and the signified, no fixed set of values to which the former must point. A family need not 'prevent the future' by 'embod[ying] the most conservative concepts available ...'; there is no reason why a constructed, non-essentialist alliance cannot reclaim the signifier for its own use.[55] What *Body of Glass* depicts, in fact, is the rearticulation of the signifier to a less reactionary signified, a different signified, a signified of difference.

The socialisation of Yod might also appear to inf(l)ect the narrative with humanism. What could be less threatening than an other that loses its alterity as it learns the law of the Family of Man? Carol Mason makes precisely this point, reading *Body of Glass* as a heterocentric, anthropocentric, reactionary calming of difference:

> Marge Piercy's novel ... neutralises, contains, and embodies any shifting definitions of gender. Mother and father figures serve to oedipalise Piercy's cyborg, which results in naturalising and heterosexualising Yod. Yod has all the traditional attributes of a man because a human male, Avram, designs him for defence, equipping him with cybernetic muscles and penis, and with software that gives him pleasure in violence ... Yod is, dialectically enough, a cyborg who synthesises the best of both sexed worlds and as such never interrogates the categories of masculinity and femininity but contains and confirms them.[56]

What Mason overlooks, however, is the manner in which the novel denaturalises the naturalisation it writes, ultimately intimating that human beings *learn* how to be human. Before she comes to view Yod as a person, Shira mocks Malkah's use of the personal pronoun when referring to the cyborg: '"You might as well believe the house is really a woman"', she declares, '"the way little kids do. Or name your cleaning robot and talk to it."'[57] Common sense tells Shira that what she is dealing with is utterly other, absolutely different from herself, an 'it'. And yet, her own words actually undermine this humanism. By observing that children make no distinction between the human and the inhuman, Shira unwittingly reveals that the faculty to tell such a difference is not innate: to become an adult, to recognise oneself as human, is to learn to reject indifference. 'Human' has no meaning without 'inhuman', and this meaning is acquired. Yod must learn how to be human, but so must humans, a point he actually makes when he remarks, following Shira's question about his compulsion to give pleasure during sex: '"Aren't you programmed too? Isn't that what socialising a child is?"'[58] The novel, in this respect, recalls a remark once made by Jean-François Lyotard:

> If humans are born humans, as cats are born cats (within a few hours), it would not be ... I don't even say desirable, which is another question, but simply possible, to educate them. That children have to be educated is a circumstance which only proceeds from the fact that they are not completely led by nature, not programmed. The institutions which constitute culture supplement this native lack.[59]

The love story at the heart of the novel might, as I have already intimated, be dismissed as yet another manifestation of humanism. But, as it describes the development of the affair, the text actually exposes the process by which 'nature' – humanism's faithful partner – is culturally constructed. When Shira first meets Yod, she finds Malkah's ritual of embracing the cyborg 'beyond bizarre'.[60] In time, however, everything changes: 'It felt quite *natural* now to touch him, the most *normal* gesture she could imagine.'[61] The unnatural has become unquestionably normal. Moreover, what was formerly natural would now be considered quite abnormal: 'nature' has changed, and in this movement *Body of Glass* sketches out nothing other than posthumanism. If Yod and Shira ultimately believe in love and a nature of intimacy, 'that final belief/Must be in a fiction',[62] in something made and made over.

The novel also brings cultural difference to bear upon romance, striking yet another blow to faith in a universal human essence. Discussing sexual attraction, Nili (who has come to Tikva from Safed) confesses to confusion:

'I don't understand this whole attraction business. ...
'I mean, at home we tend to become involved with the people we work with. *We find that natural.* ...
'Basically don't you think it's a matter of what you're used to and what's in front of you? If you raise chickens, you eat chickens and you eat eggs. You people live on fish.'[63]

Later in the narrative, disturbed by the discovery of Malkah's sexual involvement with Yod, Shira considers turning to Nili for support, but hesitates: '[She] had no idea what the norms of Nili's culture were. Nili might not be able to sympathise with [her] shame and discomfort.'[64] What appears to be natural, in other words, can be quite alien to an individual from another culture which has its own set of norms, its own conceptions of the 'natural' and 'unnatural'. This is not to say that norms are without material implications; the point, rather, is that the novel actually shows 'nature' to be a *construction* specific to a given context. It testifies to what Jean-François Lyotard would call a *différend*, 'a case of conflict between (at least) two parties, that cannot be equitably resolved for lack of a rule of judgment applicable to both arguments'.[65] What Shira finds 'natural' is 'unnatural' to Nili. There is no shared view of the world:

Nili saw the Glop differently than Shira always had. Shira realised she had been *trained automatically by her culture*, especially by corporate culture, to treat the Glop as an unimportant place where nothing consequential happened. ... But Nili turned to the New Gangs for answers. In people living off the garbage of the preceding century, Nili found much to study and admire.[66]

Although Tikva and Yakamura-Stichen continue to tell (narrate) the difference between the human and the inhuman, the real and the fake, the natural and the unnatural, the novel *itself* reveals that is impossible to tell (locate) that difference. Humanism is stalled as it is installed, re-written as it is written, deposed as it is imposed. Piercy returns to the space vacated by Haraway, repeats its claims 'in a certain way', and shows how humanism forever contains (carries within) yet cannot contain (limit) its 'post-'. Haraway's essay, to take a phrase from another manifesto, melts all that is solid into air, killing the old in the name of the new.[67] *Body of Glass*, on the other hand, draws attention to the ways in which the solid is never solid: pockets of air mean that the melting is always already happening from within. Piercy's posthumanism breathes this air.

III

My words have congregated around faith, around Haraway's hope that her cyborg will be unfaithful to its origins in humanism, around Piercy's apparent infidelity to the 'Cyborg Manifesto', and around a diffraction which might be seen as a betrayal of both figures. I mention this latter aspect of faith because, beyond the optical sense upon which I have insisted, a 'diffraction' can signify a shattering, a breaking into pieces. My diffraction, my deconstruction, should not be confused with a simple destruction or rejection of the cyborg. Like Haraway, I still believe it to be a promising monster with much to offer a theorisation of the post-humanist condition. I feel that Maurice Blanchot was right to suggest, with reference to Lévi-Strauss, that to express a certain dissatisfaction with something 'is certainly the best way of liking it and of staying loyal to it'.[68] I believe, that is to say, in blasphemous faith, in what Derrida calls 'unfaithful faithfulness'.[69] If certain promises become compromises, if certain of the cyborg's components require retuning, it does not follow that the possibility of change is terminated. Difference does not necessarily die when 'we' turn back to tradition, for Piercy's novel unearths the bones of glass which prevent humanism from constituting itself. Man breathes 'himself' to death, raises himself to ruins. Humanism forever rewrites itself as posthumanism. Like Yod, *Body of Glass* self-de(con)structs.

12

Postcards from the Posthuman Solar System

Scott Bukatman

A cyborg body is not innocent; it was not born in a garden; it does not seek unitary identity and so generate antagonistic dualisms without end (or until the world ends); it takes irony for granted.

Donna Haraway

The subject 'is [the] body and [the] body is the potentiality of a certain world', according to Maurice Merleau-Ponty (p. 106). At the intersection of cybernetics and phenomenology, the body already operates as an *interface* between mind and experience, but in contemporary SF and horror, the body is also narrated as a site of exploration and transfiguration, through which an interface with an electronically-based postmodern experience is inscribed. The body is no longer simply the repository of the soul; it has become a cyborg body, one element in an endless interface of bio-technologies. The SF text stages the superimposition of technology upon the human in all its effects: the computer alone has been figured as a prosthetic extension of the human, as an addictive substance, as a space to enter, as a technological intrusion into human genetic structures, and, finally, as a replacement for the human in a posthuman world. The obsessive restaging of the refiguration of the body posits a constant redefinition of the subject through the multiple superimposition of bio-technological apparatuses. In this epoch of human obsolescence, however, a remarkably consistent imaging/imagining of both body and subject ultimately emerges.

The cyborg performance art of Stelarc exemplifies these concerns with a techno-surrealist sense of transgression, and with an immediate emphasis upon the flesh – as paradigmatic a landscape for postmodern exploration as cyberspace itself. Stelarc, an Australian performance artist living in Japan, has filmed his bodily interior, amplified its functions, enhanced its abilities, and worked towards 'the body's transcendence of all conventional boundaries'. As cyberpunk John Shirley has written of Stelarc, 'All the signposts direct us to him' (p. 59).

Through the sonic amplification of his bodily functions, Stelarc transforms his body into 'an acoustical landscape' – an array of beats, beeps, and gurgles. Here the subject is replaced into the continuity of biological process, but this fusion is only performed through a symbiosis with electronic technology. Arthur and Marilouise Kroker note that Stelarc 'makes of his own body its own horizon of sometimes repulsive, sometimes fascinating, possibilities' (p. 25). He has explored and experimented with the 'architecture' of the body, treating the body as an 'environment which needs to be made more adaptable'. Stelarc's most recent work has moved from mapping the body, acoustically and cinematically, to extending and enhancing its capabilities. His performance, 'Event for Amplified Body, Laser Eyes, and Third Hand', features a new limb activated by his abdominal and thigh muscles, while his real left arm is 'controlled' by the random electrical impulses of a muscle stimulator. Stelarc bounces laser beams off mirrored contact lenses, 'drawing' with the light which emanates from his eyes. Shirley quotes Stelarc as stating, 'We're at the time now where we have to start redesigning the human body to match the technology we've created. ... [We] are confronted by the end of the human form as we know it.'[1]

I

J. G. Ballard's *Crash* obsessively narrates a sacrificial violence which empties the human experience of any transcendent meaning. It is a brilliantly ironic work, set in a post-industrial landscape of highways and automobiles, high rises and airports, television sets and billboards. It is a landscape in which the erotic is denied, repressed, and paved over by layers of concrete, tarmac, and chrome. Vaughan, the 'hero' of *Crash*, fantasises his death in a headlong collision with Elizabeth Taylor. The narrator, 'Ballard', is ever-increasingly drawn towards Vaughan's vision of transcendent sex and violence. Vaughan has reinvested the de-eroticised landscape with the passion of desire:

> Two months before my accident, during a journey to Paris, I had become so excited by the conjunction of an air hostess's fawn gaberdine skirt on the escalator in front of me and the distant fuselages of the aircraft, each inclined like a silver penis towards her natal cleft, that I had involuntarily touched her left buttock. (sect. 4, p. 41)

The geometrical alignment of escalator, woman's hip, and distant airplane become urgently sexualised, but only in the precise language of the engineer. Eroticism becomes a question of mathematics, of alignment. Ballard mocks the functionalist understanding of the human as a single component in a rational system; while both driver and automobile are defined in dispassionate terms as problems in engineering, both are also endowed and imbued with the irrational potentials of erotic desire and violence.

Ballard's achievement is to narrate a profoundly isolating contemporary environment within which Vaughan seeks a joyful synthesis with the very objects which distance the subjects and reinforce the discontinuous experience of being. Georges Bataille writes that 'the movement that pushes a man in certain cases to give himself (in other words, to destroy himself) not only partially but completely, so that a bloody death ensues, can only be compared, in its irresistible and hideous nature, to the blinding flashes of lightning that transform the most withering storm into transports of joy' (p. 69). In *Crash*, tragedy becomes consummation: 'Vaughan dreamed endlessly of the deaths of the famous, inventing imaginary crashes for them. Around the deaths of James Dean and Albert Camus, Jayne Mansfield and John Kennedy he had woven elaborate fantasies' (sect. 1, p. 15). Vaughan's dreamt-of crash into the movie star's limousine becomes an act of sacrifice, an *automutilation*, which reestablishes his continuity with the world by literally crashing through the separations – both physical and spectacular – to achieve the complete fusion of a technologically eroticised and *violent* death. Ballard simultaneously mocks and evokes the 'drive' towards transcendence and continuity. Few works of SF, indeed of literature, have attained such a level of transgression.[2]

Perhaps the only other SF novel to appropriate Bataille's notion of sacrificial mutilation is Bernard Wolfe's *Limbo*, first published in 1952 – an extraordinary anomaly, deriving imagery from Bataille while anticipating the cybernetic paranoia of Pynchon.[3] It is a dense, philosophical novel set in a post-apocalyptic world dominated by the functionist cybernetic paradigms of Norbert Wiener, whose theory of cybernetics provided, in the 1950s, 'simultaneously a theory of communication and a promising technology of control' (Haraway, *Primate Visions*, p. 106). The narrator, Doctor Martine, reflects that 'People, cowed by the machines that had grown bigger than themselves, could no longer think except in mechanical terms' (sect. 5, p. 51). Wolfe is explicit about the power of a managerial revolution in a cybernetically-defined society (which includes both American and Soviet cultures)[4] and the need to construct a mass culture 'welded together into a tight, quickly mobilised monolithic unit whose nerve centres were the lightning quick mass media' (sect. 11, p. 135).

In the postwar environment that Martine tours, societies perform lobotomies and amputations on their citizens, not only to prevent the possibility of war, but in order to move closer to the immobile perfections of a machine-like status. On one occasion Martine listens to a lecturer for whom 'the machine is eternally the brain's dream of fulfilment':

After the agony of the Third, the war in which the dream of perfection became a steamrollering nightmare, this brain has finally discovered how to link itself to its own projected vision – it has lopped off its animalistic tails. It has suddenly made the breathtaking discovery that the perfection of EMSIAC and other robot brains lies in the fact that they are sheer brain with no irrelevancies, no arms and legs, just lines of communication and feedbacks – and it has begun to overhaul itself in the image of the robot (sect. 12, p. 143).

In *Limbo*, sacrificial mutilation is performed in the *service* of an instrumental, managerial reason, and not – as in Bataille's examples – as a sign of madness and the end of the rational. Wolfe brilliantly demonstrates the power of the technocratic society to co-opt and assimilate the most apparently subversive doctrines and behaviours. Thus the philosophy of 'Immob':

Immob is the cyber-cyto dialectic – the dwindling distance between cybernetics and cytoarchitectonics. The bridging of the gap between the mechanical and the human – the discovery of the Hyphen between machine and man – this enabling man finally to triumph over the machine because it's *man* who has the Hyphen and not the machine (sect. 12, p. 142).

Here is religious ecstasy and fusion; here is a terminal identity which is purely a surrender to the cybernetic predictability of the machine.

It is tempting to equate the cyberpunks (or their protagonists) with the Immobs, since both are implicated in a technological sublime which substitutes the invisible cybernetic flow of the computer for the physical mobility of the human. Just as the Immobs operate in service to a machine-driven economy, so the cyberpunks ultimately serve the increasing penetration of the machine into all aspects of quotidian existence. The transgressive collisions of Ballard's *Crash* have been superseded by the kinetic appropriation of cyberspace. There is no irony in William Gibson's *Neuromancer* when the hero is presented with his brand new brand-name cyberdeck, for in *Neuromancer*, the *drive* is all, the crash is nothing.[5] Amputation and lobotomy are the analogies when he is *unable* to 'jack in' to the computer space.

But as a character in Bruce Sterling's *Schismatrix* observes, the old categories are a bit outmoded, and are breaking up. Technologies are more prevalent, but less centralised: we are already cyborgs, despite Wolfe's apprehensions. The category of instrumental reason has been superseded by a culture which seems increasingly dispersed and immersed in the process of ontological transformation.

In her striking and effective 'Cyborg Manifesto', Donna Haraway has argued for a feminist, progressive cyborg mythos constituted within a postmodern context which blurs distinctions between organism and machine in a high-stakes 'border war':

> Late twentieth-century machines have made thoroughly ambiguous the difference between natural and artificial, mind and body, self-developing and externally-designed, and many other distinctions that used to apply to organisms and machines. Our machines are disturbingly lively, and we ourselves frighteningly inert. (p. 69)

Thus, 'by the late twentieth century, our time, a mythic time, we are all chimeras, theorised and fabricated hybrids of machine and organism; in short, we are cyborgs. The cyborg is our ontology; it gives us our politics' (p. 67).

The polemical advantage of the cyborg, for Haraway, is that it resists being encoded as natural. 'The cyborg skips the step of original unity, of identification with nature in the Western sense' (p. 67). 'We cannot go back ideologically or materially' (p. 81), she writes, recalling a character in Bruce Sterling's *Schismatrix* who says, 'There's no going back. That's a game for those who still have flesh.' For both writers, the cyborg inhabits a posthuman solar system – 'posthuman' in biological terms, and in the ideological sense of 'human' as a particular mythos of 'natural' individualism. As Foucault indicated, in an oft-quoted passage, 'man is only a recent invention, a figure not yet two centuries old, a new wrinkle in our knowledge, and ... he will disappear again as soon as that knowledge has discovered a new form' (p. xxiii). There's no going back.

One finds in Haraway's writing a rejection of the instrumental forces of technocratic reason in favour of a pleasurable and utopian excess. In her discussion, the interplay of continuities and discontinuities is striking: 'So my cyborg myth is about transgressed boundaries, potent fusions, and dangerous possibilities which progressive people might explore as one part of needed political work' (p. 71). The dualisms which structure too much socialist and feminist thought need to be supplanted: 'A cyborg body is not innocent; it was not born in a garden; it does not seek unitary identity and so generate antagonistic dualisms without end (or until the world ends); it takes irony for granted' (p. 99). Haraway's cyborg mythology assails the dispassionate rationalism of power structures while it overturns discontinuities of a gender-based ideology. 'Haraway's originality', Istvan Csicsery-Ronay argues,

> in terms equally valid for critical theory and SF, is her notion of imagining utopia by moving through the 'heart' of dystopia. Recovering the cyborg from [its] role as ideological legitimator (for conservative

humanists and naive technophiles both), Haraway attempts to clear a new path for utopian rationality through the sprawl of instrumental rationalisations. (p. 12)

'Cyborg politics' opens the prospect of technological symbiosis as a progressive alternative, rather than a simple masculine fantasy of 'natural' mastery and domination. In fact, that symbiosis has already been attained: 'The boundary between science fiction and social reality is an optical illusion', she declares (p. 66).

II

Cyberpunk, a subgenre of commercial SF, remains the literary form most centrally concerned with the rhetorical production of a complex imbrication between the human subject and the electronically defined realities of the Dataist Era. The deeply influential fiction of William Gibson has been analysed *ad nauseam*, but a consideration of the movement's other 'leader', Bruce Sterling, reveals some very different strategies. Sterling has occupied the centre of cyberpunk territory since the advent of the movement, and he continues to serve as its most valuable spokesperson, editor, and polemicist. The volume of cyberpunk writings that he edited, *Mirrorshades*, has contributed more to the general understanding of cyberpunk than any text besides *Neuromancer*, while his authorial collaborations with Gibson, Lewis Shiner, and Rudy Rucker have produced fundamental texts. In fact, the coherence of cyberpunk as a movement is, to a large degree, attributable to Sterling's persistence and ubiquity.

Much of Sterling's fiction is similar to Gibson's in its dense, hyperbolised appropriation of technical languages, and in the clear recognition and acceptance of the conditions of the Information Age. As in *Neuromancer*, corporations and cartels serve as the ruling power; nations have ceased to exist. Computers, data screens, and terminals dominate here as much as in Gibson, although video is more prevalent in Sterling's diegesis, both as fact and as paradigmatic structure. These similarities are evident, but there are equally apparent differences between the two authors that undermine the stylistic consistency implied by the 'cyberpunk' label. Sterling's narrative structures are less derivative of other genres, and there is little of the literary quality of Gibson's prose, which is replete with echoes of his literary antecedents and pop-culture forerunners (such as Raymond Chandler and the Velvet Underground). His impact has also been less overtly marked; it is difficult to think of another writer who is emulating Sterling's textual formations, formations that are significantly more dense and perhaps slightly less profound (at least on the surface) than those of Gibson.

In his most characteristically cyberpunk writings, the Shaper/Mechanist series, Sterling remains entirely within the physical universe: the rhetorical and phenomenological freedoms of cyberspace are not to be had. Without the ecstatic possibilities inherent in that particular paraspace, there is in Sterling's work a more pronounced ambivalence revealed in its negotiation of the electronic and cybernetic datascape.

The Shaper/Mechanist consists of five short stories – 'Swarm' and 'Spider Row' (1982), 'Cicada Queen' (1983), 'Sunken Gardens' and 'Twenty Evocations' (1984) – and the novel *Schismatrix*.[6] The postulated future is set in a 'posthuman solar system' in which different visions of humanity's successors struggle for dominance. The Shapers are generally 'reshaped' beings with amplified intelligence, disease-free bodies, and unprecedented muscular control. Their adversaries are the Mechanists, cyborg formations whose posthuman abilities are a function of comprehensive technological augmentation. The conflicts are set amidst a solar system of asteroid mines, orbital colonies, alien traders, and an anachronistic (and unvisited) Earth. By the end of *Schismatrix*, even this dichotomy is passing:

> 'The old categories, Mechanist and Shaper–they're a bit outmoded these days, aren't they? Life moves in clades.' He smiled. 'A clade is a daughter species, a related descendant. It's happened to other successful animals, and now it's humanity's turn. The factions still struggle, but the categories are breaking up. No faction can claim the one true destiny for mankind. Mankind no longer exists.' (sect. 6, p. 183)

Within the context of a postmodern culture that has proclaimed the death of the author as well as the imminent death of 'Man', Sterling's fiction seems to be, if not exemplary, at least relevant.

The prose that presents this posthumanist future is dense, technical, jargon-ridden, and at times it approaches the indecipherable. Here Lindsay Abelard, modified human, surveys a space station:

> The grapelike cluster of cheap inflatables was hooked to an interurban tube road. He floated at once down the lacquered corridor and emerged through a filament doorway into the swollen transparent nexus of crossroads. Below was Goldreich-Tremaine, with its Besetzny and Patterson Wheels spinning in slow majesty; with the molecule-like kinks and knobs of other suburbs shining purple, gold, and green, surrounding the city like beaded yarn. At least he was still in G-T. He headed for home. (sect. 5, p. 158)

This baroque techno-babble is far from Sterling's only prose style. He has, in fact, a talent for pastiche, and several of his fantasy stories have mimicked oral and Asiatic narrative voices. His most recent novel, the near-future *Islands in the Net*, is written in a comparatively straightforward manner. One can therefore deduce that the paraspatial density of the Shaper/Mechanist fiction is a strategy deliberately designed to produce specific effects in the reader.

The compression increases from story to story: not until 'Cicada Queen' does the style approach that of *Schismatrix*. In his analysis of Sterling's Shaper/Mechanist fictions, cyberpunk writer Tom Maddox has noted that 'Swarm' and 'Spider Rose' 'use the Shaper/Mechanist context as the ground for rather traditional SF'. In the third story, however, the thematic concerns of the series are foregrounded: 'With "Cicada Queen", the trope of posthumanism acquires symbolic depth, and the Mechanist/Shaper series its own higher level of complexity' (p. 240). Maddox is primarily referring to the concepts Sterling deploys, but his observations hold true for the language of the narrative as well. There is, in fact, a strong correlation between 'the trope of posthumanism' and the rhetorical density of the Shaper/Mechanist series.

Sterling is engaged in the production of a unique textual matrix that emerges from a web (or 'net') of discourses; economics, politics, history, technology, and narrative all intersect to produce an ideolect that, at times, is hardly *narrative* at all. Instead, the effect is of a carefully developed semiotics of the future. The works are crawling with a sensory overload: colours, textures, and odours are a part of every description (the attention to colour is especially reminiscent of SF by Delany and Zelazny). Abelard has been trained as a diplomat by the shapers, and so is overtly aware of the meaning behind every gesture. The body is qualified by its signifying function, as in this observation by an alien Investor: 'In civilised Investor life [the frills] were a relic, like the human eyebrow, which had evolved to deflect sweat. Like the eyebrow, their social use was now paramount (sect. 6, p. 166).

The Shaper/Mechanist writing almost demands a deconstructive engagement through its wilfully contradictory metaphors, signs, and terms. When a character in *Schismatrix* says, 'I'm wired to the ass', the phrase is meant to be taken literally on at least one level: the character is technologically augmented to a maximal degree (today, the phrase implies a purely figurative sense of intoxication, while yet another reading might be possible in, for example, a text by William Burroughs, in which the anatomical details would be more explicit). Sterling's very title is oxymoronic: a *schismatrix* which inserts an entirely contradictory tension between the *schism*, or gap, and the *matrix*, or connective network (as in a mathematical matrix). Also, in this tale of diplomacy, betrayal, and commerce, it's difficult not to read the title as a pun on *schismatic*: one who promotes or exploits a schism. Finally, the term is perfect for the status of the information in the Dataist Era – physically dissolute, yet conversely bound more closely together than at any other moment in history.

Perhaps most strikingly, Sterling's cyborg prose is marked by an obsessive deployment of technological and biological metaphors; each is nearly always described in terms of the other. It is this tropological system, at once contradictory and appropriate, that distinguishes the paraspatial quality of the Shaper/Mechanist discourse. This imbrication of human and machine is first signalled by a deployment of insect metaphors;[7] indeed, the first three Shaper/Mechanist stories, 'Swarm', 'Spider Rose', and 'Cicada Queen', incorporate such metaphors into their very titles. In 'Sunken Gardens' machines are described in insectoid (and arachnoid) terms: 'The crawler lurched as its six picklike feet scrabbled down the slopes of a deflation pit' (p. 81); 'The crawler ran spiderlike along the crater's snowy rim' (p. 83); 'The black crawler was crouched with its periscoped head sunk downward, as if ready to pounce. Its swollen belly was marked with a red hourglass and the corporate logos of its faction' (p. 85). In these examples, the modelling of machine upon insect/arachnid is obvious and diegetic, but note also that Sterling emphasises a certain mechanical autonomy: 'The crawler worked its way up the striated channel of an empty glacier bed' (p. 82). The story presents rival factions working to create a viable biosphere on a terraformed Mars; that these scrabbling mechanical spiders and mantises should engineer such metamorphoses is typical of Sterling's deformations. Life – the flora and fauna deployed by the crawlers – seems more like an infection spread by cybernetic carriers. Insect forms also recur in *Schmismatrix* in the form of trained killer butterflies and the ubiquitous multi-coloured roaches that have accompanied humanity into space, feeding upon its detritus. 'If it weren't for the roaches, the *Red Consensus* would eventually smother in a mouldy detritus of cast-off skin and built-up layers of sweated and exhaled effluvia' (sect. 3, p. 68).

Insects are only the most evident metaphorical process conflating a number of irreconcilable terms such as *life/non-life, biology/technology, human/machine*. Throughout the Shaper/Mechanist fictions, Sterling's tropological systems become more complex, as the operations of SF syntax produce an emergent synthesis of the organic and the cybernetic – a soft machine. For example, in this description of an asteroid mining colony in *Schismatrix*, rock, biotics, and technology intersect: 'Trade secrets were secure within Dembowsha's bowels, snug beneath kilometres of rock. Life had forced itself like putty into the fracture in this minor planet: dug out its inert heart and filled it with engines' (sect. 6, p. 181). None of the metaphors Sterling uses here is particularly original, but in their aggregate, the effect is notable. Here is Abelard's mechanical arm: 'Lindsay ran his mechanical hand over his coils of grey hair. The steel knuckles glittered with inlaid seed-germs; the wire tendons sparkled with interwoven strands of fiberoptics' (sect. 5, p. 142). 'Wire tendons' is to be taken literally, but then what ought the reader to do with the 'coils' of hair? The confusion between literal and figurative languages is fundamental to the experience of *Schismatrix*, forcing the reader to negotiate among dichotomies that are no longer dichotomous. Alien recording tape *might* be alive: 'Slowly, a memory, either biological or cybernetic, took hold of it. It began to bunch and crumple into a new life form' (sect. 6, p. 188). The Shaper/Mechanist system is oxymoronic, its coherence and plausibility guaranteed only by the binding structures of language, specifically the language of SF. Sterling often achieves a kind of high-tech cyborg poetry: 'And there it was: the outside world. There was not much of it: words and pictures, lines on a screen. She ran her fingertips gently over the scalding pain in her knee' (sect. 4, p. 122).

There is, in Sterling's writing, a profound acceptance of the human as a complex network of biological, political, technological, economic, and even aesthetic forces (which recalls much of the SF produced by more explicitly feminist writers). To some degree, Sterling locates the technological as the determinant structure in defining the range of cultural systems. Even the central political struggle in the Shaper/Mechanist stories is technologically determined, as a character tells Abelard:

> The Shapers, the Mechanists – those aren't philosophies, they're technologies made into politics. The technologies are at the core of it. Science tore the human race to bits. When anarchy hit, people struggled for community. The politicians chose enemies so that they could bind their followers with hate and terror. Community isn't enough when a thousand new ways of life beckon from every circuit and test tube. (sect.6, p. 185)

If Sterling subscribes to a model of technological determinism, then that model is always tempered by the recognition of technology's imbrication with other mutually affecting forces. Like Althusser's 'in the last analysis' model of economic determinism, Sterling seems to recognise that 'the last analysis' is only an abstraction. And if there was ever an 'essential' human nature, then surely there is no longer. Neither does Sterling lament its passage (and thereby turn the Shaper/Mechanist future into a cautionary parable). Instead there is a consistent acknowledgement of the complex and conditional status of human definition.

III

What Sterling shares most deeply with Gibson and others of the cyberpunk movement (and what the cyberpunks share with the horror genre) is a surrealist perspective that revels in the deformation and destruction, the resurrection and reformation, of the human. Taking their cues from Burroughs and Pynchon as well as from Bataille and Breton and Dali and Man Ray, the technotactics of cyberpunk transform the rational structures of technological discourse to produce instead a highly poeticised, dream-like liberation. The languages of science and technology are inverted by a metaphorical system of language which effaces the borders between conscious and unconscious, physical and phenomenal realities, subject and object, individual and group, reality and simulacrum, life and death, body and subject, future and present. The Shaper/Mechanist and Cyberspace fictions construct collages, placing the subject in urbanesque cyberspaces, or within insect mechanisms in alien habitats. The human is emplaced within the machine; the human becomes an adjunct to the machine: the cyborg is a cut-up, a juxtaposition, a *bricolage* of found objects.

If these works fail to provide the surrealistically scatological pleasures of the works of Bataille or Bunuel, much less those of Burroughs or Pynchon, then this should be read in terms of the texts' intricate relation to the genre of SF. Unlike the more overtly literary mannerisms of the SF produced by the New Wave or *Dangerous Visions* groups in the 1960s and '70s – fiction with far more evident connections to both the Surrealist and Beat movements – the cyberpunk writings are not presented as subversive of the genre. These are *SF texts* which seem to exploit, and not to exceed, the language and protocols of the genre to which they belong. If '80s SF is 'more liberatory', as Fred Pfeil would have it, it is precisely because of its explicit imbrication with lived experience and its 'frenzied tryings-on of a new, cybernetic sense of identity' (p. 88). The sustained inscription of a spectacular discourse *of the body* in cyberpunk is conspicuous and remarkable.[8] In fact, it is possible to regard the 'shocking' erotic contents and stylistic tricks of the New Wave writers as more derivative and more dated. As Debord wrote in 1957, 'We now know that the unconscious imagination is poor, that automatic writing is monotonous, and the whole genre of ostentatious surrealist "weirdness" has ceased to be very surprising' (p. 19). Very little that occurred after the psychedelic rediscovery of surrealism would necessitate revising that assessment. On the other hand, cyberpunk's *technological* imagination, cut-up structures, and *cybernetic* 'weirdness' succeed in 'catalysing for a certain time the desires of an era'. In these more positive terms, cyberpunk 'endeavour[s] to define the terrain of a constructive action on the basis of the spirit of revolt and the extreme depreciation of traditional means of communication', which is how Debord characterised the emergence of surrealism (it might be noted that cyberpunk also avoids 'Futurism's puerile technological optimism' [p. 18]). I am far from arguing for the superiority of cyberpunk over the libidinal excesses of the Surrealist movement, but I *am* proposing that cyberpunk constitutes a discourse within which many concerns and techniques of surrealism again become relevant – a techno-surrealist production of new flesh, a terminal flesh. The cyberpunk narrations indeed speak with the voices of repressed desire and repressed anxiety about terminal culture. Cyberpunk negotiates a complex and delicate trajectory between the forces of instrumental reason and the abandon of a sacrificial excess. Through their construction of a cultural politics inscribed by the forces of a technological reason, and through their resistance to the constraints of that reason, the texts promise and even produce a transcendence of the human condition which is also always a surrender.

IV

To conclude, it is worth considering some postulations by Gilles Deleuze and Félix Guattari, who write extensively about the Body without Organs (or the BwO, as they would have it). The BwO, a fantasy they encounter in Artaud and other discourses of madness, is an abstraction of subject annihilation, *Being Degree Zero*: 'Where psychoanalysis says, "Stop, find your self again", we should say instead, "Let's go further still, we haven't found our BwO yet, we haven't sufficiently dismantled our self' (p. 151). The BwO is opposed to the 'depth' of the subject:

> We come to the gradual realisation that the BwO is not at all the opposite of the organs. The organs are not its enemies. The enemy is the organism. The BwO is opposed not to the organs but to that organisation called the organism ... the organic organisation of the organs. The *judgement of God*, the system of the judgement of God, the theological system, is precisely the operation of He who makes an organism. (p. 58)

The Body without Organs stands against the *telos* of theology and the order of instrumental reason. It is a heterogeneous system, and thus the BwO can be defined through the very *malleability* of the organs, rather than simply through their absence. They cite a passage from Burroughs:

> The physical changes were slow at first, then jumped forward in black klunks, falling through his slack tissue, washing away the human lines. ... In his place of total darkness mouth and eyes are one organ that leaps forward to snap with transparent teeth ... but no organ is constant as regards either function or position. ... [S]ex organs sprout everywhere ... rectums open, defecate and close ... the entire organism changes colour and consistency in split-second adjustments. (Deleuze, p. 153; *Naked Lunch*, sect. 9)

In the fantasy of the Body without Organs, the body resists the finality of the organism, of the subject. And yet, as the very term makes evident, the ideal status of the BwO, the new flesh, is not so easily attained: 'You never reach the Body without Organs, you can't reach it, you are forever attaining it, it is a limit' (Deleuze, p. 150).

This material is especially fascinating when confronting SF fantasies of *new flesh*, of *antibodies* and cyberneticised existences, of the perfection of the *machine*. The body becomes a desiring machine. 'The question posed by desire is not "What does it mean?" but rather "How does it work?"' (p. 109). The BwO 'works' against the totality of the organism; as Deleuze and Guattari observe, 'This drawing together, this reweaving is what Joyce called *re-embodying*', but the re-embodying of the Body without Organs is not an act of totalisation (p. 43). *Crash* becomes a compendium of atrocities without subsuming them to a totalising system of meaning. Vaughan seeks to crash through to attain that state of being without organs. The sounds of Sterlac's organs are amplified to become electronic music as he reforms his organs to suit a changing world. Max Wren, in David Cronenberg's film *Videodrome*, has a hand that is sometimes also a gun, and a slit that sometimes appears in his stomach ('sex organs sprout everywhere'). Wren may in fact be approaching the Body without Organs when he fires at his temple, but that's precisely the point at which the film has to end.[9] This *re-embodying* is inconceivable: even the imagination can only approach its condition.

The BwO is not alone. In dismantling the self, the body can fuse with the world: 'If the BwO is already a limit, what must we say of the totality of all BwOs? It is a problem not of the One and the Multiple but of a fusional multiplicity that effectively goes beyond any opposition between the one and the multiple' (p. 154). The disembodied fusion with the fields and arrays of electronic space, the dissolution of the body into the self-aware nöocytes of intelligent blood cells, the graphic loss of bodily organs by a half-fly/half-man, and the cybernetic existence behind the screen are all manifestations of this transcendence. Here Deleuze and Guattari simultaneously present a disembodied subject and a trajectory through a space that is defined and anchored by the machine:

[T]he points of disjunction on the body without organs form circles that converge on the desiring-machines; then the subject – produced as a residuum alongside the machine, as an appendix, or as a spare part adjacent to the machine – passes through all the degrees of the circle, and passes from one circle to another. This subject itself is not at the centre, which is occupied by the machine, but on the periphery, with no fixed identity, forever decentred, *defined* by the states through which it passes. (p. 20)

Deleuze and Guattari are cyberpunks, too, constructing fictions of terminal identity in the nearly familiar language of techno-surrealism: note
that the body is described biologically ('an appendix') and mechanically
('a spare part'). The subject is always on the periphery, on the verge of
the BwO, but always in a state of continual passage.

The Body without Organs is the state where we desire to dissolve the
body and regain the world. So the contemporary drama of the subject,
which I call *terminal flesh*, is played out upon the *surface* of the body:
'depth' is an illusion that belongs to a passing moment of a particular
subjectivity. The surface of the body becomes the arena for the dissolution of the governing instrumental reason of the organism. The flat,
affectless *oeuvre* of Andy Warhol stands as a paradigmatic aesthetic
experience in the posthuman solar system (and yet one also thinks of the
shocking photograph by Avedon of Warhol displaying his wounds, the
wounds that proved he *was* of the flesh after all). And so the last word
should be given, not to Andy Warhol exactly, but to 'Andy Warhol' – an
android copy of the original (one of many, of course) as presented in a
Neil Gaiman script for the comic book *Miracleman*.[10] 'Andy' has attained
the Body without Organs. 'Do you like this existence, Andy?' he is asked:

> 'Oh, sure. It's wonderful. I *like* being a machine.
> 'It's what I always *wanted* to be. You see, I used to carry a camera
> with me wherever I went.
> 'Now my eyes are cameras, recording all they see.
> 'I don't *need* tape recorders any more – I *am* a tape recorder.
> 'This is heaven.
> 'And the *comics*. That's what I read when I was a child.
> '*Superman* and *Popeye* and *Nancy* and *Uncle Scrooge*.
> 'And *this* is a comic book *world*.'

The posthuman solar system is a comic-book world of infinite possibilities and cyborg multiplicities, defined in and through the technologies
that now construct our experiences and therefore our *selves*.

13

Pagans, Perverts or Primitives? Experimental Justice in the Empire of Capital

Bill Readings

In characterising Lyotard's work as providing 'a rationale for lying back and enjoying late capitalism', Alex Callinicos speaks for a number of critical sociologists and Marxist cultural analysts.[1] Horrified by the prospect of a paganism that leaves him nothing to believe in and everything yet to be done, Callinicos concludes that the benefit one draws as a reader of Lyotard is the indulgence of perversions; simply that one 'may now sample the benefits of commodity fetishism without a twinge of guilt'.[2] Paganism, it seems, is the old spectre of *fin de siècle* perversion and decadence. I want to argue that Lyotard's rethinking of philosophy as a process of experimental or pagan judgement allows the question of justice to be kept alive in late capitalism. Just as paganism is not merely decadent perversion, it is not the return to primitive mysticism that Habermas claims.[3] Lyotard's insistence on the radical heterogeneity of language games provides a series of hints as to the stakes in the complete 'overhaul' of 'the meaning of the word "politician"' for which he calls in *Just Gaming*.[4]

The case requiring the exercise of experimental or pagan judgement that will be examined concerns the relations between Australia (a modern republican nation-state, officially dedicated to the Idea of humanity) and the indigenous people of the Australian continent. A brief excursus, beside marking this essay as resolutely occasional, may allow us to establish the relevance of this marginal case, at the edge of the Western Empire, to the contemporary framework of political dispute.[5] The tensions attendant on the collapse of the Soviet empire in 1989 seem to me to have less to do with the social impact of rampant acquisition of consumer durables than with newly emergent nationalisms rejecting the claim of the Soviet government that Marxist doctrine speaks for universal human nature. A series of conflicts over the extent of federalism also marks the politics of the United States, the European Economic Community and India. These struggles do not have any common political agenda, nor do they translate simply into political calculations of progressive and reactionary. Thus, for example, the United States federal government at times protects minority rights against recalcitrant local practices of discrimination in a classic paradigm of Enlightenment, at times suppresses diversity in the name of universal citizenship. The dispute common to these problems is the clash between the metanarrative of a unitary state claiming to embody universal values and more fragmentary or explicitly local communities or minoritarian groups, groups which may seem either reactionary or progressive. The central state imposes a notion of abstract citizenship in the name of a narrative of the progressive realisation of national (and ultimately, supra-national or human) destiny, erasing the specificity of local practices.

Such oppositions between the totalising and the minoritarian raise a problem for the social critic: if justice is an abstract universal, how can it reside with the explicitly local?[6] Traditional political discourse suggests that social justice is an abstract model, a set of criteria in terms of which each case can be judged. As Lyotard puts it in *Just Gaming*:

there is a type of discourse that somehow dominates the social practice of justice and that subordinates it to itself. This type of discourse is common to an entire political tradition (that includes Marx as well), in which it is presupposed that if the denotation of the discourse that describes social justice is correct, that is, if this discourse is true, then the social practice can be just insofar as it respects the distribution implied in the discourse. (*JG*, p. 20)

Tactically, one may at times support the centre against the margins (over civil rights in the USA) or the margins against the centre (resisting forced sterilisation in India). One may criticise the Soviet Union in terms of Marxism, or the USA for failing to live up to the condition of republican democracy. None the less, a model of universal justice conventionally grounds our arbitration of these disputes; one defends the minority against the totality only in the name of a higher totality, such as universal human rights. What is common to American liberal republicanism, European social democracy, Indian socialism and Soviet communism is an understanding of the nature of human society in terms of universal abstraction. In this sense, they all share a common 'modernity', proposing a metanarrative of emancipation. As Lyotard characterises the stories in *Le Postmoderne expliqué aux enfants*, Marxism will reveal the proletariat as universal subject of history, democracy will reveal human nature as the people become the subject of a universal history of humanity, the creation of wealth will free mankind from poverty through the

technological breakthroughs of free-market capitalism or the redistribu-
tive policies of state socialism.[7]

Lyotard's paganism consists in refusing to counter the evident repres-
sive force of these metanarratives (the imperialism of modernity) with
another, purer metanarrative, a new model. Lyotard's point is that such a
model would itself be an imperialising abstraction, that 'the question of
justice for a society cannot be resolved in terms of models' (*JG*, p. 25).
The claim to legitimate a prescriptive politics by appeal to a literally
describable model of universal justice necessarily totalises one narrative
of the state of things and victimises those excluded from political
performativity. Lyotard redescribes justice as the task of responding to
what he calls *différends*, points at which the framework of political representation (what counts as 'political discourse') performs a victimisation
('a damage [*dommage*] accompanied by loss of the means to prove the
damage').[8] The aim of this brief survey is to point out that *différends* occur
marginally and occasionally because they are marginal to our ways of
thinking about social justice, rather than because they are uncommon.
Différends are singular, but they are not rare. If a *différend* is 'a case of
conflict between (at least) two parties that cannot be equitably resolved
for lack of a rule of judgement applicable to both arguments' (*TD*, p. xi),
the metalanguages of our modernity consistently propose a universal
rule of justice or equity that silences any argument structured on other
principles, any heterogeneous language game.

The structural implication of such victimisation with the category of
knowledge itself in the post-Enlightenment west is amply evidenced in
the history of anthropological treatment of the Aborigine. Kenelm
Burridge's *Encountering Aborigines* offers a straightforward example of
the conceptual imperialism that dogs even the most well-meaning and
tolerationist attempt to think about Aboriginal culture within the terms
of universal humanity. Using the Australian Aborigine as a test case for
the history of anthropology itself, Burridge eschews the imperialist
myths of primitivism that animated the first anthropological studies of
the Aborigine. His insistence on 'the reach into otherness' demands that
we must learn from the Aborigines just (or almost) as much as they from
us and he explicitly links the epistemological assurance of western
modernity (the assurance that makes other cultures merely objects of
study and the western man of science into an 'impersonal' observer) to
the road to Dachau.[9] Yet Burridge singularly fails to perceive that his
notion of common humanity is itself a product of that very epistemological arrogance that the Enlightenment celebrated, that the notion of a
'common heritage' that 'we and they' might 'come in time to share' is
very much *our* notion.[10] In his concluding sentence, Burridge remains an
imperialist when he fails to recognise that 'history' is an entirely western
term, that it still spells extinction for the Aborigine:

as Aboriginal cultures melt into history, Aborigines have to explain themselves not only to themselves but to those others in the differentiated community they are joining.[11]

As we shall see, it is very little by way of differentiation if Aborigines are only permitted to be different provided that they give evidence before the imperial tribunal of world history. The argument of this essay will be that universal history is not the ground of global community but of victimisation and terror, in so far as aboriginal otherness is admitted only with the proviso that the rules of evidence of western rationality and the temporality of western historicism prevail.

Thus, in turning to Australian Aborigines in order to illustrate the pagan justice called for in Lyotard's writings I am not proposing that the Aborigines offer an identity like ours, and thence a model of paganism that we might apply universally. Rather, the *différend* between Aborigines and the liberal capitalist democracy of the Commonwealth of Australia illustrates the injustice. Justice in this case will not be an abstraction that can reside with one argument or other; the radical incommensurability between the two kinds of arguments means that neither can recognise the other as an 'argument' at all. If I am to do justice to this case, a number of caveats are necessary. First of all, within the terms of western intellectual rationality, I am not talking about Australian Aborigines at all. I shall be looking at the *différend* between the Aborigines and the west as it is witnessed in a film, Herzog's *Where the Green Ants Dream*; this is a fiction of indigenous Australia, which I hope to use by analogy to Barthes's 'fictional Japan' in *Empire of Signs* – as much of Aboriginal life as a westerner can see.[12] As such, I can claim no more than to 'write the history of our own obscurity – manifest the density of our narcissism'.[13] That is to say, these are not 'real' Aborigines, an authentic other (another identity) to western culture into which westerners can transplant themselves empathically. Rather than an alternative organic community these Aborigines (who do not *belong* to either myself or to Werner Herzog) appear to us pagans, or what Lyotard has elsewhere called 'the jews', an other to western modernity that haunts its margins.[14]

Paganism does not lie in a celebration of Aboriginal rootedness but in the fact that, whatever it is, the Aborigines' 'authenticity' or 'identity' is radically inaccessible to us. Keep the question open, imagine that I make no negative value judgement in saying, as I shall have to later in this paper, that Aborigines are not 'human', because by considering them 'human' (exemplars of an abstract nature that we share) we victimise them, make them more like us than they are. Their identity remains radically untranslatable, heterogeneous to western modernist rationality.[15] And yet it remains. It remains as that otherness which western

modernity must annihilate, whether by murder or assimilation, in realis-
ing its own universal dream. It remains in that the very energy required
for its extinction bears mute witness to a non-identity, to the imperialist
terror inherent in western notions of justice and humanity as universal
abstractions. It remains as the encounter that Herzog's film evokes, an
encounter which lacks a language that might phrase it adequately, an
encounter in which language *encounters* silence rather than silence being
simply language's absence (or vice versa).

Herzog's film centres on the dispute between an Aboriginal group and
a mining corporation (Ayers Mining). It takes place at the edge of
Empire, in the Australian desert, on a site which is at the same time
central to the political struggles currently animating the west: the rights
of indigenous peoples in the wake of Empire. In the course of the film a
radical aporia in legal arbitration appears as a structural necessity of the
modernist insistence on the representability of the human and the possibility of universal justice.

In Herzog's treatment of the Aboriginal in the face of the law, injustice
is shown to reside not in accidents or errors of the political or legal representation of rights nor in a particular structure of political or legal representation but in the exclusive rule of representation itself. *Where the Green
Ants Dream* shows that ethical responsibility demands a quasi-aesthetic
experimentation if justice is to be done to an Aboriginal claim that can
only be evoked as irrepresentable. The film, that is, simply does not
make sense, if sense is delimited by considerations of representability
(*Rücksicht auf Darstellbarkeit*, in Freud's term). And it is only by not
making sense, by evoking what we may call the 'strange beauty' of the
Aboriginal, that a sense of the injustice that is being done to the indigene
can be preserved.[16] Doing justice is a matter of experimentation rather
than of correspondence to models. The quasi-aesthetic strategies that
evoke this aporia in the political representation of justice will be
explored in order then to argue for a refiguration of the political,
specifically one that rejects the universality of the human as a category.
This is something rather more unimaginable than the orthodox post-
Althusserian attack on humanism, where 'subject' reinscribes the very
categorical universality that is denied to the liberal concept of 'human
nature'.[17]

Before discussing the film in detail, I want to establish in some
specificity the discursive co-ordinates of the modern state, which always
aspires to empire by virtue of its claim to embody the universal will of
human nature in speaking with a republican 'we'. Lyotard argues in *The
Differend* that the notion of universal human nature, and the attendant
imperialism (external and internal) of the modern nation-state, proceed
from the representational structure of the republican 'we'. *Where the
Green Ants Dream* is set in contemporary Australia, an effectively repub-

lican commonwealth. Whatever its *de jure* relation to the English crown and the historical traditions of British imperialist expansion, Australia has a long history of genocide that parallels treatment of indigenous peoples in the United States. The continued existence of the immigrant Australian Commonwealth after the dissolution of the British Empire means that Australia finds its rationale as a modern state in the Republican tradition, by analogy with France or the United States. As Lyotard points out in *The Differend*, the idea of the modern democratic republic is that of a people that becomes a people by saying 'we, the people', rather than by living together, or living in any one place, for a long time: 'In a republic, the pronoun of the first-person plural is in effect the linchpin of/for the discourse of authorisation.'[18] In the notice entitled 'Declaration of 1789', Lyotard points out the links between the republican 'we' and the notion of universal humanity, 'the Idea of man'.[19] As he puts it, 'After 1789, international wars are also civil wars'.[20] Lyotard's analysis of the republican 'we' in *The Differend* focuses on France, but its contours apply to the modern western democracy, be it Europe, the United States, or Australia.

The claim of universal humanity inherent in the republican 'we' underpins the apparent paradox that a nation like the United States, dedicated to the inalienable rights of man, should be hostage to racism, sexism and homophobia, with a long history of genocide waged against Native Americans. American hatred of difference and fear of the other is so persistent and complex precisely because Americans believe themselves to be human. Theirs is not a tolerance of difference, but of identity, of the identity of an abstract human nature. Or, to put it less provocatively, they believe that they can say 'we', and that their 'we' will stand for humanity, that it can mean 'we humans'. The Republic declares itself to be the citadel of freedom and religious tolerance freed from monarchical oppression. The United States stands today indicted of enormous crimes of intolerance towards other cultures both internally and externally, from the repression of African-Americans and the near-extermination of the indigenous peoples of central North America through to at least the Vietnam War. How can the citadel of freedom have been built with the stones of oppression and imperialism, cemented with the blood of victims rather than of martyrs? This is no accident. It has to do with the way the Republic says 'we', from its inception in the phrase 'we, the people'. That 'we' has the effect of never allowing the question 'Who are we to speak?' to arise. The American 'we' is inherently integrationist – which is why anyone can become an American, why all Americans (and Australians) are essentially immigrants. This is why fantasies of space travel such as *Star Trek* are so compelling: the site in which the modern state elaborates the understanding of the human subject as essentially immigrant.[21] The Americanness of someone who says 'we' is not grounded in anything outside the act of saying 'we', which makes America a modern country. A republic is not founded in a common tradition but in a common declaration of independence from tradition, something which the facts of colonialism and immigration underline in the United States and Australia even more than in Lyotard's France. So republics do not ask where they have come from (no aristocracy of blood) but where they are going. The republic is the nation that is modern because it is going somewhere, that is headed towards a 'we' that will be the 'we' of humanity itself. Humanity in its essence, freed from any local constraints of class, race, creed, geographic origin. Universal humanity.

Lyotard notes the paradox of the fact that the republican 'we' is self-authorising in part four of his Notice on the French Declaration of 1789.[22] The same logic applies to the American Declaration of Independence. When we say 'we, the people' in order to found a state, we presuppose the existence of a people who can say 'we', even though it is only the declaration of independence that brings that people into existence as a people capable of saying 'we', a people that understands itself as a community. The founding fathers didn't worry about this logical flaw because they understood this statement as something in the nature of a promise. The American state is dedicated to a proposition that it will be its historical project to bring into being: the proposition of a common humanity, the proposition that there is such a thing as a people out there waiting to come into being. Lyotard's vigilance reminds us that it is very dangerous to assume that we know humanity in advance, that humanity, or tomorrow, belong to us. We are never so terroristic as when destiny seems manifest.

The project of the republican 'we' is to build a consensus that defines its community as that of humanity in its freedom. As Lyotard puts it, the republic asks, 'What must we do to become ourselves', to become a freer, more American, more human society?[23] Our community is established in the suppression of difference and the revelation of the common humanity that underlies our various cultural and racial 'clothes'. The achievement of tolerance will be a consensus, the community of a homogeneous 'we', in which our association is grounded on our common humanity. But the question we don't ask, can't ask, is 'Who are we to speak?'. We cannot enquire into the 'we' that grounds the possibility of our becoming 'ourselves'.

Lyotard argues that the homogeneous 'we' is not innocent, but that its union of the 'I' and the 'you' is the domination of the sender or speaker and the suppression of the receiver or hearer. Any culture that doesn't understand itself as a 'self', or as potentially human, is silenced, suppressed. No one can speak to republics unless they understand themselves as a 'we', a people – a different people perhaps, but a people all the same. All the same: a people united by being all the same, being people. As Lyotard reminds us, acts of great terror have been committed not simply in the name of but *as a result of* the presumption of a common, abstract, universal humanity.

Herzog's film is a minute example of the paradigm of such acts of terror, focusing on a small mining station called Mintabe.[24] Hackett, a young white mining engineer, conducts blasting tests for mineral deposits on behalf of the Ayers Mining Company. His tests bring the mining company into conflict with a group of local Aborigines who wish to prevent the blasting or mining lest the 'dreaming' of the green ants be disturbed and the 'universe world' come to an end. The dispute is taken to the Supreme Court, where the Aborigines lose. An extra-legal settlement by Ayers Mining apparently 'pacifies' the Aborigines by giving them a large green ant-like aeroplane (an RAAF Caribou) in which the tribal elder and an alcoholic Aboriginal ex-pilot fly off east in the direction of the annual migration of the green ants, apparently crashing in the mountains. Disgusted by the conduct of the mining company, the engineer Hackett goes off into the bush to live as a kind of hermit. The film does not explain whether or not the world would have ended had not the mimetic sacrifice been made.[25]

Where the Green Ants Dream can therefore be viewed as an attempt to negotiate with the terms of Lyotard's call for a quasi-aesthetic experimentation as the grounds of doing justice: 'let us wage a war on totality; let us be witnesses to the unpresentable; let us activate the differences and save the honour of the name'.[26] The film does not represent an other so much as bear witness to an otherness to representation, a *différend*. The task of witnessing requires, according to Lyotard, a series of paralogical experiments which displace the governing frame of representation. Such experiments are 'pagan' in that they seek to do justice rather than represent the truth in their interventions. If the problem of cultural transformation is that of how the weak can be made strong, paganism resists the Marxist piety which claims that the oppressed are really, truly, strong, and that we need merely to strip away the veils of ideological illusion to reveal the proletariat as historical destiny. There is no true strength to the Aborigines that western discourse can represent, yet a tendency to be exterminated is not the mark of some internal flaw. Paganism does not aim to represent the truth of the Aborigines, to show them as truly strong; rather it employs ruses so that their *weakness* may overcome the strength of their oppressors. I call these ruses, tricks and experiments quasi-aesthetic, following Lyotard's insistence on the paralogical nature of postmodern aesthetic experimentation (as opposed to modernist aesthetic innovation).[27]

Don't represent the Aborigines; testify to their *différend* with representation as the voicing of an identity. The opening sequence jump cuts between the diagonal slash of a conveyer belt and that of a digeri-doo, between the booming of a digeridoo and the grinding of machin-ery, between the conical pile of the anthill and that of the slag-heap. All of the film is wagered on the possibility that these are not differences within a representational frame but marks of a *différend* with represent-ation itself.[28] Thus, the opening shot of Mintabe exacerbates the visual effect of heat haze to the point where the filmic surface seems to buckle. The titles supervene, extended in the two-dimensional virtual space of 'textuality' (as described by Lyotard in *Discours, figure*) evoking the incommensurability of this landscape of the green anthills with the rational discourse that seeks to map and name it. This incommensura-bility is that of the *différend* between the modern republic, founded on the Idea of man, and the Aborigines. From the strange relation of the Aborigines to electromagnets to the final sacrifice, the film consistently hints that the Aborigines are in some sense closer to the ants than to the white men. In making this comparison I do not mean that ants are or should be in any way anthropomorphised, or that Aborigines are animals. Rather, the western inability to consider Aborigines except as animals or plants marks the obscurity of our pretended 'enlightenment' and the limited 'universality' of the western concept of the 'human'.[29]

The array of white characters in the film embodies a multiplicity of des-tinies for modernity. Ferguson, the executive vice-president of the Ayers Mining Company, makes the claim of universalism, that 'what we take out of the ground was meant for everyone'. The liberal capitalist claim for emancipation by means of the creation of wealth is backed by a negotiat-ing strategy in which communication and domination are inextricably linked. Ferguson immediately demands 'Who is your spokesman?', insist-ing that the Aborigines isolate an individual speaking subject authorised to produce a republican 'we' analogous to that of the white man. When the Aborigines reply by indicating that they have a group of 'tribal elders' and 'a giver of song' rather than a single voice, he reminds them that:

> Until today we've lacked a contact, or at least one official person to address … All of us, including you, are subject to the binding stric-tures of the Land Rights Act of the Commonwealth of Australia.

This rigid insistence of the universality of the law of the white man, in this case the law that claims to take note of Aboriginal rights, is mocked when Ferguson plaintively demands that the Aborigines produce someone au-thorised to sign for receipt of the aeroplane. The Aborigines ignore him, just as they refuse the company's offers. The litany of negotiation, in which Ferguson progressively raises the stakes, charts the history of exploitation and assimilation of the indigenous people. First, in return for the right to mine, the company offers technological toys: a pumping station and a school bus. Then Ferguson switches to the strategy of assimilation rather than robbery: a small percentage of profits. His final offer underlines the link between representation and death for the Aborigines: funding for an Aboriginal art museum. Kenelm Burridge's 'melting into history' of the Aborigine appears clearly as an oppressive move, offering the Aborigines the chance to turn their culture into an object of western historical representation and a commodity for exchange among white men.[30]

Hackett, the young geologist, figures the heroic phase of modern capitalist man, the youthful explorer who conducts tests despite the initial opposition of the hidebound traditionalists of the mining corporation. His general liberalism links the emancipatory or even rebellious spirit of modernity to imperialist expansion. His main companion on the site is a supervisor called Cole, who calls Aborigines 'black bastards' and makes Nazi jokes referring to Hackett as 'mein Kapitän' or 'mein Kommandant'. The liberal and the thuggish faces of modernity are accompanied by an old lady, named Miss Stralow (Australia?), who exhibits a naïve faith in modern technology's capacity to find her dog, Benjamin Franklin, lost in the mine workings. Technological invention proves inadequate, and poor Benjamin Franklin remains 'out in the tunnel, in the darkness', helpless despite the ingenuity of his namesake's epigones.[31]

In contrast, the Aborigines remain largely silent and impassive. Most of their statements in the first part of the film are made in their tribal language and then translated into English. As if to underline the issue of translation, those who at times act as translators in turn require their own statements to be translated by others. Like the green ants, which possess a susceptibility to magnetic fields and always align themselves on a north-south axis, the Aborigines seem to possess a peculiar relation to electronics, repeatedly causing elevators and digital watches to malfunction. As is later pointed out in court, their relation to time and number is entirely alien to the abstract enumeration that characterises western rationality, evidenced in the following dialogue:

Hackett: How long have you been waiting?
Daipu: A little long while.
Hackett: Ten minutes?
Daipu: Yes.
Hackett: One hour?
Daipu: Yes.
Hackett: Since yesterday evening sundown?
Daipu: Yes.

The truth of each response marks a stoic refusal to conceive of time in chronological terms. Each question is answered in response to the immediate situation in which it is posed, rather than according to any commonly held metalanguage of universal temporality.[32] This is paralleled by a relation to space which is not that of the western cartographic tradition, which is not organised by abstract dimensional co-ordinates. Thus the land exists as an apparently random series of sacred sites or dreamings, which mark pathways in an ahistorical temporality.[33] Importantly, however, the film does not mark this alterity as a mystical identity but insists upon its otherness. Thus, the Aboriginal critique of western man appears entirely incongruous in its failure to evoke the organic rootedness that is the usual object of western nostalgia:

> You white men are lost. You don't understand the land. Too many silly questions. You have no sense, no purpose, no direction.

The *différend*, the heterogeneity of Aboriginal to western argument, appears here in the very *congruity* of this statement with the western criticism of the Aborigines (who at one point steal transmission fluid in order to get high by drinking it). Each side speaks a different language, and the film refuses to identify the Aborigines as simply the inchoate or primitive *opposite* of the rationality of technological man. They are not an opposite, an other that the west might represent, they are different, irrepresentable.

This *différend* appears most clearly in the representation of the Supreme Court hearing in *Where the Green Ants Dream*, on which I want to focus. The plaintiff and the defendant do not merely speak different languages, they participate in utterly incommensurable language games. As Lyotard's analysis of Auschwitz in *The Differend* establishes, the assumption of common humanity and the goal of tolerant consensus, which has universal human understanding as its horizon, grounds the claim of western liberal democracies that all difference can be overcome and that we can understand each other. Thus, if we are truly human, truly tolerant, then everyone may speak and no one will be silenced. Each community may speak a different language but all languages can be translated into each other so that understanding may be reached. The goal of republican tolerance, the tolerance of identity, is to find the universal language, the 'common law' of humanity that will arbitrate all disputes in reference to what is human, to what constitutes human liberation. The variant idioms of plaintiff and defendant will then be translated into this common language, this common law, so that a justice may be done which respects human freedom. Differences arising from cultural diversity are referred to the universal language of human liberty and freedom so that difference may be overcome.

In this case, the judge is a kindly old man who professes himself sympathetic to the Aborigines, and Herzog makes it clear that he is not biased in favour of the mining company. The injustice done to the Aborigines is not the effect of a biased white man's law. Rather, injustice is the effect of the very fairness of the white man's law, its blank, bleached, abstract humanity – its claim to be 'common law'. Common – both traditional and universally reasonable. That is to say, the silencing of the Aboriginal voices is not the product of an external censorship, a repression that we might denounce as unfair. The Aborigines are killed with kindness, by the assumption that they are the same kind of people as the white Australians; they are silenced by the very fact of being let speak.

The question of silencing structures the entire court hearing, as Aborigines are silenced in the very act of being ushered into court to speak. The scene begins with an usher, who calls out for 'silence', so that 'all persons ... shall be heard'. The possibility of being heard depends on a dismissal of noise, of a certain multiplicity of voices that characterises Aboriginal tribal discussions. There is only one kind of voice, the 'we' of abstract human nature discovering itself. And the Aborigines do not speak with that unitary 'we'; their resolutely ungrammatical 'we' marks the inception of a multiple patchwork of stories, what Lyotard would call 'little narratives': 'We're going to tell you about the land. The land that we is living on.'

During the court hearing, the Aborigines produce as 'evidence' certain sacred objects. But the sacred objects that will show and prove 'what the land is belong and belong to the land is' can only be recorded as an utter blank: 'wooden object, carved, with marking, the markings indecipherable. The significance of the markings not plain to this court'. Unlike the flag that Governor Phillips erected in 1788 to lay claim to the land at about the same time as the burial of the sacred objects, these markings are untranslatable into any language. They are inhuman, it seems. And their untranslatability is a structural principle: the court must be cleared lest they be seen and the world die (we never see them in the film).

It could be argued, however, that the Aboriginal markings could be translated if only we learnt the language. The heterogeneity of the aboriginal language game is underlined by the appearance of a witness known as 'the mute', Mr Balai-La. Balai-La speaks out of turn, and the judge is bemused because Balai-La was introduced to the court as a mute. He is 'mute' because he is the only one left alive who speaks 'his' language.[34] He doesn't speak any other languages, even if it were not a sin for him to teach the secrets of his tribe's language to a foreigner. He is mute because there is no one left on earth who can understand what he says. And yet we realise that he does speak a language, but one which we will never be able to understand.[35] The mute is the strong figure for the condition of all Aboriginal discourse in the court: the ability to speak is merely a sham. Just because you have a voice doesn't mean you're not mute.

In this dispute 'between (at least) two parties, that cannot be equitably resolved for lack of a rule of judgment applicable to both arguments', whose claim is just?[36] Governor Phillips raised his flag in 1788, around 200 years ago, more or less when the Aboriginal sacred objects were buried. But they weren't buried at the same time, since they weren't buried in the same history. The problem is not just that there are two different histories, one of 'discovery' and one of 'invasion', but that the flag is raised in western historical time and the objects are buried in a time that is not historical in any sense we might recognise. We are dealing with 'unthinkably ancient times' as an anthropologist witness puts it: time which cannot be thought by western science.[37] This is not so much because it is so old as because its cumulation is not organised by counting but by a kind of remaining, as evidenced in the conversation quoted above, so that even to try to write an Aboriginal counter-history would be a kind of imperialism. This radical heterogeneity of languages is replayed not simply in time, but in space as well.

Thus the Solicitor-General, appearing for the mining company, mocks the Aboriginal testimony that delineates territorial space by means of a gesture, or the phrase 'a little long way', asking sarcastically 'Can you please translate that into English?'. The judge's reprimand of this discourtesy does nothing to alter the discounting of the radical heterogeneity of this language game to that of rational evidence. These are not just two different concepts of the 'same' space but understandings of space that are in one case conceptual and in the other not even linked to conceptual abstractions. As the other anthropologist, the white man who dwells beside the Aborigines, points out: there is no abstract enumeration in Aboriginal culture, only the sequence of numbers from one to three followed by 'many'. Yet, he adds, this is not merely incoherent, since a cattleman will know at a glance if one cow is missing from a corral of six hundred or more.

It might seem therefore that Aboriginal evidence is funny. It's not obviously evidence. But common law is flexible: as the judge points out, enough hearsay may 'condense into a palpable truth'. After all, we are all human, and the dignity and eloquence of the judge is exemplary. But what is condensation, here, if not a form of 'abstraction', as Marx analyses it, the point at which sheer quantity is translated into quality, when material becomes commodity, when materials become exchangeable, when they speak the common language of money?[38] This is the structure of evidence in the white man's law, even when it doesn't conform to formal rules. Thus the judge's tolerance extends to admitting that the rough weight of speech acts, 'hearsay', may achieve a mysterious transformation into the supposedly 'universal' language of evidence – 'palpable truth',[39] but only by becoming universally exchangeable, palpable; the tolerance that admits Aboriginal evidence, that lets it speak in court, silences the Aboriginal in its translation. In gaining value as evidence, the Aboriginal voice is abstracted from its locality just as the mining company gives land value in abstracting minerals from their location. In order to become evidence, Aboriginal language must be 'mined'. And of course the voice of the Aborigines is an attempt to speak the land in a way that resists any such mining. As the giver of song introduces the Aboriginal case to the court, 'We're going to tell you about the land ... the land that we're living on'. The sacred land, where green ants dwell. The green ants cannot emigrate. If the land is not there for them to return to in season, then they cannot return and the world will be destroyed. And the Aborigines 'belong the land' in the same way. Not belong *to* the land: there is no possibility of even a thought of separation or abstraction. They can't be transplanted, immigrate elsewhere. They have no *abstract human nature* that would survive in another place, anywhere else.

How then can this case be resolved? What 'we' can judge it? Each claimant is right in their own terms, and the application of a notion of universal justice, the appeal to an abstract human nature as the ground of a solution, is unjust to the Aborigines, victimises them. The Aborigines 'belong' (to) a land which cannot be abstracted, transferred, translated (*trans-latio*, lift across, move, transfer); it is not a land *on* which humans live, which they exploit, but a land to which humans and non-humans belong in ways that cannot be mapped conceptually. To put it another way, Aborigines are not candidates for the next casting call on *Star Trek*. Abstraction from the land into a virtual space organised by rational co-ordinates (mapped land, legal property), produces death.[40] How can one (a knowing subject) begin to translate, to transpose and take away into another place, the chiasmatic interpenetration of the Aboriginal task of witnessing to 'What the land is belong, and belong to the land is'? It is a land that cannot be 'mined' for its truth, that is destroyed in being made 'evidence'.

Thus, the injustice that arises is not that of a simple collusion between the language of the mining company and that of the court. The mining company might as well be French, or American, or multinational. Translation would be possible, in principle, between these languages. Injustice in the proceedings of translation comes not from the fact of simply speaking a different language but from the fact that the language of the Aborigines is untranslatable into the language of the court, heterogeneous to the language of common law, of common humanity. An encounter takes place, it happens, but no language is available to phrase it, for the Aboriginal language is insistently local, rooted in the land from which it comes; it cannot become multinational. It cannot, that is, become modern: no one can immigrate into Aboriginal culture. Hence the white man who dwells beside the Aborigines repeatedly remarks that he knows nothing of their culture, insisting that the mining company should go away rather than assimilating to the Aborigines. The vagrant anthropologist who lives at the edge of the bush (or *pagus*), like Hackett who goes to dwell beside him, becomes pagan; he does not become an Aboriginal tribesman.[41]

The Aborigines retain their difference. The pagan tolerance of difference does not mean an identification with the other but an endurance of that unbearable difference without trying to appropriate it. The suggestion that all cultures are fundamentally the same is the trade mark of the imperialism of modernity, which seeks to erase rootedness and difference, to reduce everyone to a blank abstract humanity, a bleached-out indifference. To put it bluntly, saying that we are all just human is an act of imperialism, because it means we are all white under the skin. The last freedom, the power of the enslaved, lies in the refusal to relinquish the experience of difference to the cultural tourism of the oppressor.[42]

Hence Lyotard's paganism is not a politics of despair, though it may reject the confidence of political piety that has traditionally animated Marxism. If this is a loss of confidence, the confidence is that of the imperialist. Rather than a relinquishment of political agency, it is a chance to think liberation otherwise than as an abstraction into ever more splendid (more universal) isolation, a refusal to think freedom as self-domination. Lyotard calls for a rethinking of the notion of community under a horizon of dissensus rather than of consensus, a dissensus distinct from atomistic individualism.[43] The horizon of consensus is the production of a total subject who will serve as the end of narrative, whether 'man' (humanism) or 'the proletariat as subject of history' (Marxism). It aims at the revelation of a total 'we'. To ask, as I have done, 'Who are we to speak?' is not to entrench that 'we' more firmly but to displace it. To say that we speak radically heterogeneous language games (even to 'ourselves') is not a recipe for isolation or solipsism – but a thought of our interaction otherwise than in terms of consensus, unity and self-domination.

What this film portrays is not an incidental act of injustice, a casual imperialism, but the necessary, structurally implicit terror that accompanies the encounter of a people that says 'we' with a community that is not modern, that doesn't think itself as a people. Australia is a republic, however much the Crown is mentioned, and the Aborigines are up against 'common law', not an artificial set of rules, a code, but a law that bases itself in the understanding of a 'reasonable man', in a common humanity. The paradox that arises is that neither side is wrong. There is simply no common humanity between the two sides. Rather, it is unjust to the cultural diversity of the Aborigines to presume that they are human, that the law can understand them. It is unjust to think that they are human. What if thinking diversity lay not in affirming a common humanity, but in actually thinking difference, rather than oscillating between the poles of identity and non-existence? This would mean that doing justice to the difference of the Aborigines lay in westerners recognising the possibility that their 'we' had nothing in common with them, that differences cannot be overcome either by our uniting with them in common humanity or exterminating them.

Thinking this multiplicity and difference is not a matter of fine-tuning the intersections of race, class and gender in order to liberate a new 'we' but a matter of rethinking what struggle and liberation may have to come to be in the light of the radicality of cultural difference. The acknowledgement of the opposition of the 'we' to cultural diversity means that politics, the play of dispute and difference, *doesn't end* – there is no universal community, no city on a hill. Or as Lyotard puts it in *Just Gaming*, 'there is no just society'.[44] It is very hard to think this, since most politicians simply want to put an end to politics, to argument, to dispute. Lyotard's acknowledgement that politics is everywhere, that 'everything is political if politics is the possibility of the differend on the occasion of the slightest linkage [of phrases]' means that politics is not about getting it right.[45]

'We' have no way of saying who is *right* here, the mining company or the Aborigines. No 'we' can pronounce once and for all on their dispute. All we can do, and it is a very difficult task, is to try to tell another story, after these two, one that doesn't seek to synthesise or assimilate them but to keep dispute and the difference an open question, that avoids the injustice of victimisation, that doesn't speak with a 'we'. This does not mean resolving the dispute within the terms of western rationality but preventing its suppression, keeping difference in question. It is the difficult task of opening western language to silence (which is *not* the same thing as giving voices to the silent); it is to recognise that this encounter with the mute voice of the Aboriginal happens, although no translation is possible, although it cannot be spoken in any obvious sense, since language would only kill the silence in speaking (of) it. As Lyotard says, 'Let us ... activate the differences'.[46] The struggle must go on, in order that the *différend* of the Aboriginal cannot be erased by the pretensions to abstract universality of the white man's discourse. This involves a guerrilla struggle to prevent totalising abstraction, which is also a struggle in this case to prevent mining. Of course this is not because the Aboriginal land claim is *more true* in any simple sense. One can't clear up the question of who owns the land, since the Aboriginal way would be silenced even granting them ownership in 'our' terms (prepositional 'property'). Here, then, is Lyotard's paganism. It is not that 'we' have to learn to live with cultural difference; rather, an attention to difference, a living in diversity, explodes the indifferent domination exercised by the consensual 'we'. It is important to understand that in making this claim I am not simply providing a recipe for giving up the power and pleasure of the dominating 'we'. I am not romanticising Aboriginal culture, or saying with Burridge that 'we have much to learn from them'. 'We', in so far as we think ourselves as 'we', cannot learn anything – for to learn in that way would be to perform one more act of cultural 'mining'. Rather, the force of their silent accusation is to make us ask 'Who are we to speak?', to give up the unquestioned assumption of our common humanity and to force us to think community and freedom otherwise. Ceasing to think community in terms of a universal 'we' gives us the chance to relinquish our enslavement to our own power, to transform a culture in which we only feel ourselves to be 'men' in so far as we silence what we cannot understand. bell hooks has pointed out that feminism is not a threat to African-American masculinity, but perhaps the only hope of young black men in an American culture that leads them to murder each other in pursuit of manhood.[47] Likewise, to struggle against ourselves, to attempt to think the multiplicity and diversity of culture without recourse to totalitarian notions of the universal, may be the best hope for avoiding total destruction in a world where the dream of consensus stands revealed as the nightmare of mutual annihilation.

The injustice perpetrated on indigenes is not a racism accidental to modernism which might be prevented by including them within a wider concept of human nature. Rather, the assumption of universal human nature, like all modernist metanarratives, lights the way to terror even as it upholds the torch of human rights. The problem of averting genocide demands a respect for difference, a deconstructive ethics, that is prepared to relinquish the concept of the human, to separate liberty from fraternity. Deconstruction rephrases the political, not by adding race along with gender and class to the categories by which we calculate oppression but by invoking an incalculable difference, an unrepresentable other, in the face of which any claim to community must be staked.

14

Can Thought Go On Without a Body?

Jean-François Lyotard

HE

You philosophers ask questions without answers, questions that have to remain unanswered to deserve being called philosophical. According to you answered questions are only technical matters. That's what they were to begin with. They were mistaken for philosophical questions. You turn to other questions that seem completely impossible to answer: which by definition resist every attempt at conquest by the understanding. Or what amounts to the same thing: you declare if the first questions were answered, that's because they were badly formulated. And you grant yourselves the privilege of continuing to regard as unresolved, that is as well formulated, questions that technical science believes it answered but in truth only inadequately dealt with. For you solutions are just illusions, failures to maintain the integrity due to being – or some such thing. Long live patience. You'll hold out forever with your incredulity. But don't be surprised if all the same, through your irresolution, you end up wearing out your reader.

But that's not the question. While we talk, the sun is getting older. It will explode in 4.5 billion years. It's just a little beyond the halfway point of its expected lifetime. It's like a man in his early forties with a life expectancy of eighty. With the sun's death your insoluble questions will be done with too. It's possible they'll stay unanswered right up to the end, flawlessly formulated, though now both grounds for raising such questions as well as the place to do this will no longer exist. You explain: it's impossible to think an end, pure and simple, of anything at all, since the end's a limit and to think it you have to be on both sides of that limit. So what's finished or finite has to be perpetuated in our thought if it's to be thought of as finished. Now this is true of limits belonging to thought. But after the sun's death there won't be a thought to know that its death took place.

That, in my view, is the sole serious question to face humanity today. In comparison everything else seems insignificant. Wars, conflicts, political tension, shifts in opinion, philosophical debates, even passions –

everything's dead already if this infinite reserve from which you now draw energy to defer answers, if in short thought as quest, dies out with the sun. Maybe death isn't the word. But the inevitable explosion to come, the one that's always forgotten in your intellectual ploys, can be seen in a certain way as coming before the fact to render these ploys posthumous – make them futile. I'm talking about what's X'd out of your writings – matter. Matter taken as an arrangement of energy created, destroyed and recreated over and over again, endlessly. On the corpuscular and/or cosmic scale I mean. I am not talking about the familiar, reassuring terrestrial world or the reassuring transcendent immanence of thought to its objects, analogous to the way the eye transcends what's visible or *habitus* its *situs*. In 4.5 billion years there will arrive the demise of your phenomenology and your utopian politics, and there'll be no one there to toll the death knell or hear it. It will be too late to understand that your passionate, endless questioning always depended on a 'life of the mind' that will have been nothing else than a covert form of earthly life. A form of life that was spiritual because human, human because earthly – coming from the earth of the most living of living things. Thought borrows a horizon and orientation, the limitless limit and the end without end it assumes, from the corporeal, sensory, emotional and cognitive experience of a quite sophisticated but definitely earthly existence – to which it's indebted as well.

With the disappearance of earth, thought will have stopped – leaving that disappearance absolutely unthought of. It's the horizon itself that will be abolished and, with its disappearance, your transcendence in immanence as well. If, as a limit, death really is what escapes and is deferred and as a result what thought has to deal with, right from the beginning – this death is still only the life of our minds. But the death of the sun is a death of mind, because it is the death of death as the life of the mind. There's no sublation or deferral if nothing survives. This annihilation is totally different from the one you harangue us about talking about 'our' death, a death that is part of the fate of living creatures who think. Annihilation in any case is too subjective. It will involve a change in the condition of matter: that is, in the form that energies take. This change is enough to render null and void your anticipation of a world after the explosion. Political science-fiction novels depict the cold desert of our human world after nuclear war. The solar explosion won't be due to human war. It won't leave behind it a devastated human world, dehumanised, but with none the less at least a single survivor, someone to tell the story of what's left, write it down. Dehumanised still implies human – a dead human, but conceivable: because dead in human terms, still capable of being sublated in thought. But in what remains after the solar explosion, there won't be any humanness, there won't be living creatures, there won't be intelligent, sensitive, sentient earthlings to bear witness to it, since they and their earthly horizon will have been consumed.

Assume that the ground, Husserl's *Ur-Erde*, will vanish into clouds of heat and matter. Considered as matter, the earth isn't at all originary since it's subject to changes in its condition – changes from further away or closer, changes coming from matter and energy and from the laws governing Earth's transformation. The *Erde* is an arrangement of matter/energy. This arrangement is transitory – lasting a few billion years more or less. Lunar years. Not a long time considered on a cosmic scale. The sun, our earth and your thought will have been no more than a spasmodic state of energy, an instant of established order, a smile on the surface of matter in a remote corner of the cosmos. You, the unbelievers, you're really believers: you believe much too much in that smile, in the complicity of things and thought, in the purposefulness of all things! Like everyone else, you will end up victims of the stabilised relationships of order in that remote corner. You'll have been seduced and deceived by what you call nature, by a congruence of mind and things. Claudel called this a *'co-naissance'*, and Merleau-Ponty spoke of the chiasmus of the eye and the horizon, a fluid in which mind floats. The solar explosion, the mere thought of that explosion, should awaken you from this euphoria. Look here: you try to think of the event in its *quod*, in the advent of 'it so happens that' before any quiddity, don't you? Well, you'll grant the explosion of the sun is the *quod* itself, no subsequent assignment being possible. Of that death alone, Epicurus ought to have said what he says about death – that I have nothing to do with it, since if it's present, I'm not, and if I'm present, it's not. Human death is included in the life of human mind. Solar death implies an irreparably exclusive disjunction between death and thought: if there's death, then there's no thought. Negation without remainder. No self to make sense of it. Pure event. Disaster. All the events and disasters we're familiar with and try to think of will end up as no more than pale simulacra.

Now this event is ineluctable. So either you don't concern yourself with it – and remain in the life of the mind and in earthly phenomenality. Like Epicurus you say 'As long as it's not here, I am, and I continue philosophising in the cosy lap of the complicity between man and nature.' But still with this glum afterthought: *après moi le déluge*. The deluge of matter. You'll grant there's a significant point of divergence between our thinking and the classical and modern thought of Western civilisation: the obvious fact of there being no nature, but only the material monster of *D'Alembert's Dream*, the *chôra* of the *Timaeus*. Once we were considered able to converse with Nature. Matter asks no questions, expects no answers of us. It ignores us. It made us the way it made all bodies – by chance and according to its laws.

Or else you try to anticipate the disaster and fend it off with means belonging to that category – means that are those of the laws of the transformation of energy. You decide to accept the challenge of the extremely likely annihilation of a solar order and an order of your own thought. And then the only job left you is quite clear – it's been underway for some time – the job of simulating conditions of life and thought to make thinking remain materially possible after the change in the condition of matter that's the disaster. This and this alone is what's at stake today in technical and scientific research in every field from dietetics, neurophysiology, genetics and tissue synthesis to particle physics, astrophysics, electronics, information science and nuclear physics. Whatever the immediate stakes might appear to be: health, war, production, communication. For the benefit of humankind, as the saying goes.

You know – technology wasn't invented by us humans. Rather the other way around. As anthropologists and biologists admit, even the simplest life forms, infusoria (tiny algae synthesised by light at the edges of tidepools a few million years ago) are already technical devices. Any material system is technological if it filters information useful to its survival, if it memorises and processes that information and makes inferences based on the regulating effect of behaviour, that is, if it intervenes on and impacts its environment so as to assure its perpetuation at least. A human being isn't different in nature from an object of this type. Its equipment for absorbing data isn't exceptional compared to other living things. What's true is that this human being is omnivorous when dealing with information because it has a regulating system (codes and rules of processing) that's more differentiated and a storage capacity for its memory that's greater than those of other living things. Most of all: it's equipped with a symbolic system that's both arbitrary (in semantics and syntax), letting it be less dependent on an immediate environment, and also 'recursive' (Hofstadter), allowing it to take into account (above and beyond raw data) the way it has of processing such data. That is, itself. Hence, of processing as information its own rules in turn and of inferring other ways of processing information. A human, in short, is a living organisation that is not only complex but, so to speak, replex. It can grasp itself as a medium (as in medicine) or as an organ (as in goal-directed activity) or as an object (as in thought – I mean aesthetic as well as speculative thought). It can even abstract itself from itself and take into account only its rules of processing, as in logic and mathematics. The opposite limit of this symbolic recursiveness resides in the necessity by which it is bound (whatever its *meta*-level of operation) at the same time to maintain regulations that guarantee its survival in any environment whatsoever. Isn't that exactly what constitutes the basis of your transcendence in immanence? Now, until the present time, this environment has been terrestrial. The survival of a thinking-organisation requires exchanges with that environment such that the human body can perpetuate itself there. This is equally true of the quintessential *meta-function* – philosophical thought. To think, at the very least you have to breathe, eat, etc. You are still under an obligation to 'earn a living'.

The body might be considered the hardware of the complex technical device that is human thought. If this body is not properly functioning, the ever so complex operations, the meta-regulations to the third or fourth power, the controlled deregulations of which you philosophers are so fond, are impossible. Your philosophy of the endless end, of immortal death, of interminable difference, of the undecidable, is an expression, perhaps the expression *par excellence*, of meta-regulation itself. It's as if it took itself into account as *meta*. Which is all well and good. But don't forget – this faculty of being able to change levels referentially derives solely from the symbolic and recursive power of language. Now language is simply the most complex form of the (living and dead) 'memories' that regulate all living things and make them technical objects better adjusted to their surroundings than mechanical ensembles. In other words your philosophy is possible only because the material ensemble called 'man' is endowed with very sophisticated software. But also, this software, human language, is dependent on the condition of the hardware. Now: the hardware will be consumed in the solar explosion taking philosophical thought with it (along with all other thought) as it goes up in flames.

So the problem of the technological sciences can be stated as: how to provide this software with a hardware that is independent of the conditions of life on earth.

That is: how to make thought without a body possible. A thought that continues to exist after the death of the human body. This is the price to be paid if the explosion is to be conceivable, if the death of the sun is to be a death like other deaths we know about. Thought without a body is the prerequisite for thinking of the death of all bodies, solar or terrestrial, and of the death of thoughts that are inseparable from those bodies.

But 'without a body' in this exact sense: without the complex living terrestrial organism known as the human body. Not without hardware, obviously.

So theoretically the solution is very simple: manufacture hardware capable of 'nurturing' software at least as complex (or replex) as the present-day human brain, but in non-terrestrial conditions. That clearly means finding for the 'body' envisaged a 'nutrient' that owes nothing to biochemical components synthesised on the surface of the earth through the use of solar energy. Or: learning to effect these syntheses in other places than on earth. In both cases then this means learning to manufacture a hardware capable of nourishing our software or its equivalent, but one maintained and supported only by sources of energy available in the cosmos generally.

It's clear even to a lay person like myself that the combined forces of nuclear physics, electronics, photonics and information science open up a possibility of constructing technical objects, with a capacity that's not just physical but also cognitive, which 'extract' (that is select, process and distribute) energies these objects need in order to function from forms generally found everywhere in the cosmos.

So much for the hardware. As for the software such machines are to be equipped with – that's a subject for research in the area of artificial intelligence and for the controversies surrounding such research. You philosophers, writers and artists are quick to dismiss the pathetic track record of today's software programs. True – thinking or 'representing' machines (Monique Linard's term) are weaklings compared to ordinary human brains, even untrained ones.

It can be objected that programmes fed into such computers are elementary and that progress can be expected in information science, artificial languages and communications science. Which is likely. But the main objection concerns the very principle of these intelligences. This objection has been summed up in a line of thought proposed by Hubert L. Dreyfus. Our disappointment in these organs of 'bodiless thought' comes from the fact that they operate on binary logic, one imposed on us by Russell's and Whitehead's mathematical logic, Turing's machine, McCulloch's and Pitts's neuronal model, the cybernetics of Wiener and von Neumann, Boolian algebra and Shannon's information science.

But as Dreyfus argues, human thought doesn't think in a binary mode. It doesn't work with units of information (bits), but with intuitive, hypothetical configurations. It accepts imprecise, ambiguous data that don't seem to be selected according to pre-established codes or readability. It doesn't neglect side effects or marginal aspects of a situation. It isn't just focused, but lateral too. Human thought can distinguish the important from the unimportant without doing exhaustive inventories of data and without testing the importance of data with respect to the goal pursued by a series of trials and errors. As Husserl has shown, thought becomes aware of a 'horizon', aims at a 'noema', a kind of object, a sort of non-conceptual monogram that provides it with intuitive configurations and opens up 'in front of it' a field of orientation and expectation, a 'frame' (Minsky). And in such a framework, perhaps more like a scheme, it moves towards what it looks for by 'choosing', that is, by discarding and recombining the data it needs, but none the less without making use of pre-established criteria determining in advance what's appropriate to choose. This picture inevitably recalls the description Kant gave of a thought process he called reflective judgement: a mode of thought not guided by rules for determining data, but showing itself as possibly capable of developing such rules afterwards on the basis of results obtained 'reflexively'.

This description of a reflective thought opposed to determinate thought does not hide (in the work of Husserl or Dreyfus) what it owes to perceptual experience. A field of thought exists in the same way that there's a field of vision (or hearing): the mind orients itself in it just as the eye does in the field of the visible. In France, this analogy was already central to Wallon's work, for example, and also to Merleau-Ponty's. It is 'well known'. None the less it has to be stressed this analogy isn't extrinsic, but intrinsic. In its procedures it doesn't only describe a thought analogous with an experience of perception. It describes a thought that proceeds analogically and only analogically – not logically. A thought in which therefore procedures of the type – 'just as ... so likewise ...' or 'as if ... then' or again 'as p is to q, so r is to s' are privileged compared to digital procedures of the type 'if ... then ...' and 'p is not non-p'. Now these are the paradoxical operations that constitute the experience of a body, of an 'actual' or phenomenological body in its space-time continuum of sensibility and perception. Which is why it's appropriate to take the body as model in the manufacture and programming of artificial intelligence if it's intended that artificial intelligence not be limited to the ability to reason logically.

It's obvious from this objection that what makes thought and the body inseparable isn't just that the latter is the indispensable hardware for the former, a material prerequisite of its existence. It's that each of them is analogous to the other in its relationship with its respective (sensible, symbolic) environment: the relationship being analogical in both cases. In this description there are convincing grounds for not supporting the hypothesis (once suggested by Hilary Putnam) of a principle of the 'separability' of intelligence, a principle through which he believed he could legitimate an attempt to create artificial intelligence.

SHE

Now that's something to leave us satisfied as philosophers. At least something to assuage a part of our anxiety. A field of perception has limits, but these limits are always beyond reach. While a visual object is presenting one side to the eye, there are always other sides, still unseen. A direct, focused vision is always surrounded by a curved area where visibility is held in reserve yet isn't absent. This disjunction is inclusive. And I'm not speaking of a memory brought into play by even the simplest sight. Continuing vision preserves along with it what was seen an instant before from another angle. It anticipates what will be seen shortly. These syntheses result in identifications of objects, identifications that never are completed, syntheses that a subsequent sighting can always unsettle or undo. And the eye, in this experience, is indeed always in search of a recognition, as the mind is of a complete description of an object it is trying to think of: without, however, a viewer ever being able to say he recognises an object perfectly since the field of presentation is absolutely unique every time, and since when vision actually sees, it can't ever forget that there's always more to be seen once the object is 'identified'. Perceptual 'recognition' never satisfies the logical demand for complete description.

In any serious discussion of analogy it's this experience that is meant, this blur, this uncertainty, this faith in the inexhaustibility of the perceivable, and not just a mode of transfer of the data onto an inscription-surface not originally its own. Similarly, writing plunges into the field of phrases, moving forward by means of adumbrations, groping towards what it 'means' and never unaware, when it stops, that it's only suspending its exploration for a moment (a moment that might last a lifetime) and that there remains, beyond the writing that has stopped, an infinity of words, phrases and meanings in a latent state, held in abeyance, with as many things 'to be said' as at the beginning. Real 'analogy' requires a thinking or representing machine to be *in* its data *just as* the eye is in the visual field or writing is in language (in the broad sense). It isn't enough for these machines to simulate the results of vision or of writing fairly well. It's a matter (to use the attractively appropriate locution) of 'giving body' to the artificial thought of which they are capable. And it's that body, both 'natural' and artificial, that will have to be carried far from earth before its destruction if we want the thought that survives the solar explosion to be something more than a poor binarised ghost of what it was beforehand.

From this point of view we should indeed have grounds not to give up on techno-science. I have no idea whether such a 'programme' is achievable. Is it even consistent to claim to be programming an experience that defies, if not programming, then at least the programme – as does the vision of the painter or writing? It's up to you to give it a try. After all, the problem's an urgent one for you. It's the problem of a comprehension of ordinary language by your machines. A problem you encounter especially in the area of terminal/user interface. In that interface subsists the contact of your artificial intelligence with the naïve kind of intelligence borne by so-called 'natural' languages and immersed in them.

But another question bothers me. Is it really another question? Thinking and suffering overlap. Words, phrases in the act of writing, the latent nuances and timbres at the horizon of a painting or a musical composition as it's being created (you've said this yourselves) all lend themselves to us for the occasion and yet slip through our fingers. And even inscribed on a page or canvas, they 'say' something other than what we 'meant' because they're older than the present intent, overloaded with possibilities of meaning – that is, connected with other words, phrases, shades of meaning, timbres. By means of which precisely they constitute a field, a 'world', the 'brave' human world you were speaking about, but one that's probably more like an opaqueness of very distant horizons that exist only so that we'll 'brave' them. If you think you're describing thought when you describe a selecting and tabulating of data, you're silencing truth. Because data aren't given, but givable, and selection isn't choice. Thinking, like writing or painting, is almost no more than letting a givable come towards you. In the discussion we had last year at Siegen, in this regard, emphasis was put on the sort of emptiness that has to be obtained from mind and body by a Japanese warrior-artist when doing calligraphy, by an actor when acting: the kind of suspension of ordinary intentions of mind associated with *habitus*, or arrangements of the body. It's at this cost, said Glenn and Andreas (and you can imagine how quickly I agreed, helped out by Dôgen, Diderot and Kleist), that a brush encounters the 'right' shapes, that a voice and a theatrical gesture are endowed with the 'right' tone and look. This soliciting of emptiness, this evacuation – very much the opposite of overweening, selective, identificatory activity – doesn't take place without some suffering. I won't claim that the grace Kleist talked about (a grace of stroke, tone or volume) has to be merited: that would be presumptuous of me. But it has to be called forth, evoked. The body and the mind have to be free of burdens for grace to touch us. That doesn't happen without suffering. An enjoyment of what we possessed is now lost.

Here again, you will note, there's a necessity for physical experience and a recourse to exemplary cases of bodily ascesis to understand and make understood a type of emptying of the mind, an emptying that is required if the mind is to think. This obviously has nothing to do with *tabula rasa*, with what Descartes (vainly) wanted to be a starting from scratch on the part of knowing thought – a starting that paradoxically can only be a starting all over again. In what we call thinking the mind isn't 'directed' but suspended. You don't give it rules. You teach it to receive. You don't clear the ground to build unobstructed: you make a little clearing where the penumbra of an almost-given will be able to enter and modify its contour. An example of this work is found *mutatis mutandis* in Freudian *Durcharbeitung*. In which – though I won't labour the point – the pain and the cost of the work of thought can be seen. This kind of thinking has little to do with combining symbols in accordance with a set of rules. Even though the act of combining, as it seeks out and waits for its rule, can have quite a lot to do with thought.

The pain of thinking isn't a symptom coming from outside to inscribe itself on the mind instead of in its true place. It is thought itself resolving to be irresolute, deciding to be patient, wanting not to want, wanting, precisely, not to produce a meaning in place of what *must* be signified. This is a tip of the hat to a *duty* that hasn't yet been named. Maybe that duty isn't a debt. Maybe it's just the mode according to which what doesn't yet exist, a word, a phrase, a colour, *will emerge*. So that the suffering of thinking is a suffering of time, of what happens. To sum up – will your thinking-, your representing-machines suffer? What will be their future if they are just memories? You will tell me this scarcely matters if at least they can 'achieve' the paradoxical relationship to the said 'data', which are only quasi-givens, givables, which I've just described. But this is a hardly credible proposition.

If this suffering is the mark of true thought, it's because we think in the already-thought, in the inscribed. And because it's difficult to leave something hanging in abeyance or take it up again in a different way so what hasn't been thought yet can emerge and what *should be* inscribed *will be*. I'm not speaking just about words lacking in a superabundance of available words, but about ways of assembling these words, ways we should accept despite the articulations inspired in us by logic, by the syntax of our languages, by constructions inherited from our reading. (To Sepp Gumbrecht, who was surprised that any and all thought, according to me, should require and involve inscription, I say: we think in a world of inscriptions already there. Call this culture if you like. And if we think, this is because there's still something missing in this plenitude and room has to be made for this lack by making the mind a blank, which allows the something else remaining to be thought to happen. But this can only 'emerge' as already inscribed in its turn.) The unthought hurts because we're comfortable in what's already thought. And thinking, which is accepting this discomfort, is also, to put it bluntly, an attempt to have done with it. That's the hope sustaining all writing (painting, etc.): that at the end, things will be better. As there is no end, this hope is illusory. So: the unthought would have to make your machines uncomfortable, the uninscribed that remains to be inscribed would have to make their memory suffer. Do you see what I mean? Otherwise why would they ever *start* thinking? We need machines that suffer from the burden of their memory. (But suffering doesn't have a good reputation in the technological megalopolis. Especially the suffering of thinking. It doesn't even incite laughter anymore. The idea of it doesn't occur, that's all. There's a trend towards 'play', if not performance.)

Finally, the human body has a gender. It's an accepted proposition that sexual difference is a paradigm of an incompleteness of not just bodies, but minds too. Of course there's masculinity in women as well as femininity in men. Otherwise how would one gender even have an idea of the other or have an emotion that comes from what's lacking? It's lacking because it's present deep inside, in the body, in the mind. Present like a guard, restrained, off to the side, at the edge of your vision, present on some horizon of it. Elusive, impossible to grasp. Again we're back at transcendence in immanence. The notion of gender dominant in contemporary society wants this gap closed, this transcendence toppled, this powerlessness overcome. Supposed 'partners' (in a pleasure arrangement) draw up a contract for purposes of common 'enjoyment' of sexual difference itself. The contract provides that neither party suffer from this association and that at the first sign of lack (whether through failure to perform or not), of defocalisation, of lack of control and transcendence, the parties break the contract – though that's still too strong a phrase, they'll just let it lapse. And even if from time to time fashion gives 'love' its place back among the inventory of objects that circulate, it's as a 'top of the line' sexual relationship, reserved for superstars and advertised as an enviable exception. I see in this arrangement a sign that techno-science conditions thought to neglect the different it carries within.

I don't know whether sexual difference is ontological difference. How would a person *know*? My unassuming phenomenological description still doesn't go far enough. Sexual difference isn't just related to a body as it feels its incompleteness, but to an unconscious body or to the unconscious as body. That is, as separated from thought – even analogical thought. This difference is *ex hypothesi* outside our control. Maybe (because as Freud showed in his description of deferred action, it inscribes effects without the inscription being 'memorised' in the form of recollection) it's the other way around? And this difference is what initially sets up fields of perception and thought as functions of waiting, of equivocations, as I've stated? This quite probably defines suffering in perceiving and conceiving as produced by an impossibility of unifying and completely determining the object seen. To that which without gendered difference would only be a neutral experience of the space-time of perceptions and thoughts, an experience in which this feeling of incompleteness would be lacking as unhappiness, but only an experience producing a simple and pure cognitive aesthetic, to this neutrality gendered difference adds the suffering of abandonment because it brings to neutrality what no field of vision or thought can include, namely a demand. The faculty to transcend the given that you were talking about, a faculty lodged in immanence indeed finds a means to do this in this recursiveness of human language – although such a capacity isn't just a possibility but an actual force. And that force is desire.

So: the intelligence you're preparing to survive the solar explosion will have to carry that force within it on its interstellar voyage. Your thinking machines will have to be nourished not just on radiation but on the irremediable differend of gender.

And here is where the issue of complexity has to be brought up again. I'm granting to physics theory that technological-scientific development is, on the surface of the earth, the present-day form of a process of negentropy or complexification that has been underway since the earth began its existence. I'm granting that human beings aren't and never have been the motor of this complexification, but an effect and carrier of this negentropy, its continuer. I'm granting that the disembodied intelligence that everything here conspires to create will make it possible to meet the challenge to that process of complexification posed by an entropic tidal wave which from that standpoint equates with the solar explosion to come. I agree that with the cosmic exile of this intelligence a locus of high complexity – a centre of negentropy – will have escaped its most probable outcome, a fate promised any isolated system by Carnot's second law – precisely because this intelligence won't have let itself be left isolated in its terrestrial-solar condition. In granting all this, I concede that it isn't any human desire to know or transform reality that propels this technoscience, but a cosmic circumstance. But note that the complexity of that intelligence exceeds that of the most sophisticated logical systems, since it's another type of thing entirely. As a material ensemble, the human body hinders the separability of this intelligence, hinders its exile and therefore survival. But at the same time the body, our phenomenological, mortal, perceiving body is the only available *analogon* for thinking a certain complexity of thought.

Thought makes lavish use of analogy. It does this in scientific discovery too of course 'before' its operativity is fixed in paradigms. On the other hand its analogising power can also return, bringing into play the spontaneous analogical field of the perceiving body, educating Cézanne's eye, Debussy's ear, to see and hear givables, nuances, timbres that are 'useless' for survival, even cultural survival.

But once again that analogising power, which belongs to body and mind analogically and mutually and which body and mind share with each other in the art of invention, is inconsequential compared to an irreparable transcendence inscribed on the body by gender difference. Not only calculation, but even analogy cannot do away with the remainder left by this difference. This difference makes thought go on endlessly and won't allow itself to be thought. Thought is inseparable from the phenomenological body: although gendered body is separated from thought, and launches thought. I'm tempted to see in this difference a primordial explosion, a challenge to thought that's comparable to the solar catastrophe. But such is not the case, since this difference causes infinite thought – held as it is in reserve in the secrecy of bodies and thoughts. It annihilates only the One. You have to prepare post-solar thought for the inevitability and complexity of this separation. Or the pilot at the helm of spaceship *Exodus* will still be entropy.

Summaries and Notes

1. NEIL BADMINGTON, INTRODUCTION: APPROACHING POSTHUMANISM

Notes

1. *Time*, 3 January 1983, p. 3. I was led to this source by a passing reference in James Flint's posthumanist novel, *Habitus* (London, 1998), p. 390. For readers' responses to the Machine of the Year award, see the *Time* letters page of 24 January 1983.
2. Martin Heidegger, 'Letter on Humanism', *Basic Writings*, revised edn, ed. David Farrell Krell (London, 1993), p. 219.
3. I place this term in quotation marks because, as William V. Spanos has pointed out, the 'naturalised "we"' is one of the hallmarks of humanism. William V. Spanos, *The End of Education: Toward Posthumanism* (Minneapolis and London, 1993), p. 3. For more on this question, see Bill Readings, 'Pagans, Perverts or Primitives? Experimental Justice in the Empire of Capital', in this volume, essay 13.
4. Umberto Eco, 'On the Crisis of the Crisis of Reason', *Travels in Hyperreality: Essays*, trans. William Weaver (New York, 1990), p. 126.
5. Ihab Hassan, 'Prometheus as Performer: Toward a Posthumanist Culture? A University Masque in Five Scenes', *Georgia Review*, 31 (1977), 843.
6. Kate Soper, *Humanism and Anti-Humanism* (London, 1986) and Tony Davies, *Humanism* (London and New York, 1997).
7. Quoted in Davies, *Humanism*, p. 1.
8. Soper, *Humanism and Anti-Humanism*, p. 9.
9. Ibid., pp.11–12.
10. Bertrand Russell, *A History of Western Philosophy*, 2nd edn (1961) (London, 1979), p. 542.
11. René Descartes, *Discourse on the Method of Rightly Conducting One's Reason and Seeking the Truth in the Sciences* (1637), *Descartes: Selected Philosophical Writings*, ed. and trans. John Cottingham, Robert Stoothoff and Dugald Murdoch (Cambridge and New York, 1988), p. 36. The use of gender-specific language runs throughout; I draw attention to it merely in this first instance.
12. Descartes, *Discourse on the Method*, p. 20.
13. Ibid., p. 36. Translation modified. Although the *Discourse* was originally written in French, this famous phrase is frequently given in Latin as 'Cogito, ergo sum'.
14. Ibid, pp.44–5.
15. This phrase forms part of the title of the ninth chapter of Louis Althusser and Etienne Balibar, *Reading Capital*, trans. Ben Brewster (1968) (London, 1970).
16. Karl Marx and Friedrich Engels, *The German Ideology: Critique of Modern German Philosophy According to its Representatives Feuerbach, B. Bauer and*

Stirner, and of German Socialism According to its Various Prophets, Collected Works, 48 vols (London, 1975–99), vol. 5, p. 23.

17. Ibid., p. 37.
18. Louis Althusser, 'Marxism and Humanism' in this volume, essay 6.
19. Sigmund Freud, 'The Question of a *Weltanschauung*', *New Introductory Lectures on Psychoanalysis*, ed. James Strachey and Angela Richards, trans. James Strachey, Pelican Freud Library, vol. 2 (Harmondsworth, 1973), p. 217.
20. Jacques Lacan, *Ecrits: A Selection*, trans. Alan Sheridan (London, 1977), p. 166.
21. Sigmund Freud, *Psychopathology of Everyday Life*, trans. A. A. Brill (1901) (Harmondsworth, 1938), p. 71.
22. Ibid, p. 77.
23. Sigmund Freud, *Beyond the Pleasure Principle* (1920), *On Metapsychology: The Theory of Psychoanalysis*, ed. Angela Richards, trans. James Strachey, Penguin Freud Library, vol. 11 (Harmondsworth, 1991), p. 295.
24. Sigmund Freud, 'Fixation to Traumas – The Unconscious', *Introductory Lectures on Psychoanalysis*, ed. James Strachey and Angela Richards, trans. James Strachey, Pelican Freud Library, vol. 1 (1916–17) (Harmondsworth, 1973), p. 326.
25. Lacan, *The Seminar of Jacques Lacan, Book I: Freud's Papers on Technique 1953–1954*, ed. Jacques-Alain Miller, trans. John Forrester (1975) (New York and London, 1991), p. 166.
26. Lacan, *Ecrits*, p. 1.
27. Ibid., p. 114.
28. Jacques Lacan, *The Seminar of Jacques Lacan, Book II: The Ego in Freud's Theory and in the Technique of Psychoanalysis 1954–1955*, ed. Jacques-Alain Miller, trans. Sylvana Tomaselli (1978) (New York and London, 1991), p. 13.
29. Lacan, *Ecrits*, p. 324.
30. Soper, *Humanism and Anti-Humanism*, p. 99.
31. Jean-François Lyotard, 'Adorno as the Devil', trans. Robert Hurley, *Telos*, 19 (1974), 137. The subject of the original sentence is Hegel, not Man. The American alien invasion narratives of the 1950s have habitually been read as a 'reflection' of Cold War paranoia about communist infiltration; I am suggesting that there may be still more at stake.
32. Istvan Csicsery-Ronay, Jr, 'The SF of Theory: Baudrillard and Haraway', *Science-Fiction Studies*, 18.3 (1991), 389.
33. Manfred E. Clynes and Nathan S. Kline, 'Cyborgs and Space', *Astronautics* (September 1960), 26–7, 74–6.
34. Jean Baudrillard, 'Simulacra and Science Fiction', *Simulacra and Simulation*, trans. Sheila Faria Glaser (1981) (Ann Arbor, MI, 1994), p. 121.
35. Maurice Blanchot, *The Writing of the Disaster*, trans. Ann Smock (1980) (Lincoln, NE, and London, 1986), p. 43.
36. For a wonderful account of posthumanism which moves seamlessly between the spaces of technology and fiction, see N. Katherine Hayles, *How We Became Posthuman: Virtual Bodies in Cybernetics, Literature, and Informatics* (Chicago and London, 1999). I would have loved to include something from this text in the present volume but I did not become aware of Hayles' book until *Posthumanism* was in the final stages of production.
37. This subject is considered at some length in Jacques Derrida, 'The Ends of Man', *Margins of Philosophy*, trans. Alan Bass (1972) (Hemel Hempstead, 1982), pp.109–36.

38. Jacques Derrida, *Positions*, trans. Alan Bass (1972) (London, 1981), p. 12.
39. Jacques Derrida, *Of Grammatology*, trans. Gayatri Chakravorty Spivak (1967) (Baltimore and London, 1976), p. 24.
40. Hayles, *How We Became Posthuman*, p. 246.
41. Douglas Coupland, *Polaroids from the Dead* (London, 1996), p. 85.

2. ROLAND BARTHES, 'THE GREAT FAMILY OF MAN'
(From *Mythologies*, ed. and trans. Annette Lavers (London, 1993), pp.100–2. The full text of *Mythologies* was originally published in French in 1957.)

Summary

Is there really a human essence that can be captured on paper, canvas or film? Edward Steichen's *The Family of Man*, a collection of photographs first exhibited in the mid-1950s (and since published by the New York Museum of Modern Art, 1986), claims to reveal a basic human consciousness beneath the cultural differences of the individuals it depicts. Barthes views the very notion of a Family of Man as an ambiguous myth which suppresses the importance of history, implying that culture and politics have no effect upon an individual's sense of self. He proceeds to call for a 'progressive humanism' which would, unlike classical humanism, recognise that the implications of difference invalidate the belief that there is an unchanging human essence.

3. ROSALIND COWARD, 'THE INSTINCT'
(From *Female Desire: Women's Sexuality Today* (London, 1984), pp.233–43.)

Summary

Common sense tells 'us' that 'we' behave the way 'we' do because of natural instincts. Humans, according to this account, cannot help the way they act and organise. This essay takes issue with such a claim, suggesting that it is misleading to explain the relationship between the sexes in this manner. The distribution of power is not an effect of nature, but of specific cultural circumstances: it is, in other words, *constructed*. To resort to a general notion of instinct is to overlook alternatives and to limit the extent to which change can be imagined. Where instinct is, difference cannot be (and vice versa).

Notes

1. Not all societies create a surplus which is then distributed inequitably. Certain societies produce surplus resources which are then distributed equitably between the whole society.
2. See Richard Dawkins, *The Selfish Gene* (London, 1978).
3. For a useful summary of the kinds of families currently living in Britain see *Families in the Future* from the Study Commission on the Family (1983). This

document makes it clear that the 'typical' family is not typical, that Britain has a diversity of 'household forms' – single parents, elderly people on their own, and different ethnic family forms.

4. 'FRANTZ FANON, 'THE WRETCHED OF THE EARTH'
(Extract from chapter in *The Wretched of the Earth*, trans. Constance Farrington (Harmondsworth, 1967), pp.251–5. *The Wretched of the Earth* was originally published in French in 1961.)

Summary

Humanism is a distinctly European phenomenon, inseparable from imperialism. Implicit in humanism's will to see sameness wherever it looks is a desire to *make* sameness, to impose a partial world-view as a universal truth. Humanism, therefore, is responsible for a series of atrocities: those who cannot be assimilated must be destroyed. The Third World must not seek to imitate Europe; it must, rather, look beyond the parameters of classical (European) humanism. Only when this is recognised will it be possible to begin a new stage in Man's development in which Europe is no longer the naturalised norm.

5. MICHEL FOUCAULT, 'THE ORDER OF THINGS: AN ARCHAEOLOGY OF THE HUMAN SCIENCES'
(Extract from chapter in *The Order of Things: An Archaeology of the Human Sciences* (London and New York 1989), pp.385–7. *The Order of Things* was originally published in French in 1966.)

Summary

Having shown elsewhere in *The Order of Things* precisely how the humanist figure of Man was constituted at a certain historical moment, Foucault proceeds to suggest that Man must therefore be understood as a recent invention, and not – *pace* humanism – an eternal, naturally occurring phenomenon. Made possible by a certain reorganisation of knowledge, Man could, therefore, disappear if a further epistemic shift were to take place.

6. LOUIS ALTHUSSER, 'MARXISM AND HUMANISM'
(Extract from chapter in *For Marx*, trans. Ben Brewster (London and New York, 1996), pp.227–31. *For Marx* was originally published in French in 1965.)

Summary

The 'mature' writings of Karl Marx articulated a 'theoretical anti-humanism' which challenged humanism's belief in the Family of Man. After 1845, Marx distanced himself from the notion that there is a universal human essence, recognising instead that human subjectivity is a *social construct*. The self – *pace* humanism – is not a given, but an effect of social conditions. Humanism is henceforth understood to be an *ideology*, which amounts to saying that it can never be scientific, can never provide knowledge of things as they really are.

Notes

1. The whole, fashionable, theory of 'reification' depends on a projection of the theory of alienation found in the early texts, particularly the *1844 Manuscripts*, on to the theory of 'fetishism' in *Capital*. In the *1844 Manuscripts*, the objectification of the human essence is claimed as the indispensable preliminary to the reappropriation of the human essence by man. Throughout the process of objectification, man only exists in the form of an objectivity in which he meets his own essence in the appearance of a foreign, non-human, essence. This 'objectification' is not called 'reification' even though it is called *inhuman*. Inhumanity is not represented *par excellence* by the model of a 'thing': but sometimes by the model of animality (or even of pre-animality – the man who no longer even has simple animal relations with nature), sometimes by the model of the omnipotence and fascination of transcendence (God, the State) and of money, which is, of course, a 'thing'. In *Capital* the only social relation that is presented in the form of a *thing* (this piece of metal) is *money*. But the conception of money as a *thing* (that is, the confusion of value with use-value in money) does not correspond to the reality of this 'thing': it is not the brutality of a simple 'thing' that man is faced with when he is in direct relation with money; it is a *power* (or a *lack* of it) over things and men. An ideology of reification that sees 'things' everywhere in human relations confuses in this category 'thing' (a category more foreign to Marx cannot be imagined) every social relation, conceived according to the model of a money-thing ideology.

7. JEAN BAUDRILLARD, 'PROPHYLAXIS AND VIRULENCE'
(From *The Transparency of Evil: Essays on Extreme Phenomena*, trans. James Benedict (London and New York, 1994), pp.60–70. *The Transparency of Evil* was originally published in French in 1990.)

Summary

Contemporary cultures which have reached a highly advanced state of technological development tend to view human beings as little more than bits of information within the total system of society. As humans become increasingly dependent upon technology, the idea of a 'natural' human condition becomes increasingly archaic: 'we' are all becoming like the Boy in the Bubble, whose every need (including defence against disease) is met by technology. The only form of resistance to this state of affairs comes in the form of strange viruses that develop within the closed system, interrupting the efficiency of that system. These viruses are, paradoxically, an attempt by the human to survive a culture of total transparency.

8. PAULA RABINOWITZ, 'SOFT FICTIONS AND INTIMATE DOCUMENTS: CAN FEMINISM BE POSTHUMAN?'
(From Judith Halberstam and Ira Livingston (eds), *Posthuman Bodies* (Bloomington and Indianapolis, 1995), pp. 97–112.)

Summary

The exclusion of women from the epic tale of Man means that women's stories have existed beyond the realm of human knowledge. Women have never been human, and posthumanist feminism need not seek to remedy this. There is a sense in which feminism, together with the women it addresses, is always already posthumanist. But if articulation is possible only through recourse to humanism, how can the posthumanist subject speak? The posthumanist feminism articulated in Chick Strand's film, *Soft Fiction*, is forced to evade truth claims, to draw upon fantasy, exaggeration and lies. Although Strand's text claims to be ethnographic, it does not reveal the truth about the subjects depicted. Fiction enters the frame in the form of performance, for identities are seen to be constructed rather than given. Even the most personal secrets are, once narrated or even experienced in patriarchy, somewhat public. Feminism must recognise this, just as it must attend to its own historical contingency. The essay concludes by addressing several problems with *Soft Fictions*: its whiteness, its heterocentricity, and its more general engagement with ethnography.

Notes

1. See the work of Nancy Armstrong, Mary Poovey, Denise Riley, Anita Levy, Cathy N. Davidson, among others.
2. Gayatri Chakravorty Spivak, 'Can the Subaltern Speak?' *Marxism and the Interpretation of Culture*, ed. Cary Nelson and Lawrence Grossberg (Urbana, IL, 1988), pp. 271–313.
3. I should note that in 'Changes: Thoughts on Myth, Narrative and Historical Experience', Mulvey reconsiders the spectacle/spectator model, situating it as a polemical intervention made at a precise moment in the political histories of feminism and film. *Visual and Other Pleasures* (Bloomington, IN, 1989), pp. 159–76.
4. Patricia Mellencamp describes the strategies of 'heterogeneity' in recent feminist film and video: '(1) the emphasis on enunciation and address to women *as subjects* ... (2) the telling of "stories" rather than "novels" ... (3) the inextricable bricolage of personal and theoretical knowledge; (4) the performance of parody or the telling of jokes ... (4) an implicit or explicit critique and refashioning of theories of subjectivity constructed by vision; and (6) a transgression of boundaries between private and public spaces and experiences', *Indiscretions* (Bloomington, IN, 1990), pp. 130–1. *Soft Fiction* employs virtually all of these strategies.
5. This was how Strand described *Soft Fiction* in a public lecture before its screening. Ann Arbor, MI, November 1979.
6. Karl Heider, *Ethnographic Film* (Austin, TX, 1976) states: 'A basic principle of ethnography is holism. ... From this principle come the related dicta of "whole bodies", "whole people", and "whole acts"' (p. 7).
7. Strand, 'Notes on Ethnographic Film by a Film Artist', *Wide Angle* (1978), 45–50. This is precisely the same point Trinh T. Minh-ha has made about her

controversial 'documentary' about Senegal, *Reassemblage* (1982). 'I knew very well what I did not want', she says of making the film, 'but what I wanted came with the process. ... My approach is one which avoids any sureness of signification ... the strategies of *Reassemblage* question the anthropological knowledge of the "other".' Constance Penley and Andrew Ross, 'Interview with Trinh T. Minh-ha', *Camera Obscura* (Spring–Summer, 1985), 89, 93.

8. *Canyon Cinema Catalogue*, 6, 221–3.
9. Judith Butler, *Gender Trouble: Feminism and the Subversion of Identity* (New York, 1989), p. 140.
10. This goes back to Robert Flaherty's re-enactments of the whale kill in *Nanook of the North* (1925).
11. Marsha Kinder, '*Soft Fiction*', *Film Quarterly*, 33 (Spring 1980), 50.
12. Thanks to Jane Gallop for this pun which she made in response to the panel, 'En/Countering Censorship: Feminist Transgressions', at the 1990 ASA Convention in New Orleans at which I presented a version of this paper.
13. 'Chick Strand at the Cinematheque', *Cinemanews*, 3/4/5 (1980), 11.
14. Anne Koedt, 'The Myth of the Vaginal Orgasm', *Notes from the Second Year* (New York, 1970). See Linda Williams, *Hard Core: Pleasure, Power and the 'Frenzy of the Visible'* (Berkeley, CA, 1989) for a full analysis of the genre of feature-length porn films.
15. See Ann Snitow, 'Mass Market Romance: Pornography for Women Is Different' in *Powers of Desire*, ed. Snitow, Stansell, and Thompson (New York, 1983), pp. 245–63.
16. See Snitow, 'Mass Market Romance'; Tania Modleski, *Loving with a Vengeance* (New York, 1986), and Janice Radway, *Reading the Romance* (Chapel Hill, NC, 1987).
17. 'Chick Strand at the Cinematheque', *Cinemanews*, 11.
18. Ibid., 1.
19. Ibid., 14.
20. Adena Rosmarin, *The Power of Genre* (Minneapolis, 1987).
21. However, in the question-and-answer session after screening *Soft Fiction*, Strand outed the woman in the kitchen, saying, 'She's fine, she's a lesbian now'. Public lecture Ann Arbor, MI, November 1979.
22. See Kaja Silverman on the 'sophisticated' feminist films of the avant-garde. *Soft Fiction* is not among them. *The Acoustic Mirror* (Bloomington, IN, 1988), p. 153.

9. JUDITH HALBERSTAM, 'SKINFLICK: POSTHUMAN GENDER IN JONATHAN DEMME'S *THE SILENCE OF THE LAMBS*'
(From *Camera Obscura*, 27 (1991), 37–52.)

Summary

Can there be a gender beyond the human? The subplot of Jonathan Demme's film, *The Silence of the Lambs*, concerns the attempt to track down a serial killer – Buffalo Bill – who skins his (female) victims in order to construct a 'woman suit'. Bill longs to exist beyond the limits of humanism, in that he wants a body that is beyond identity, gender, and the known. He desires, in other words, a posthuman gender. The author resists a feminist reading of the film which would simply condemn a violently aestheticised misogyny; she similarly refuses to dismiss *The Silence of the Lambs* as homophobic. Bill, she suggests, does not believe himself to be in the wrong body, but the wrong *skin*. The film, accordingly, stages posthumanism in the realm of gender, for it separates sex from gender/nature, shifting attention to the surface of the body. Bill is neither transsexual (for he is not seeking to change his genitals) nor homosexual (object choice is not an issue). He is posthuman because *skin* is what is at stake. Identity is no longer innate or internal; it is, rather, a surface effect, something stitched together, a costume acquired.

Notes

1. Hannah Arendt, *Eichmann in Jerusalem* (New York, 1963), p. 276.
2. See Laura Mulvey, 'Visual Pleasure and Narrative Cinema', *Screen*, 16.3 (Autumn 1975), 14.
3. Franco Moretti, *Signs Taken for Wonders: Essays in the Sociology of Literary Forms*, trans. Susan Fischer, David Forgacs and David Miller (London, 1983), pp. 84–5.
4. Sigmund Freud, 'The Uncanny' (1919) in *On Creativity and the Unconscious*, intro. Benjamin Nelson (New York and London, 1958), p. 151.
5. In the novel *The Silence of the Lambs* by Thomas Harris (New York, 1988), Buffalo Bill works for a leather company called Mr Hide.
6. Michel Foucault, *The History of Sexuality I: An Introduction*, trans. Robert Hurley (New York, 1980), p. 129.
7. As an interesting note on the theme of blindness as a fear blocker, in another film made from a Thomas Harris novel, *Manhunter* (1988), the female would-be victim is also blind and her blindness also aids her in her escape from a murderer. In this film, the murderer's predilection is to take posed photographs of his victims after he has killed them. He works in a dark room developing film, furthermore, and this is where he meets the blind woman. Obviously, Harris is making connections between vision and the production of horror – what you cannot see will not hurt you seems to be the message, and the dark is always to the woman's advantage. This may be read as a kind of postmodern rewriting of the feminist slogan 'take back the night'.

10. DONNA J. HARAWAY, 'A CYBORG MANIFESTO: SCIENCE, TECHNOLOGY, AND SOCIALIST-FEMINISM IN THE LATE TWENTIETH CENTURY'

(Extract from chapter in *Simians, Cyborgs, and Women: The Reinvention of Nature* (London, 1991) pp.149–81. The 'Cyborg Manifesto' was originally published under a slightly different title in 1985.)

Summary

The inability to divorce everyday life from technology renders the classical humanist framework (in which the human and the inhuman, the natural and the unnatural, are held in binary opposition) obsolete. Rather than continuing to see ourselves as humans, it makes better sense to claim that we are cyborgs (cybernetic organisms, a mixture of the organic and the inorganic). This does not mark the end of political agency; on the contrary, socialist-feminism has much to gain from abandoning the familiar appeal to a natural state of unity. While the cyborg has its roots in patriarchy and humanism (the figure was developed during the 1960s as a means to conquer outer space), there is always the possibility that it could be rearticulated to a radical political agenda which would celebrate multiplicity, unnatural connections, and permanent contradiction. Cyborg politics, from this latter perspective, is about living with difference in a space free from humanism, where gender and essence are things of the past.

Notes

1. Research was funded by an Academic Senate Faculty Research Grant from the University of California, Santa Cruz. An earlier version of the paper on genetic engineering appeared as 'Lieber Kyborg als Göttin: für eine sozialistisch-feministische Unterwanderung der Gentechnologie', in Bernd-Peter Lange and Anna Marie Stuby (eds) (Berlin, 1984), pp. 66–84. The cyborg manifesto grew from my 'New machines, new bodies, new communities: political dilemmas of a cyborg feminist', 'The Scholar and the Feminist X: The Question of Technology', Conference, Barnard College, April 1983.

    The people associated with the History of Consciousness Board of UCSC have had an enormous influence on this paper, so that it feels collectively authored more than most, although those I cite may not recognise their ideas. In particular, members of graduate and undergraduate feminist theory, science, and politics, and theory and methods courses contributed to the cyborg manifesto. Particular debts here are due Hilary Klein (1989), Paul Edwards (1985), Lisa Lowe (1986), and James Clifford (1985).

    Parts of the paper were my contribution to a collectively developed session, 'Poetic Tools and Political Bodies: Feminist Approaches to High Technology Culture', 1984 California American Studies Association, with History of Consciousness graduate students Zoe Sofoulis, 'Jupiter space'; Katie King, 'The pleasures of repetition and the limits of identification in feminist science fiction: reimaginations of the body after the cyborg'; and Chela Sandoval, 'The construction of subjectivity and oppositional consciousness in feminist film and video'. Sandoval's (n. d.) theory of oppositional consciousness was published as 'Women respond to racism: A Report on the National Women's Studies Association Conference'. For Sofoulis's semiotic-psychoanalytic readings of nuclear culture, see Sofia (1984). King's unpublished papers ('Questioning tradition: canon formation and the veiling of power'; 'Gender and genre: reading the science fiction of Joanna Russ'; 'Varley's *Titan* and *Wizard*: feminist parodies of nature, culture, and hardware') deeply informed the cyborg manifesto.

    Barbara Epstein, Jeff Escoffier, Rusten Hogness, and Jaye Miller gave extensive discussion and editorial help. Members of the Silicon Valley Research Project of UCSC and participants in SVRP conferences and workshops were very important, especially Rick Gordon, Linda Kimball, Nancy Snyder, Langdon Winner, Judith Stacey, Linda Lim, Patricia Fernandez-Kelly, and Judith Gregory. Finally, I want to thank Nancy Hartsock for years of friendship and discussion on feminist theory and feminist science fiction. I also thank Elizabeth Bird for my favourite political button: 'Cyborgs for Earthly Survival'.

2. Useful references to left and/or feminist radical science movements and theory and to biological/biotechnical issues include: Bleier (1984, 1986), Harding (1986), Fausto-Sterling (1985), Gould (1981), Hubbard *et al.* (1982),

Keller (1985), Lewontin *et al.* (1984), *Radical Science Journal* (became *Science as Culture* in 1987), 26 Freegrove Road, London N7 9RQ; *Science for the People*, 897 Main St, Cambridge, MA 02139.

3. Starting points for left and/or feminist approaches to technology and politics include: Cowan (1983), Rothschild (1983), Traweek (1988), Young and Levidow (1981, 1985), Weizenbaum (1976), Winner (1977, 1986), Zimmerman (1983), Athanasiou (1987), Cohn (1987a, 1987b), Winograd and Flores (1986), Edwards (1985), *Global Electronics Newsletter*, 867 West Dana St, 204, Mountain View, CA 94041; *Processed World*, 55 Sutter St, San Francisco, CA 94104; ISIS, Women's International Information and Communication Service, PO Box 50 (Cornavin), 1211 Geneva 2, Switzerland, and Via Santa Maria Dell'Anima 30, 00186 Rome, Italy. Fundamental approaches to modern social studies of science that do not continue the liberal mystification that it all started with Thomas Kuhn, include: Knorr-Cetina (1981), Knorr-Cetina and Mulkay (1983), Latour and Woolgar (1979), Young (1979). The 1984 Directory of the Network for the Ethnographic Study of Science, Technology, and Organisations lists a wide range of people and projects crucial to better radical analysis; available from NESSTO, PO Box 11442, Stanford, CA 94305.

4. A provocative, comprehensive argument about the politics and theories of 'postmodernism' is made by Fredric Jameson (1984), who argues that postmodernism is not an option, a style among others, but a cultural dominant requiring radical reinvention of left politics from within; there is no longer any place from without that gives meaning to the comforting fiction of critical distance. Jameson also makes clear why one cannot be for or against postmodernism, an essentially moralist move. My position is that feminists (and others) need continuous cultural reinvention, postmodernist critique, and historical materialism; only a cyborg would have a chance. The old dominations of white capitalist patriarchy seem nostalgically innocent now: they normalised heterogeneity, into man and woman, white and black, for example. 'Advanced capitalism' and postmodernism release heterogeneity without a norm, and we are flattened, without subjectivity, which requires depth, even unfriendly and drowning depths. It is time to write *The Death of the Clinic*. The clinic's methods required bodies and works; we have texts and surfaces. Our dominations don't work by medicalisation and normalisation any more; they work by networking, communications redesign, stress management. Normalisation gives way to automation, utter redundancy. Michel Foucault's *Birth of the Clinic* (1963), *History of Sexuality* (1976), and *Discipline and Punish* (1975) name a form of power at its moment of implosion. The discourse of biopolitics gives way to technobabble, the language of the spliced substantive; no noun is left whole by the multinationals. These are their names, listed from one issue of *Science*: Tech-Knowledge, Genentech, Allergen, Hybritech, Compupro, Genen-cor, Syntex, Allelix, Agrigenetics Corp., Syntro, Codon, Repligen, MicroAngelo from Scion Corp., Percom Data, Inter Systems, Cyborg Corp., Statcom Corp., Intertec. If we are imprisoned by language, then escape from that prison-house requires language poets, a kind of cultural restriction enzyme to cut the code; cyborg heteroglossia is one form of radical cultural politics. For cyborg poetry, see Perloff (1984); Fraser (1984). For feminist modernist/postmodernist 'cyborg' writing, see HOW(ever), 871 Corbett Ave, San Francisco, CA 94131.

5. The US equivalent of Mills & Boon.

6. Baudrillard (1983). Jameson (1984, p. 66) points out that Plato's definition of the simulacrum is the copy for which there is no original, i.e., the world of advanced capitalism, of pure exchange. See *Discourse*, 9 (Spring/Summer

1987) for a special issue on technology (cybernetics, ecology, and the post-modern imagination).

7. A practice at once both spiritual and political that linked guards and arrested anti-nuclear demonstrators in the Alameda County jail in California in the early 1980s.

8. Powerful developments of coalition politics emerge from 'Third World' speakers, speaking from nowhere, the displaced centre of the universe, earth: 'We live on the third planet from the sun' – *Sun Poem* by Jamaican writer, Edward Kamau Braithwaite, review by Mackey (1984). Contributors to Smith (1983) ironically subvert naturalised identities precisely while constructing a place from which to speak called home. See especially Reagon (in Smith, 1983, pp. 356–68). Trinh T. Minh-ha (1986–87).

9. hooks, (1981, 1984); Hull *et al.* (1982). Bambara (1981) wrote an extraordinary novel in which the women of colour theatre group, The Seven Sisters, explore a form of unity. See analysis by Butler-Evans (1987).

10. On orientalism in feminist works and elsewhere, see Lowe (1986); Said (1978); Mohanty (1984); *Many Voices, One Chant: Black Feminist Perspectives* (1984).

11. This chart was published in 1985. My previous efforts to understand biology as a cybernetic command-control discourse and organisms as 'natural-technical objects of knowledge' were Haraway (1979, 1983, 1984). The differences indicate shifts in argument.

12. Service Employees International Union's office workers' organisation in the US.

13. The convention of ideologically taming militarised high technology by publicising its applications to speech and motion problems of the disabled/differently abled takes on a special irony in monotheistic, patriarchal, and frequently anti-semitic culture when computer-generated speech allows a boy with no voice to chant the Haftorah at his bar mitzvah. See Sussman (1986). Making the always context-relative social definitions of 'ableness' particularly clear, military high-tech has a way of making human beings disabled by definition, a perverse aspect of much automated battlefield and Star Wars R&D. See Welford (1 July 1986).

Bibliography

Athanasiou, Tom (1987) 'High-tech politics: the case of artificial intelligence', *Socialist Review*, 92, 7–35.

Bambara, Toni Cade (1981) *The Salt Eaters* (New York).

Baudrillard, Jean (1983) *Simulations*, trans. P. Foss, P. Patton, P. Beitchman (New York).

Bleier, Ruth (1984) *Science and Gender: A Critique of Biology and Its Themes on Women* (New York)

—— (ed.) (1986) *Feminist Approaches to Science* (New York).

Butler-Evans, Elliott (1987) 'Race, gender and desire: narrative strategies and the production of ideology in the fiction of Toni Cade Bambara, Toni Morrison and Alice Walker', University of California at Santa Cruz, PhD thesis.

Clifford, James (1985) 'On ethnographic allegory', in James Clifford and George Marcus (eds), *Writing Culture: The Poetics and Politics of Ethnography* (Berkeley, CA).

Cohn, Carol (1987a) 'Nuclear language and how we learned to pat the bomb', *Bulletin of Atomic Scientists*, 17–24.

—— (1987b) 'Sex and death in the rational world of defense intellectuals', *Signs*, 12(4), 687–718.

Cowan, Ruth Schwartz (1983) *More Work for Mother: The Ironies of Household Technology from the Open Hearth to the Microwave* (New York).

de Waal, Frans (1982) *Chimpanzee Politics: Power and Sex among the Apes* (New York).

Edwards, Paul (1985) 'Border wars: the science and politics of artificial intelligence', *Radical America*, 19(6), 39–52.

Fausto-Sterling, Anne (1985) *Myths of Gender: Biological Theories about Women and Men* (New York).

Foucault, Michel (1963) *The Birth of the Clinic: An Archaeology of Medical Perception*, trans. A. M. Smith (New York, 1975).

—— (1975) *Discipline and Punish: The Birth of the Prison*, trans. Alan Sheridan (New York, 1979).

—— (1976) *The History of Sexuality*, Vol. 1: *An Introduction*, trans. Robert Hurley (New York, 1978).

Fraser, Kathleen (1984) *Something. Even Human Voices. In the Foreground, a Lake* (Berkeley, CA).

Gould, Stephen, J. (1981) *Mismeasure of Man* (New York).

Haraway, Donna J. (1979) 'The biological enterprise: sex, mind, and profit from human engineering to sociobiology', *Radical History Review*, 20, 206–37.

—— (1983) 'Signs of dominance: from a physiology to a cybernetics of primate society', *Studies in History of Biology*, 6, 129–219.

—— (1984) 'Class, race, sex, scientific objects of knowledge: a socialist-feminist perspective on the social construction of productive knowledge and some political consequences', in Violet Haas and Carolyn Perucci (1984) *Women in Scientific and Engineering Professions* (Ann Arbor, MI), pp. 212–29.

Harding, Sandra (1986) *The Science Question in Feminism* (Ithaca, NY).

Hogness, E. Rusten (1983) 'Why stress? A look at the making of stress, 1936–56', unpublished paper available from the author, 4437 Mill Creek Rd, Healdsburg, CA 95448.

hooks, bell (1981) *Ain't I a Woman* (Boston).

—— (1984) *Feminist Theory: From Margin to Center* (Boston).

Hubbard, Ruth, Henifin, Mary Sue, and Fried, Barbara (eds) (1979) *Women Look at Biology Looking at Women: A Collection of Feminist Critiques* (Cambridge, MA).

—— (eds) (1982) *Biological Woman, the Convenient Myth* (Cambridge, MA).

Hull, Gloria, Scott, Patricia Bell, and Smith, Barbara (eds) (1982) *All the Women Are White, All the Men Are Black, But Some of Us Are Brave* (Old Westbury).

Jameson, Fredric (1984) 'Post-modernism, or the cultural logic of late capitalism', *New Left Review*, 146, 53–92.

Keller, Evelyn Fox (1985) *Reflections on Gender and Science* (New Haven, CT).

Klein, Hilary (1989) 'Marxism, psychoanalysis, and mother nature', *Feminist Studies*, 15(2), 255–78.

Knorr-Cetina, Karin (1981) *The Manufacture of Knowledge* (Oxford).

—— and Mulkay, Michael (eds) (1983) *Science Observed: Perspectives on the Social Study of Science* (Beverly Hills, CA).

Lange, Bernd-Peter and Stuby, Anna Marie (eds) (1984) *1984* (Berlin).

Latour, Bruno and Woolgar, Steve (1979) *Laboratory Life: The Social Construction of Scientific Facts* (Beverly Hills, CA).

Lewontin, R. C., Rose, Steven, and Kamin, Leon J. (1984) *Not in Our Genes: Biology, Ideology, and Human Nature* (New York).

Lowe, Lisa (1986) 'French literary Orientalism: The representation of "others" in the texts of Montesquieu, Flaubert and Kristeva', University of California at Santa Cruz, PhD thesis.

Mackey, Nathaniel (1984) 'Review', *Sulfur*, 2, 200–5.

Many Voices, One Chant: Black Feminist Perspectives (1984) *Feminist Review*, 17, special issue.

Mohanty, Chandra Talpade (1984) 'Under western eyes: feminist scholarship and colonial discourse', *Boundary 2*, 3 (12/13), 333–58.

Ong, Aihwa (1987) *Spirits of Resistance and Capitalist Discipline: Factory Workers in Malaysia* (Albany, NY).

—— (1988) 'Colonialism and modernity: feminist representations of women in non-western societies', *Inscriptions*, 3/4, 79–93.

Perloff, Marjorie (1984) 'Dirty language and scramble systems', *Sulfur*, 11, 178–83.

Reagon, Bernice Johnson (1983) 'Coalition politics: turning the century', in Smith (1983) pp. 356–68.

Rothschild, Joan (ed.) (1983) *Machina ex Dea: Feminist Perspectives on Technology* (New York).

Said, Edward (1978) *Orientalism* (New York).

Sandoval, Chela (1984) 'Dis-illusionment and the poetry of the future: the making of oppositional consciousness', University of California at Santa Cruz, PhD qualifying essay.

—— (n. d.) *Yours in Struggle: Women Respond to Racism, a Report on the National Women's Studies Association* (Oakland, CA).

Smith, Barbara (ed.) (1983) *Home Girls: A Black Feminist Anthology* (New York).

Sofia, Zoe (also Zoe Sofoulis) (1984) 'Exterminating fetuses: abortion, disarmament, and the sexo-semiotics of extra-terrestrialism', *Diacritics*, 14(2), 47–59.

Sofoulis, Zoe (1984) 'Jupiter Space', paper delivered at the American Studies Association, Pomona, CA.

—— (1987) 'Lacklein', University of California at Santa Cruz, unpublished essay.

—— (1988) 'Through the lumen: Frankenstein and the optics of re-origination', University of California at Santa Cruz, PhD thesis.

Sussman, Vic (1986) 'Personal tech. Technology lends a hand', *The Washington Post Magazine*, 9 November, pp. 45–56.

Traweek, Sharon (1988) *Beamtimes and Lifetimes: The World of High Energy Physics* (Cambridge, MA).

Trinh T. Minh-ha (1986–7) 'Introduction', and 'Difference: "a special third world women issue"', *Discourse: Journal for Theoretical Studies in Media and Culture*, 8, 3–38.

Weizenbaum, Joseph (1976) *Computer Power and Human Reason* (San Francisco, CA).

Welford, John Noble (1 July 1986) 'Pilot's helmet helps interpret high speed world', *New York Times*, pp. 21, 24.

Winner, Langdon (1977) *Autonomous Technology: Technics out of Control as a Theme in Political Thought* (Cambridge, MA).

—— (1980) 'Do artifacts have politics?' *Daedalus*, 109(1), 121–36.

—— (1986) *The Whale and the Reactor* (Chicago).

Winograd, Terry and Flores, Fernando (1986) *Understanding Computers and Cognition: A New Foundation for Design* (Norwood, NJ).

Young, Robert M. (1979, March) 'Interpreting the production of science', *New Scientist*, 29, 1026–8.

Young, Robert M. and Levidow, Les (eds) (1981, 1985) *Science, Technology and the Labour Process*, 2 vols (London).

Zimmerman, Jan (ed.) (1983) *The Technological Woman: Interfacing with Tomorrow* (New York).

11. NEIL BADMINGTON, 'POSTHUMANIST (COM)PROMISES: DIFFRACTING DONNA HARAWAY'S CYBORG THROUGH MARGE PIERCY'S *BODY OF GLASS*'

(A longer version of this essay formed part of my PhD thesis, *A Crisis of Versus: Postmodernity and Fictions of the Inhuman*, Cardiff University, 1998.)

Summary

This essay looks at the way in which Marge Piercy's *Body of Glass* both entertains and interrogates Donna Haraway's posthumanist cyborg. While much of the novel's narrative revolves round a cyborg, the societies depicted preserve a strict hierarchy between the human and the inhuman. The exit from humanism proposed in the 'Cyborg Manifesto' has not occurred (in fact, this essay turns to the work of Jacques Derrida in order to call the very notion of a radical break into question). In complete opposition to Haraway's vision, Piercy's characters continue to think of themselves and their machines according to a distinctly humanist logic. And yet the essay argues that the apparent return to humanism is a critical one, for it actually reveals how humanism is forever calling itself into question. Because 'we' cannot simply step outside humanism once and for all, it does not necessarily follow that 'we' are simply confined to tradition. 'We' can (and must) show how humanism is always and everywhere failing, rewriting itself as posthumanism.

Notes

1. Allucquere Rosanne Stone, 'Will the Real Body Please Stand Up?: Boundary Stories about Virtual Cultures', *Cyberspace: First Steps*, ed. Michael Benedikt (Cambridge, MA, and London, 1991), p. 108.
2. Hugh Gusterson, 'Short Circuit: Watching Television with a Nuclear-Weapons Scientist', *The Cyborg Handbook*, ed. Chris Hables Gray, Heidi J. Figueroa-Sarriera and Steven Mentor (New York and London, 1995), p. 109.
3. Donna J. Haraway, 'A Cyborg Manifesto: Science, Technology, and Socialist-Feminism in the Late Twentieth Century', in this volume, essay 10.
4. Marge Piercy, *Body of Glass* (Harmondsworth, 1992). The original American edition of the novel was published in 1991 under the title *He, She and It*. The only differences between the two versions appear to be: (1) The opening chapters carry slightly different titles; (2) Certain signifiers are modified in *Body of Glass* in accordance with the conventions of British-English; (3) A passage in chapter 20 describing the experiences of Shira and Yod in cyberspace is rendered, in the American edition, as two parallel columns of text, whereas the British edition utilises two ordinary paragraphs, printed in a slightly smaller typeface. I thank Emma Mason for providing me with a copy of *He, She and It*.
5. Piercy, *Body of Glass*, p. 584. For more on the circuit that connects the two texts, see John R. R. Christie, 'A Tragedy for Cyborgs', *Configurations*, 1.1 (1992), 171–96.
6. Haraway, 'A Cyborg Manifesto', p. 77 this volume. Emphasis added.
7. Ibid., p. 78.
8. Ibid.

9. Ibid., p. 84.
10. For an abridged translation, see *Madness and Civilization: A History of Insanity in the Age of Reason*, trans. Richard Howard (London, 1971).
11. Jacques Derrida, 'Cogito and the History of Madness', *Writing and Difference*, trans. Alan Bass (1967) (London, 1978), p. 33. Derrida has returned to Foucault's book in the more recent '"To Do Justice to Freud": The History of Madness in the Age of Psychoanalysis', *Resistances of Psychoanalysis*, trans. Peggy Kamuf, Pascale-Anne Brault and Michael Naas (1996) (Stanford, CA, 1998), pp.70–118.
12. Derrida, 'Cogito and the History of Madness', p. 34.
13. Ibid., p. 36.
14. Jacques Derrida, 'Violence and Metaphysics: An Essay on the Thought of Emmanuel Levinas', *Writing and Difference*, trans. Alan Bass (1967) (London, 1978), p. 111.
15. Jacques Derrida, *Of Grammatology*, trans. Gayatri Chakravorty Spivak (1967) (Baltimore and London, 1976), p. 24. Emphasis in original.
16. Derrida, 'Cogito and the History of Madness', p. 32.
17. Jacques Derrida, *Of Spirit: Heidegger and the Question*, trans. Geoffrey Bennington and Rachel Bowlby (1987) (Chicago and London, 1989) p. 31.
18. Bill Readings, 'Pagans, Perverts or Primitives? Experimental Justice in the Empire of Capital', in this volume, essay 13. I take the notion of quotation marks functioning as pincers from Jacques Derrida, 'Du Tout', *The Post Card: From Socrates to Freud and Beyond*, trans. Alan Bass (1980) (Chicago and London, 1987), p. 517.
19. Haraway, 'A Cyborg Manifesto', p. 70 this volume. Emphasis added.
20. Jacques Derrida, 'The Ends of Man', *Margins of Philosophy*, trans. Alan Bass (1972) (Hemel Hempstead, 1982), p. 121. It would be unfair at this point to fail to mention an interview in which Haraway reconsiders her use of the term 'we'. See 'Cyborgs at Large: Interview with Donna Haraway', *Technoculture*, ed. Constance Penley and Andrew Ross (Minneapolis and Oxford, 1991), pp.12–13.
21. Haraway, 'A Cyborg Manifesto', pp. 81, 77 this volume.
22. Although the novel consists of two historically distinct narratives – one concerned with the struggle over a cyborg in the twenty-first century; the other with Rabbi Loew's golem – I will only engage with the former. This is not to imply that the second tale is unimportant, or that the two strands of the text can be easily separated; I merely wish to concentrate upon the cyborg.
23. Donna J. Haraway, 'The Promises of Monsters: A Regenerative Politics for Inappropriate/d Others', *Cultural Studies*, ed. Lawrence Grossberg, Cary Nelson and Paula A. Treichler (New York and London, 1992), p. 300.
24. I owe this translation to Alan Grossman, and thank him for his willingness to explain many of the novel's allusions to Jewish culture.
25. Kerstin W. Shands, *The Repair of the World: The Novels of Marge Piercy* (Westport and London, 1994), p. 147.
26. Piercy, *Body of Glass*, pp.48–9.
27. Ibid., pp.547–8.
28. Ibid., p. 10.
29. Ibid., p. 192.
30. Ibid. Ellipsis in original.
31. Haraway, 'Cyborgs at Large', p. 18.
32. Haraway, 'A Cyborg Manifesto', p. 71 this volume.
33. Piercy, *Body of Glass*, p. 437.

34. Ibid., p. 524.
35. Donna Haraway, 'The Actors are Cyborg, Nature is Coyote, and the Geography is Elsewhere: Postscript to "Cyborgs at Large"', *Technoculture*, ed. Constance Penley and Andrew Ross (Minneapolis and Oxford, 1991), p. 21.
36. I have summarised the Laws from Isaac Asimov, 'Runaround' (1942), *The Complete Robot* (London, 1982), pp.269–70.
37. Piercy, *Body of Glass*, p. 282.
38. Ibid., p. 233.
39. Peter Fitting, 'Beyond the Wasteland: A Feminist in Cyberspace', *Utopian Studies*, 5.2 (1994), 5.
40. See Brian Stableford, 'Cyborgs', *The Encyclopedia of Science Fiction*, ed. John Clute and Peter Nicholls (London, 1993), pp.290–1.
41. See Manfred E. Clynes and Nathan S. Kline, 'Cyborgs and Space', *Astronautics* (September 1960), 26–7, 74–6. This article was responsible for coining the term 'cyborg'.
42. More strangely, perhaps, Fitting's model would not permit the character played by Arnold Schwarzenegger in *The Terminator* and *Terminator 2: Judgment Day* to be called a cyborg, precisely because the figure in question was never human.
43. See Isaac Asimov, 'The Bicentennial Man' (1976), *The Complete Robot* (London, 1982), pp.635–82.
44. Piercy, *Body of Glass*, p. 558.
45. For instance: their physical movements are deemed similar (p.257); both are bewildered by the Glop (p.339), the 'spiral dance' (an allusion to the final sentence of Haraway's manifesto) (p.330), and the concept of sexual attraction (Yod actually attempts to explain heterosexuality to Nili on one occasion) (pp.345, 376); both are intended to serve and protect Tikva; and, finally, Nili's trick of clicking her fingers is mimicked by Yod (p.546).
46. François Truffaut, *Hitchcock*, rev. edn, trans. Helen Scott (London, 1978), pp.157–8.
47. Piercy, *Body of Glass*, p. 258.
48. Ibid., p. 259.
49. Ibid.
50. See June Deery, 'Ectopic and Utopic Reproduction: *He, She and It*', *Utopian Studies*, 5.2 (1994), 39–40.
51. See Piercy, *Body of Glass*, pp.126, 489, for instance.
52. Ibid., p. 257.
53. Ibid., pp.421, 412 (emphasis added), 308.
54. Ibid., p. 485.
55. Juliet Mitchell, *Woman's Estate* (Harmondsworth, 1971), p. 156.
56. Carol Mason, 'Terminating Bodies: Toward a Cyborg History of Abortion', *Posthuman Bodies*, ed. Judith Halberstam and Ira Livingston (Bloomington and Indianapolis, 1995), pp.240–1, n.3.
57. Piercy, *Body of Glass*, p. 103.
58. Ibid., p. 435.
59. Jean-François Lyotard, 'Introduction: About the Human', *The Inhuman: Reflections on Time*, trans. Geoffrey Bennington and Rachel Bowlby (1988) (Cambridge, 1991), p. 3. Ellipsis in original.
60. Piercy, *Body of Glass*, p. 127.
61. Ibid., p. 324. Emphasis added.
62. Wallace Stevens, 'Asides on the Oboe', *Selected Poems* (London, 1965), p. 72.
63. Piercy, *Body of Glass*, pp.345–6. Emphasis added.

64. Ibid., p. 478.
65. Jean-François Lyotard, *The Differend: Phrases in Dispute*, trans. George Van Den Abbeele (1983) (Manchester, 1988), p. xi.
66. Piercy, *Body of Glass*, p. 488. Emphasis added.
67. See Karl Marx and Friedrich Engels, *Manifesto of the Communist Party*, trans. Samuel Moore (1848) (Harmondsworth, 1967), p. 83. As Catherine Belsey has pointed out to me, the image in question is an allusion to *The Tempest*, ed. Frank Kermode (London, 1954), IV.i.148–50.
68. Maurice Blanchot, 'Man at Point Zero', *Friendship*, trans. Elizabeth Rottenberg (1971) (Stanford, CA, 1997), pp.74–5.
69. Jacques Derrida, 'De l'hospitalité', *Sur parole: instantanés philosophiques* (Paris, 1999), p. 64. My translation.

12. SCOTT BUKATMAN, 'POSTCARDS FROM THE POSTHUMAN SOLAR SYSTEM'
(From *Science-Fiction Studies*, 18.3 (1991), 343–57.)

Summary

Contemporary science fiction has been responsible for articulating new ways of thinking about what it means to be human, if such a term is still meaningful, in a technological society. Visions of subjectivity and embodiment which depart from the principles of humanism proliferate as the genre stages how the humanist subject is pushed into the space of posthumanism. In the fictions of Bernard Wolfe, J. G. Ballard, and (above all) Bruce Sterling, as well as in the theories of Gilles Deleuze and Félix Guattari, there is a marked emphasis on the way in which the category of the human has been replaced by the cyborg. All of these writers despatch postcards from the posthuman solar system.

Notes

1. As Shirley notes, this is strikingly similar to 'ideas explored by Bruce Sterling in *Schismatrix* and Samuel R. Delany in *Nova*' (59).
2. 'Warm Leatherette', an early electronic dance record produced by The Normal in the late 1970s, adapted Ballard's imagery:

    A tear of petrol is in your eye/
    The handbrake penetrates your thigh/
    Quick/Let's make love/Before you die/
    On warm/Leatherette.

    The song was later recorded by androgynous disco queen, Grace Jones.

3. Wolfe, a fascinating figure, was at one time a bodyguard of Trotsky's in Mexico. J. G. Ballard, incidentally, has called *Limbo* the finest American SF novel.
4. The rationalist drive of the superpower's supercomputers to merge into one global unit had, in fact, precipitated the global conflict, as desperate humans pitted the machines against each other.
5. 'Drives' and 'crashes' are both familiar to computer users.
6. Page references for these stories are to Sterling's *Crystal Express*.

7. Insect metaphors also pervade the writings of William Burroughs, especially in *The Soft Machine* (1966), in which insects obviously represent an evil empire of slavish devotion – a hive mentality of entirely programmed functions. Insects also clearly connote decay and putrescence, emphasising the organic limitations of bodily flesh. At the same time, insects are frequently linked with technology in these texts. The linking of insect with machine is not Burroughs's innovation, nor is it restricted to his work. One recalls the intercutting of grasshopper and scythe in Serge Eisenstein's film *Old and New* (1928) – an evocative rhyme that suggests, first, an equivalence, and then finally man's superior control over the forces of nature. And in Cronenberg's *The Fly*, Brundle's transformation to Brundle-fly is only a preparation for the final biotechnological horror as Brundle merges with the blue metal transporter itself.
8. It is also worth remembering the backlash which quickly characterised the genre's response to cyberpunk. Writers and fans were quick to reject what was perceived as a 'trendy' and anti-humanist discourse (that SF perhaps *ought* to be trendy, and that its trendiness might be significant, were not widely debated).
9. See my 'Who Programs You? The Science Fiction of the Spectacle' in Kuhn, *Alien Zone*, for more about *Videodrome* and representation.
10. The artwork, by Mark Buckingham, is a sophisticated pastiche of Warhol's serial lithography, and there is a full cognisance of these techniques being returned to the 'low culture' form that originally inspired them. *Miracleman*, once an older (and somewhat forgettable) British comic-book series, had been revived in the 1980s by writer Alan Moore. It became a vehicle for exploring the nature of the superhero power-fantasy before becoming a broader exploration of the ramifications of utopia.

Bibliography

Ballard, J. G., *Crash.*, 1973 (New York, 1985).

Bataille, Georges, 'Sacrifices', *Visions of Excess: Selected Writings, 1927–1939*, trans. Allan Stoerl (Minneapolis, 1985), pp. 130–6.

Burroughs, William, *Naked Lunch* (New York, 1959).

Csicsery-Ronay, Jr, Istvan, 'The Science Fiction of Theory: Baudrillard and Haraway', Paper given at the Indiana University 1991 conference on Interdisciplinarity: Science, Literature, and the University.

Debord, Guy, 'Report on the Construction of Situations and on the International Situationist Tendency's Conditions of Organisation and Action', *Situationist International Anthology* (Berkeley, CA, 1977), pp. 17–25.

Deleuze, Gilles & Félix Guattari, *A Thousand Plateaus: Capitalism and Schizophrenia* (Minneapolis, 1987).

Foucault, Michel, *The Order of Things: An Archeology of the Human Sciences* (New York, 1987).

Gaiman, Neil & Mark Buckingham, 'Notes from the Underground', *Miracleman*, 19 (Nov. 1991) (London, 1991).

Gibson, William, *Neuromancer* (New York, 1984).

Haraway, Donna, 'A Manifesto for Cyborgs: Science, Technology and Socialist Feminism in the 1980s', *Socialist Review*, (1985), 65–107.

——, *Primate Visions: Gender, Race and Nature in the World of Modern Science* (New York, 1989).

Kroker, Arthur & Marilouise Kroker, 'Theses on the Disappearing Body in the Hyper-Modern Condition', *Body Invaders: Panic Sex in America* (New York, 1987).

Kuhn, Annette (ed.), *Alien Zone: Cultural Theory and Contemporary Science Fiction Cinema* (London and New York, 1990).

Maddox, Tom, 'The Wars of the Coin's Two Halves: Bruce Sterling's Shaper/Mechanist Narratives', *Mississippi Review*, 16 (1988), 237–44.

Merleau-Ponty, Maurice, *Phenomenology of Perception*, trans. Colin Smith (London, 1962).

Pfeil, Fred, 'These Disintegrations I'm Looking Forward To', *Another Tale to Tell: Politics and Narrative on Postmodern Culture* (London, 1990).

Shirley, John, 'Stelarc and the New Reality', *Science Fiction Eye*, 1.2 (Aug. 1990), 56–61.

Sterling, Bruce, *Schismatrix* (New York, 1985).

——, *Crystal Express* (Saux City, WI, 1989).

Wolfe, Bernard, *Limbo* (New York, 1987). Same pagination as in the undated Ace A-3 edition.

13. BILL READINGS, 'PAGANS, PERVERTS OR PRIMITIVES? EXPERIMENTAL JUSTICE IN THE EMPIRE OF CAPITAL'
(From Andrew Benjamin (ed.), *Judging Lyotard* (London and New York, 1992), pp.168–91.)

Summary

Who are 'we' to say 'we', to say that others are like 'us', to say that 'you' and 'I' make a 'we'? This essay takes Werner Herzog's *Where the Green Ants Dream* as a starting point for an investigation into the encounter between two radically different parties: the Australian Commonwealth and the indigenous Aboriginal population. Drawing on Jean-François Lyotard's account of the *différend*, Readings points out that the former commits an injustice when it believes that it can fairly settle a dispute with the Aborigines in an official court of law (which is founded upon a describable model of universal justice). What the Australian state overlooks is the *différend* between itself and the indigenous population which renders any appeal to a universal human nature an act of oppression. The state should not even presume that the Aborigines are 'human', because this would be to reduce the other to the familiarity and fraternity of the same. This signifies neither a drift into nihilism nor the restoration of imperialism. Readings calls for a radical rethinking of politics, ethics, and representation, in which *différends* are never silenced in the name of unity. 'We' can no longer say 'we' without repeating humanism's injustices.

Notes

1. Alex Callinicos, 'Reactionary postmodernism?', in Roy Boyne and Ali Rattansi (eds), *Postmodernism and Society* (New York, 1990), p. 114.
2. Ibid.
3. Habermas finds poststructuralism to be 'neoconservative' because it wavers between a decadent postmodernity or a primitivist 'return to some form of

premodernity' ('Modernity: an incomplete project', in *The Anti-Aesthetic*, ed. Hal Foster [Seattle, 1983], p. 8).

4. Jean-François Lyotard and Jean-Loup Thébaud, *Just Gaming*, trans. Wlad Godzich (Minneapolis, 1985), p. 55.
5. My usage of the term 'western' is cultural rather than geographical throughout – referring to the rule of European modernism.
6. The Eritreans are a good example of this problem for the Marxist critic. When opposing Haile Selassie, the Eritreans were freedom fighters, upholding the torch of liberty against capitalist monarchy. However, once the Marxist Mengistu regime was established in Ethiopia, the Eritreans became forces of ignorance and superstition, preserving oppressive tribal values against universal human freedom as incarnated in the communist government of Ethiopia. This volte-face is not simply the hypocrisy of *realpolitik*, it is the perfectly logical outcome of the privileging of a universal abstract model of justice. See also Kurdistan.
7. J. -F. Lyotard, *Le Postmoderne expliqué aux enfants* (Paris, 1986), pp. 53–5.
8. J. -F. Lyotard, *The Differend: Phrases in Dispute*, trans. G. van den Abbeele (Minneapolis, 1988), p. 5.
9. Kenelm Burridge, *Encountering Aborigines* (New York, 1973), pp. 6, 42.
10. Ibid., p. 84.
11. Ibid., p. 243.
12. Roland Barthes, *Empire of Signs*, trans. Richard Howard (New York, 1979). As Barthes puts it (p. 3):

> Hence Orient and Occident cannot be taken here as 'realities' to be compared and contrasted historically, philosophically, culturally, politically. I am not lovingly gazing toward an Oriental essence – to me the Orient is a matter of indifference, merely providing a reserve of features whose manipulation – whose invented interplay – allows me to 'entertain' the idea of an unheard of symbolic system, one altogether detached from our own. What can be addressed, in the consideration of the Orient, are not other symbols, another metaphysics, another wisdom (though the latter might appear thoroughly desirable); it is the possibility of a difference ...

I share Barthes's reserve as to epistemic authority, if not the infelicitous implication that the possibility of difference can be a 'matter of indifference'.
13. Ibid., p. 4.
14. See *Heidegger and 'the jews'*, trans. Andreas Michel and Mark Roberts, intro. David Carroll (Minneapolis, 1990). Carroll's introduction offers a helpful statement, as much of a generalisation as is possible this side of totalisation, of the kind of dispersal and heterogeneity that this lower-case plural word names:

> For Lyotard, justice demands that 'the people' be thought in terms of 'the jews', that is, in perpetual exodus, both from themselves and from the Law to which they attempt to respond but to which they can never adequately respond. The community of 'the jews' is without a project for its unification (either in terms of a mythical origin or end). 'The jews' are an 'unfashioned,' 'unworked' community, a community without a single foundation or identity, a profoundly heterogeneous linkage of the non-identical. (*Htj*, p. xxxiii)

Herzog's German origins, and his long interest in the question of empire (*Aguirre, Wrath of God, Fitzcarraldo*) are not coincidental to this analogy; however, we should remember Lyotard's caveat:

I use quotation marks to avoid confusing these 'jews' with real Jews. What is most real about real Jews is that Europe, in any case, does not know what to do with them: Christians demand their conversion; monarchs expel them; republics assimilate them; Nazis exterminate them. 'The jews' are the object of a dismissal with which Jews, in particular, are afflicted in reality. (*Htj*, p. 3)

15. I risk the pleonasm of 'radically untranslatable' in order to mark the extent to which this is not merely a horizontal difficulty incidental to the translation between languages but also a kind of vertical impossibility of translation analogous to that which governs the (non-)relation between consciousness and the Freudian Unconscious. On the vertical impossibility of translation, see J. Derrida, *Writing and Difference*, trans. Alan Bass (London, 1987), pp. 210–11.
16. I draw the term 'strange beauty' from the lexicon of particle physics.
17. Thus *Reading Capital* replaces the 'young Marx's' humanist contrast of the free producer within a unified community to the alienated subject of capitalism with a distinction between the subject hailed to illusory individuality by ideology and the proletariat as universal subject of history. L. Althusser and E. Balibar, *Reading Capital*, trans. Ben Brewster (London, 1970).
18. Lyotard, *The Differend*, p. 98.
19. Ibid., p. 145.
20. Ibid., p. 146.
21. *Star Trek: The Next Generation* proves that even Klingons can immigrate (become human), as long as space still provides a trackless waste within which mankind may wander and which it may dominate.
22. Lyotard, *The Differend*, p. 146.
23. Ibid., pp. 147–8.
24. Since the film script is currently unavailable and the videocassette version of the film in the United States does not list the *dramatis personae* on the credits, all my spellings of proper names are approximations.
25. A similar effect, whereby what looks like myth turns out to be at least as 'real' as narrative, occurs at the conclusion of Peter Weir's *The Last Wave* (1977).
26. J.-F. Lyotard, *The Postmodern Condition: A Report on Knowledge*, trans. G. Bennington and B. Massumi (Minneapolis, 1984), p. 82.
27. For a detailed discussion of postmodern experimentation, see chapter 2 of Bill Readings, *Introducing Lyotard: Art and Politics* (London, 1991).
28. It is worth noting the demand of paralogical experimentation in order to testify to the irrepresentable is a far cry from the more programmatic demands that Lyotard makes in 'Acinema', in *The Lyotard Reader*, ed. Andrew Benjamin (Oxford, 1989). There he lays down a set of rules, a model for the destruction of the representational model. As such, 'Acinema' remains a modernist critique of film rather than a postmodern experiment; indeed, in many respects *Where the Green Ants Dream* fails to conform to its requirement of pure seriality of sterile moments of singular jouissance, whilst remaining a singular film.
29. Something of the force of this *différend* might be witnessed by pointing out that in speaking of Aborigines within the terms of western rationality, one turns for example to the language of plants in attempting to indicate their habitat-specific existence.
30. This risk establishes just what the stakes are in my present attempt to write about the Aborigines. The celebration of Aboriginal identity as offering a model of paganism for us would be entirely complicit with this move by the mining company.

31. Herzog gives short shrift to Christianity's claim to be the conscience of capitalist expansion. After an encounter with the deep mystery of the Aboriginal relation to the land, which leads a group to sit in a supermarket on the site where a tree once stood, in order to 'dream' their children, Hackett visits a mission station. There an enthusiastic priest teaches Aborigines to sing Christian songs saying 'I am happy' in English and Aboriginal language. The ludicrous quality of Christianity's claim to be a universal faith is nowhere more apparent than in the contrast between the minister's sweaty enthusiasm and the silent dignity of the Aboriginal 'giver of song'. The minister asks 'Can I help you?'; Hackett simply replies 'No, not really' and walks away.
32. This kind of discursive fragmentation is an example of the constellation of 'little narratives' by which Lyotard characterises both the postmodern condition and pagan justice.
33. Bruce Chatwin's *The Songlines* (Harmondsworth, 1987) offers a fascinating account of as much of the pathwork of 'dreamings' with which a westerner might come to terms.
34. I place 'his' in quotation marks in order to make clear that this instance does not fall foul of Wittgenstein's argument against private languages; it is the language of the victim, not the individual will. Balai-La's words have always already been spoken elsewhere, in a time and place lost to representation. Balai-La thus corresponds to the opening question that *The Differend* poses to referential discourse, alluding to Auschwitz:

    1 You are informed that human beings endowed with language were placed in a situation such that none of them is now able to tell about it. Most of them disappeared then, and the survivors rarely speak about it. (p. 3)

35. Nor is this case simply external to us, taking place beyond the margins of our culture, in the nether or outer, savage or primitive world. Freud named this the problem of the Unconscious: a force, radically alien to consciousness and yet linked to it, which western rational discourse must seek unsuccessfully to excise.
36. Lyotard, *The Differend*, p. xi.
37. The court hears from two anthropologists. The expert anthropologist produces a structural description of 'mata/mala' exogamic traditions. Another man, who lives in a shack in the bush, informs the court of the impossibility of understanding the Aborigines in western terms.
38. Karl Marx, *Capital: A Critique of Political Economy*. Trans. Ben Fowkes (New York, 1977), vol. 1, book 1, 1–3.
39. The judge refers to legal precedents in Africa and North America where 'Evidence relating to tribal customs and practices, though founded in hearsay, was given in such overwhelming numbers and with such consistency by the tribal witnesses, as to condense into a palpable truth.'
40. Death in a very real sense. Extermination of Aborigines continues today by the apparently 'neutral' act of gaoling them. Aborigines die in gaol not solely because of occasional brutality but because they are marked as individual subjects of the Australian commonwealth, 'free and equal' before the law, abstracted from the land into the virtual space of the legal system.
41. This vagrant anthropologist is thus a kind of 'métèque', the peripatetic foreign teacher with whom Lyotard identifies in *Instructions païennes* (Paris, 1977), and *Pacific Wall*, trans. Brian Boone (Venice, Los Angeles, 1990). Lyotard explains the distinction between pagan and primitive in *Just Gaming*:

    And then there is a third ordering that is popular, properly pagan, 'peasant' in the sense of pagan (and not the reverse): the people of the *pagus* (who are not the people of the village), who do any telling only inasmuch as it has been told, and under the form of ethnology, of folklore, with the idea that it is a primitive state of discourse from which we have managed to get out by means of some well-known operations, basically Platonic ones – I am thinking here of the (unsuccessful) repression of poets and myths attempted in the Republic (p. 38).

The pagan is 'peasant' is the sense that s/he is denigrated with all the force of the word as an insult in French. Yet s/he is not 'peasant' in the sense that s/he dwells in an organic or rooted community, a 'village'.

42. By analogy, the feminism that really frightens men is not simply the feminism that provides a coherent and exhaustive political platform of articulated demands. It is the feminism that makes its demands felt without ever giving in to the plea of the anxious patriarchy that Freud articulated so strongly, 'What do women want?'. The patriarchy wants to know that answer in order to (i) do away with the woman question once and for all by giving them what they want – which can't be everything; (ii) overcome feminism by forcing female desire to articulate by analogy with the end-directedness of male desire – which is another way of saying, show that women were men, all along, under the skin.

43. Lyotard, *Postmodern Condition*, p. 81.
44. Lyotard, *Just Gaming*, p. 25.
45. Lyotard, *The Differend*, p. 139.
46. Lyotard, *Postmodern Condition*, p. 82.
47. bell hooks, 'Representations: Feminism and black masculinity', in *Yearning: Race, Gender, and Cultural Politics* (Toronto, 1990).

14. JEAN-FRANÇOIS LYOTARD, 'CAN THOUGHT GO ON WITHOUT A BODY?'
(From *Discourse*, 2.1 (1987), trans. Bruce Boone and Lee Hildreth.)

Summary

In 4.5 billion years, the sun will explode. This event will mark the end of the human race, the end of philosophy. And yet no one will be able to think this end, precisely because to experience it would be to die. Thought cannot survive or think this disaster. The human race will die without witness. Unless, that is, scientists can create machines capable of simulating life and thought in a post-solar condition. The essay – voiced by two narrators: one male, the other female – begins to ask questions concerning the precise form of such machines. If human thought is embodied, the technology will need to recreate a sense of embodiment without, of course, being able to employ matter in the traditional way. It will also be required to address the unthought in order to ensure that the machines – aware of the fact that their knowledge is incomplete, that there remains something to be thought – even begin to think (why think if you already [think you] know everything?). Finally, the second voice insists that the machines be gendered, be aware of how this difference affects and perhaps even inaugurates thought.

Glossary

Base/superstructure   Metaphor used by Marx and Engels, notably in the former's preface to *A Contribution to a Critique of Political Economy*, to describe the relationship between the economic foundation of society (the base) and the elements – politics, law, art, philosophy, religion – which rise from, and depend upon it. The base determines the superstructure – only when the former changes can the latter develop – although Marxist critics continue to disagree over the specificities of the relationship between the two. In Althusserian theory, for instance, the superstructure possesses a degree of 'relative autonomy'.

Cartesian   Relating to the philosophy of René Descartes.

Cyberpunk   Movement within science fiction which became visible during the early- to mid-1980s with the appearance of films such as *Blade Runner* and *The Terminator*, and the writings of authors like William Gibson, Bruce Sterling, John Shirley, and Richard Kadrey. Cyberpunk is characterised by a fascination with how everyday life is inseparable from high technology, body modification, drugs, and loud music. Some critics have celebrated the genre for its posthumanism and postmodernity; others have identified a distinctly humanist logic at work.

Differend   In the work of Jean-François Lyotard, a differend exists when a conflict between two or more parties cannot be settled or even discussed in a language that does justice to all sides. To bear witness to a differend is to recognise that there is no universal language into which all others may be translated without some kind of loss. To ignore differends is, for Lyotard, to deny difference and justice.

Durcharbeitung   Usually translated as 'working through'. In Freud's account, 'working through' is the potentially arduous process of coming to terms with a new state of affairs. Mourning, for instance, requires that an individual 'work through' his or her attachments to the loved one who is no longer present, gradually acknowledging the reality of this absence.

Episteme   Term used by Michel Foucault to describe a regime of knowledge. When he writes of the 'modern *episteme*', therefore, he is referring to a way of thinking specific to the modern period, governing the limits of what can be thought.

Epistemology   The theory of knowledge; the study of what it is possible to know. Forms, with *ontology*, a crucial element of philosophy.

Heimoerotic   Neologism used by Judith Halberstam to describe the meeting of the homoerotic and Freud's notion of the uncanny (*unheimlich*). Because the relationship between Buffalo Bill and Hannibal Lecter described in *The Silence of the Lambs* is both *unheimlich* and homoerotic, it is said to be 'heimoerotic'.

Idealism   Whereas the historical materialism formulated by Marx and Engels insists that ideas are determined by the material conditions of existence (and, as such, cannot change without a shift in the economic base), idealism gives priority to the mind. Although their entire career depended upon a resistance to idealism, Marx and Engels lay out their opposition with particular vigour in *The German Ideology*.

Ideology   In 'Marxism and Humanism', Louis Althusser describes ideology as 'a system ... of representations (images, myths, ideas or concepts, depending on the case) endowed with a historical existence and role within a given society'. His later essay, 'Ideology and Ideological State Apparatuses (Notes Towards an Investigation)', offers a more nuanced and extremely influential understanding of the term in question.

Metanarrative   In the work of Jean-François Lyotard, a metanarrative is a grand, totalising story which claims explanatory power. In its will to universality, a metanarrative subsumes smaller narratives, claiming at the same time to reveal the truth of the latter. Examples of metanarratives would include: Marxism's metanarrative of dialectical or historical materialism, the Enlightenment notion of progress, and the story of universal patriarchy told by certain forms of feminism. For Lyotard, postmodernity is the moment at which metanarratives begin to lose their credibility. This is not, contrary to the claims of some, the same as saying that postmodernity is the absence of metanarratives or, indeed, narratives.

Ontology   The theory of being; the study of what exists. Forms, with *epistemology*, a crucial element of philosophy.

Orientalism   Term popularised by Edward Said to describe the way in which the West views the East as a monolithic, ahistorical Other. Orientalism, for Said, is an imperialism, for, as a system of knowledge, it portrays an inferior, backward East that has no basis in reality.

Phallogocentrism   Compound of phallocentrism (the privileging of male knowledge and power) and logocentrism (the privileging of ideas over language).

Sign, Signified, Signifier   In the linguistic theory of Ferdinand de Saussure, a sign is the combination of a signifier (the acoustic sound or written mark) and a signified (the meaning).

Simulacrum (plural: *simulacra*)   Term, derived from the tenth book of Plato's *Republic*, used to describe a copy of a copy, a copy for which there is no original. In recent years, the concept has come to be associated with the work of Jean Baudrillard.

Weltanschauung   World-view.

Suggestions for Further Reading

Balsamo, Anne, *Technologies of the Gendered Body: Reading Cyborg Women* (Durham, NC and London, 1996).

Bukatman, Scott, *Terminal Identity: The Virtual Subject in Postmodern Science Fiction* (Durham, NC and London, 1993).

Cadava, Eduardo, Peter Connor, and Jean-Luc Nancy (eds), *Who Comes After the Subject?* (New York and London, 1991).

Csicsery-Ronay, Istvan, Jr, 'The SF of Theory: Baudrillard and Haraway', *Science-Fiction Studies*, 18.3 (1991), 387–404.

Davies, Tony, *Humanism* (London and New York, 1997).

Derrida, Jacques, 'The Ends of Man', *Margins of Philosophy*, trans. Alan Bass (1972) (Hemel Hempstead, 1982), pp. 109–36.

Farnell, Ross, 'Posthuman Topologies: William Gibson's "Architexture" in *Virtual Light* and *Idoru*', *Science-Fiction Studies*, 25.3 (1998), 459–80.

Featherstone, Mike and Roger Burrows (eds), *Cyberspace/Cyberbodies/Cyberpunk: Cultures of Technological Embodiment* (London, 1995).

Foster, Thomas, '"The Sex Appeal of the Inorganic": Posthuman Narratives and the Construction of Desire', *Centuries' Ends, Narrative Means*, ed. Robert Newman (Stanford, CA, 1996), pp. 276–301.

Gray, Chris Hables, 'The Ethics and Politics of Cyborg Embodiment: Citizenship and Hypervalue', *Cultural Values*, 1.2 (1997), 252–8.

——, Heidi J. Figueroa-Sarriera and Steven Mentor (eds), *The Cyborg Handbook* (New York and London, 1995).

Halberstam, Judith and Ira Livingston (eds), *Posthuman Bodies* (Bloomington and Indianapolis, 1995).

Haraway, Donna J., 'Cyborgs at Large: Interview with Donna Haraway', *Technoculture*, ed. Constance Penley and Andrew Ross (Minneapolis and Oxford, 1991), pp. 1–20.

——, 'Ecce Homo, Ain't (Ar'n't) I a Woman, and Inappropriated Others: The Human in a Post-Humanist Landscape', *Feminists Theorize the Political*, ed. Judith Butler and Joan W. Scott (New York and London, 1992), pp. 86–100.

——, 'When Man™ is on the Menu', *Incorporations*, ed. Jonathan Crary and Sanford Kwinter (New York, 1992), pp. 38–43.

Hassan, Ihab, 'Prometheus as Performer: Toward a Posthumanist Culture? A University Masque in Five Scenes', *Georgia Review*, 31 (1977), 830–50.

Hayles, N. Katherine, *How We Became Posthuman: Virtual Bodies in Cybernetics, Literature, and Informatics* (Chicago and London, 1999).

Hays, K. Michael, *Modernism and the Posthumanist Subject: The Architecture of Hannes Meyer and Ludwig Hilberseimer* (Cambridge, MA and London, 1992).

Heidegger, Martin, 'Letter on Humanism' (1947), *Basic Writings*, revised edn, ed. David Farrell Krell (London, 1993), pp. 213–65.

Lyotard, Jean-François, 'A Postmodern Fable', *Postmodern Fables*, trans. George Van Den Abbeele (1993) (Minneapolis and London, 1997), pp. 83–101.

McCracken, Scott, 'Cyborg Fictions: The Cultural Logic of Posthumanism', *Socialist Register 1997*, ed. Leo Panitch (London, 1997), pp. 288–301.

Pearson, Keith Ansell, 'Life Becoming Body: On the "Meaning" of Post Human Evolution', *Cultural Values*, 1.2 (1997), 219–40.

Pepperell, Robert, *The Post-Human Condition*, 2nd edn (Exeter, 1997).

Rutsky, R.L., *High Technē: Art and Technology from the Machine Aesthetic to the Posthuman* (Minneapolis and London, 1999).

Soper, Kate, 'Feminism, Humanism and Postmodernism', *Radical Philosophy*, 55 (Summer 1990), 11–17.

——, *Humanism and Anti-Humanism* (London, 1986).

Spanos, William V., *The End of Education: Toward Posthumanism* (Minneapolis and London, 1993).

Wolfe, Cary, 'In Search of Post-Humanist Theory: The Second-Order Cybernetics of Maturana and Varela', *Cultural Critique*, 30 (1995), 33–70.

Notes on Contributors

Louis Althusser, who died in 1990, taught philosophy at the Ecole Normale Supérieure, Paris. His publications include: *For Marx* (1965), *Reading Capital* (with Étienne Balibar, 1968), and *Lenin and Philosophy and Other Essays* (1971).

Neil Badmington is a Lecturer at the Centre for Critical and Cultural Theory, Cardiff University, where he teaches Cultural Criticism and English Literature. He has published articles on critical theory, cinema, and techno-culture, and is currently working on a book provisionally entitled *Becoming Posthuman*.

Roland Barthes was, at the time of his death in 1980, Professor of Literary Semiology at the Collège de France, Paris. His many publications include: *Writing Degree Zero* (1953), *Mythologies* (1957), *S/Z* (1970), *Roland Barthes by Roland Barthes* (1975) and *Camera Lucida: Reflections on Photography* (1980).

Jean Baudrillard taught sociology at the University of Paris X (Nanterre) from 1966 to 1987. His many publications include: *Symbolic Exchange and Death* (1976), *Seduction* (1979), *America* (1986), *The Gulf War Did Not Take Place* (1991), and *The Perfect Crime* (1995).

Scott Bukatman is Assistant Professor of Film Studies at Stanford University. He is the author of *Terminal Identity: The Virtual Subject in Postmodern Science Fiction* (1993) and *Blade Runner* (1997).

Rosalind Coward is a Senior Research Fellow at Nene College, Northampton. She is the author of *Language and Materialism* (with John Ellis, 1977), *Patriarchal Precedents* (1983), *Female Desire* (1984), *The Whole Truth* (1989), *Our Treacherous Hearts: Why Women Let Men Get Their Way* (1992), and *Sacred Cows* (1999). She also writes as a columnist for the *Guardian*.

Frantz Fanon, who died in 1961, was a psychiatrist and activist in the Algerian struggle for independence. His publications include: *Black Skin, White Masks* (1952), *The Wretched of the Earth* (1961), and *Toward the African Revolution* (1964).

Michel Foucault was Professor of History of Systems of Thought at the Collège de France, Paris. His numerous publications include: *The Order of Things: An Archaeology of the Human Sciences* (1966), *The Archaeology of Knowledge* (1969), *Discipline and Punish: The Birth of the Prison* (1977), and three volumes of a project, unfinished at the time of his death in 1984, entitled *The History of Sexuality* (1976–84).

Judith Halberstam teaches queer studies, film, gender and nineteenth-century literary studies at the University of California, San Diego. She is the author of *Skin Shows: Gothic Horror and the Technology of Monsters* (1995), *Female Masculinity* (1998) and *The Drag King Book* (with Del LaGrace Volcano, 1999). She also edited, with Ira Livingston, *Posthuman Bodies* (1995).

168

Donna Haraway teaches science studies, feminist theory, and women's studies at the University of California, Santa Cruz. Her publications include: *Crystals, Fabrics, and Fields: Metaphors of Organicism in 20th Century Developmental Biology* (1976), *Primate Visions: Gender, Race, and Nature in the World of Modern Science* (1989), *Simians, Cyborgs, and Women: The Reinvention of Nature* (1991), and *Modest_Witness@Second_Millennium.FemaleMan©_Meets_OncoMouse*™: *Feminism and Technoscience* (1997).

Jean-François Lyotard was, at the time of his death in 1998, Professor Emeritus at the University of Paris and Professor of French at Emory University. His many publications include: *Discours, Figure* (1971), *The Postmodern Condition* (1979), *The Differend: Phrases in Dispute* (1983) and *Postmodern Fables* (1993).

Paula Rabinowitz teaches cultural studies at the University of Minnesota. She is the author of *Labor and Desire: Women's Revolutionary Fiction in Depression America* (1991) and *They Must Be Represented: The Politics of Documentary* (1994) and editor, with Charlotte Nekola, of *Writing Red: An Anthology of American Women Writers, 1930–1940* (1988).

Bill Readings was Associate Professor in the Department of Comparative Literature at the University of Montréal, Quebec, until his untimely death in 1994. He taught in Switzerland and the United States and published on philosophy, literary theory, Renaissance studies and art history. He was the author of *Introducing Lyotard: Art and Politics* (1991) and *The University in Ruins* (1996). He also edited, with Bennet Schaber, *Postmodernism Across the Ages: Essays for a Postmodernity that Wasn't Born Yesterday* (1993) and, with Stephen Melville, *Vision and Textuality* (1995).

Index

CPSIA information can be obtained
at www.ICGtesting.com
Printed in the USA
LVHW110058150819
627635LV00003B/320/P